# B. F. Skinner
# A Reappraisal

## Marc N. Richelle

*University of Liège, Belgium*

 LAWRENCE ERLBAUM ASSOCIATES, PUBLISHERS
Hove (UK)                                    Hillsdale (USA)

Lawrence Erlbaum Associates Ltd., Publishers
27 Palmeira Mansions
Church Road
Hove
East Sussex, BN3 2FA
U.K.


**British Library Cataloguing in Publication Data**

Richelle, Marc N.
  B. F. Skinner: Reappraisal
  I. Title
  150.92

ISBN 0-86377-283-8 (Hbk)


Typeset by Litho Link Ltd., Welshpool, Powys, Wales.
Printed and bound in the United Kingdom by BPCC Wheatons Ltd., Exeter.

# Contents

# Acknowledgements

A large part of this book was written during a sabbatic leave spent in Spanish Universities, with the support of the Fonds National de La Recherche Scientifique of Belgium. I am most grateful to them and to the Rector of the University of Liège, Professor Arthur Bodson, for providing me with a fruitful break in my academic activities.

I am especially grateful to the numerous host universities and individuals in Spain, but their part in my reflection deserves special mention with respect to the content, and is therefore evoked at the end of the Preface.

Some material included has been adapted from a book in French published earlier by Pierre Mardaga, Publisher in Brussels-Liège, under the title *Skinner ou le péril behavioriste* (1976). I thank Pierre Mardaga, who took over the publishing house started by another friend, the late Charles Dessart, for his permission, and also for having contributed to the propagation of Skinner's writings in French.

I have abundantly quoted from Skinner's writings, because this is the best way to provide the reader with objective evidence of his thought, which has been so frequently misrepresented. Quotations from Skinner, 1938, 1957, 1968, 1972, are reproduced with permission given by the B. F. Skinner Foundation (Mrs Julie Vargas, President), which I thank for its courtesy. Quotations from Skinner, 1953, are reproduced with permission courteously granted by Macmillan Publishing Co, and quotations from Skinner 1948 with permission by the same publisher.

I am grateful to Lawrence Erlbaum Associates, England, for welcoming one more continental author, with all its implications for editorial work load : in spite of my efforts, the text cannot really compare with the standard of native English-speakers. I am most grateful to the publisher and to the anonymous referee for their valuable assistance in improving my style. Remaining imperfections are, of course, my own.

Finally, the requirements made by modern publishers could not have been met without the help of my secretary, Mrs Andrée Houyoux. I thank her for her patient and expert exploitation of the word processor.

M. R.
October, 1992

# Preface

When this book was in the process of being written, in the summer of 1990, Burrhus Frederic Skinner died in Cambridge, Massachusetts, on Saturday 18 August, at the age of 86. He had been informed, several months earlier, that he suffered from leukaemia. He continued to work serenely on his manuscripts until the day before he died.

Skinner's career as a psychologist had covered almost 60 years. He had gained exceptional influence, and had been named among the few most prominent psychologists of our century. He had also been by far the most controversial. He has been attacked from the most opposed sides of psychology, of science at large and of political ideologies. He has often been depicted as the last representative of the behaviourist school, and as such, presented as a sort of fossil, or, in the last 25 years of his life, as the obsolete and unique surviving specimen of an otherwise extinct species, now replaced by the new phylum known as *cognitivism*. He has been made responsible for keeping psychology, over more than 50 years, in the "long and boring night of behaviourism", as one famous philosopher put it.[1]

Echoing characterisations often heard in scientific circles, Skinner's obituaries have, once again, pictured him as the fancy experimenter who would waste his time teaching pigeons how to play ping-pong or as the dangerous scientific dictator who would have ruled society by coercion and punishment, had he been offered the chance to enter political practice. Fortunately, he was not offered such an opportunity, and new trends in psychology arrived in due time to neutralise the dragon.

Why, in that context, a book on Skinner? Can the man and his work be of any interest, except to historians of psychology?

It might be enough to answer: for the sake of truth, since any contributor to scientific or philosophical thought deserves an honest reading of his words, and if they have been widely misrepresented, the reasons should be analysed and a more correct appraisal should eventually be reached. The issue, however, is not just a matter of giving justice to an unjustly decried author. It has relevance to the current debates within psychology. By discovering or rediscovering Skinner and Skinner's views as they really are, psychologists could also put their own current reflections in proper perspective: that is, correctly appraise the roots of present research and theorising in the past, identify the problems that have remained unsolved in spite of the change in paradigm—as the cognitivist school is often thought of—and perceive those seminal aspects of Skinner's work which open new avenues of research or converge with most promising contemporary approaches. For some reason, psychologists tend to think of the history of their science as a sequence of *revolutions* rather than *evolution*: they like to emphasise ruptures rather than build on continuities. They seem concerned to attach their name to a theory that will replace previous views, and, to that end, they occasionally indulge in the strategy of building a straw man. Skinner has been a favoured target of that strategy. But in misrepresenting his ideas, his opponents have missed most of his genuine contributions to psychology, and have completely overlooked the fact that in many areas of theory and of practice, he was indeed a forerunner.

This book is about Skinner, not about the Skinnerians. The difference is an important one, since most of the controversies surrounding Skinner involve a permanent confusion between the two. As a school of thought, as an organised movement, often identified with the "behaviour analysts", the disciples of Skinner, or some of them, have had a quite distinct history in American psychology. Among other things, they have isolated themselves from the rest of scientific psychology by creating their own journals and societies, by closing themselves to open dialogue with other trends and developing a sense of orthodoxy, which has never proved to be fruitful in the progress of a science or in the dissemination of a theory.[2] Some of them have focused on the implementation of Skinner's social philosophy, with a mixture of naïve idealism and sect-like militantism. The links between Skinner and these movements are complex, but it is clear that he cannot endorse all that has been done or said with reference to his name. Anyhow, this book is not intended to give an historical account of the behaviourist movement and its ramifications.[3]

Nor is it intended to give an historical presentation of Skinner's life and work. I leave to other people the honour of linking their name to Skinner's as his recognised biographer, as Ernest Jones' is linked to Freud. Although I shall have to put some of Skinner's ideas into adequate historical context, in order to appraise their relevance to scientific debate as it progresses through time, the organisation of this book does not obey the historical course. It is, on the contrary, a selection of themes, which appear to me as most illustrative of Skinner's contribution, or as especially misunderstood although crucial in his theory, or as generally neglected, because other, less important points have, for some reason, been emphasised.

The selection is, admittedly, a personal one. It is a selection by a *European* psychologist, with his idiosyncratic background. Maybe *European* is not a sufficient qualification: *Continental*, and even *French-speaking* should be added. Without indulging in autobiographical notes, I owe the readers some information so they can better understand my choice. After graduating in Philosophy and Letters in my home country, I took a degree in Psychology at the University of Geneva, whose Institute of Psychology was quite legitimately at that time considered as one of the best on the Continent. It was dominated by the figure of Piaget, although other names, such as Rey or Lambercier or Inhelder, deserve mention. When I came across Skinner and his work, to be precise at Harvard in 1958–59, I inevitably read it through the lenses of my own intellectual education, and I was naturally brought to confront it with major works in the European tradition. This has led me to locate major limitations in Skinner's views— limitations he might share with the North-American psychological tradition as a whole—to point to complementarities rather than contradictions or oppositions, to unveil unsuspected convergencies, to bring into quite different perspective some of the occasionally violent debates that took place around Skinner's conceptions, for example concerning verbal behaviour (in the debate initiated by Chomsky[4]) or ethology (in a rather harsh exchange involving one of Skinner's closest co-workers, Herrnstein[5]). I shall give ample space in the following pages to this exercise in confrontation and integration of two different psychological traditions. I only hope that the American reader will find the approach informative and stimulating. It is a widespread feeling among European psychologists that American psychology (with the exception of a few professional historians of the field), in spite of its outstanding development, or maybe because of it, has been ignoring most of the European major contributions to our science in this century, except for that part that has further developed on the other side of the Atlantic because of the emigration from Europe of some individuals,[6] or that part which has been transferred due to, often quite delayed, translations.[7]

As the way one reads an author's writings, be they scientific or literary, can obviously be influenced by the fact that one is personally acquainted with him, I admit that my own reading of Skinner might be biased by my personal encounters with him. It was my privilege to approach him first when I was a graduate student-fellow at Harvard, and later as a colleague, especially on the occasion of the first translation of some of his books into French, which I undertook with Graulich in the 1960s.[8]

Although what counts essentially, for all scientific purposes, are the ideas and empirical contributions as expressed in written words, I could not help being shocked by the *ad hominem* attacks addressed to Fred Skinner. For those who have approached him in his lifetime, it is difficult to understand how some of his scientific opponents could resort to accusations of power-searching. In my long experience as a student, in which I was happy enough to be taught by a number of outstanding people, including men who have shaped scientific psychology in our century, namely Piaget and Skinner, I can testify that the latter is by far the least directive teacher I have ever met. I felt it appropriate to insist on that personal detail when I gave an interview to a Spanish news reporter the day after Skinner's death was announced, while I was staying at San Lorenzo del Escorial.[9] She got the message, and the title of her report referred to "the least authoritarian teacher" Richelle had ever had.[10] At least that particular Spanish daily paper did not convey, on that occasion, the usual distorted picture of Skinner.

I am especially grateful to the reporter for that: it appeared to me as predictive of the favourable context that Spain would offer me to complete this book during the winter of 1990–91. The prediction was confirmed beyond expectation, and I heartily acknowledge my debt to Spanish psychologists who have provided me with an ideally fitting environment for efficient, quiet writing, as well as with stimulating interactions, on the occasion of lectures, seminars and symposia on various aspects of Skinner's work and other themes.[11] A list of names would be too long and expose me to omissions. The following list of host universities will allow each of these colleagues and friends to capture my message: Granada and its Jaen campus, Madrid Complutense, Madrid Autonoma, Madrid UNED, Barcelona Central, Barcelona Autonoma and its campus of Gerona, Valencia, Sevilla, Oviedo, Salamanca, Santiago de Compostela, and, out of Spain but in the peninsula, Lisbon and Coïmbra. The universities of Granada and of Madrid Complutense deserve special mention for having provided me with all desirable facilities for periods of four months each.

# NOTES

1. Bunge, M. (1980).
2. Skinner himself was aware of the self-isolation of behaviour analysts, which he traced to the difficulty in having papers on individual subjects accepted in scientific journals in the early 1950s and in finding places for gathering together if there was no officially allotted space and time at scientific meetings (see Skinner, 1989, Chapter 12). Proctor and Weeks (1990) have argued against that interpretation. See my review of their book (Richelle, 1991).
3. For the interested reader, various sources are available, including A. Schorr, 1984.
4. See Chapter 10.
5. See Chapter 6.
6. For example, the contributions of exiled Gestaltists, such as Max Wertheimer, before they left Europe, remained largely unknown in the US.

7. Piaget's work, starting in the early 1920s, was very little known in the US until some of his books were translated. Vigotsky's work, terminated by his untimely death in 1934, was brought to attention thanks to J. Bruner's initiative in 1962. Other prominent psychologists, such as P. Janet and H. Wallon, to mention only two examples in the French area, have been completely ignored until now, in spite of the importance of their work, probably matching Freud's and Vigotsky's respectively.

8. B. F. Skinner (1969a), *La révolution scientifique de l'enseignement,* and (1971), *L'analyse expérimentale du comportement,* Bruxelles, Mardaga, translations of *The technology of teaching* and *Contingencies of reinforcement,* respectively.

9. The occasion was a summer course, organised by the University Complutense of Madrid, on the theme "Freud and after Freud", in which I was due to deliver a lecture on Freud and scientific psychology, mainly devoted to Freud in Skinner's writings. This coincidence (Skinner would have noted: he was always fascinated by coincidences) brought me in contact with the Madrid press, in search of firsthand information on the late American scientist. A revised version of the talk delivered during that session has been used as part of Chapter 4.

10. *El Pais,* 22 August 1990.

11. There have probably been more papers published and more meetings on Skinner's work organised in Spain, in the year following his death, than in any other European country. As an example, see Roales-Nieto, Luciano Soriano and Pérez Alvarez, 1992. For a European approach to the experimental analysis of behaviour and to Skinner's work, see Lowe et al., 1985; Blackman and Lejeune, 1990 and Richelle, 1985.

# CONTROVERSIAL ISSUES AND UNQUESTIONABLE CONTRIBUTIONS

# 1 A Matter of Controversy

## A CONTROVERSIAL SCIENTIST

Burrhus Frederic Skinner was born on 20 March 1904 in Susquehana, a small town in Pennsylvania. He died on 18 August 1990, in Cambridge, Massachusetts. His will undoubtedly remain among the dozen great minds who have shaped twentieth-century psychology, side by side with his contemporaries, Piaget and Lorenz, or with Pavlov, Thorndike and Watson, his elders. He has been a leading figure of a school of thought, *behaviourism*, that has dominated the scene for more than half a century. His name is associated with a procedure designed to study the behaviour of animals in the laboratory, often labelled the "Skinner box" but more appropriately named a "conditioning chamber"; with a concept, *operant conditioning*, that is now part of familiar categories in a psychologist's mind; with a theoretical endeavour, aimed at the explanation of behaviour, be it in animals or in humans, in terms of *control by consequences*; and with a *social philosophy*, grounded, at least in Skinner's own view, in scientific evidence that has been largely overlooked, and is still overlooked today, to mankind's misfortune.

These various contributions to the science of psychology and to its philosophical by-products will be described and discussed at length throughout this book. It would seem at first sight that one can proceed with introducing Skinner's work as one would do for any other great psychologist, or, for that matter, any other great scientist: usually, one would have to describe a methodological approach, to recount an empirical or a conceptual breakthrough, or both—since it is rarely the case that facts are discovered independently from concepts—to evaluate a theory, and eventually to discuss attempts at deriving

3

some general philosophical view from the scientific work proper. To remain within the limits of psychology, all four levels of activity can be found in Pavlov's, Piaget's or Lorenz' long and impressive work, just as they are in Skinner's.

There seems to be something special about the latter, however, something that is not easy to capture and characterise, but that is reflected in the numerous and various expressions of hostility towards Skinner's ideas and person. Of course, scientific ideas, like other ideas, are exposed to criticism, and no one expects complete agreement on scientific issues, especially in a field still as precarious as psychology. But criticisms addressed to Skinner have been unusually violent and passionate. Their authors are not exclusively psychologists, presumably competent to appraise a colleague's work; many intellectuals pertaining to other fields of science, as well as laymen with very different, even opposite, ideological backgrounds, have crusaded against him.

A complete list of relevant quotations would cover more than half the present volume. A sample of selected opinions will suffice to illustrate the general spirit. The following are drawn from European and American sources, newspapers, political discourses, scientific journals or books. They were written or pronounced at various times of Skinner's life, or in obituaries shortly after his death:

> On behalf of a so-called "neo-behaviourist" psychology, exclusively focused on pure behaviour, a man called Skinner, a psychologist at Harvard, calls for robotisation.
> All radios make it a point of honour to invite this dangerous fool, close to Soviet Pavlovians, who asserts that man is no special state of nature; that he is but one animal among others; and that, as such, he must be trained in such a way as to react, as other animals do, to a number of external stimuli of the environment. Forget man. Consider only the animal. Analyse its conditioning by having the environment act upon it. Find out the most efficient of them and multiply them . . . Skinner calls that "operant conditioning". There is another word for it: it is Nazism.
>
> *Michel Lancelot*[1]

> Clearly, we in France are more cool-headed. Skinner's book [i.e. *Beyond freedom and dignity*] does not seem to have filled many here with enthusiasm or shock . . . This conception calls for strengthening of order; it provides an answer to criticisms against culture and society. It recommends control in order to ensure survival, hence reproduction of what exists. In contrast, freedom and dignity—core ideas of extremists—appear as bubbles of the past, based on prescientific theories. The America of Mr Nixon and Mr Agnew must take care of its own salvation, it must dare to punish and reward where and when it is needed.
>
> *Serge Moscovici*[2]

> America as a society was founded on respect of the individual and an unshakable belief in his worth and dignity . . . Skinner attacks the very precepts on which our

society is based saying that "Life, liberty and the pursuit of happiness" were once valid goals, but have no place in 20th-century America or in the creation of a new culture as he proposes.

*Spiro Agnew*[3]

. . . consider a well-run concentration camp with inmates spying on one another and the gas ovens smoking in the distance, and perhaps an occasional verbal hint as a reminder of the meaning of this reinforcer. It would appear to be an almost perfect world . . . Within Skinner's scheme there is no objection to this social order. Rather, it seems close to ideal.

*Noam Chomsky*[4]

What accounts for the success of Skinner's views in spite of all their logical pitfalls? In my opinion, it is their adherence to a set of American values that are largely exported by the government of the USA along with other goods.

*J. Jacques Vonèche*[5]

[the Skinner box] has been described as a bloodless method of decerebrating the animal. Some think the same could be said of the effects of Skinnerian theory on his adherents . . .

*The Guardian, 28 August 1990*

Finally, I do not deny that there are a few remaining Skinnerians; after all if you count fossils, there are still many dinosaurs in the world.

*Stuart Sutherland*[6]

While psychoanalysts believe in the complexity of the individual, and therefore in his freedom, behaviourists are not concerned with consciousness, and prefer to stick at scientific observable data, rediscovering altogether the virtues of authority and the recipes of the carrot and the stick. However, thanks to his cage, Skinner had yet succeeded in teaching birds how to play piano and dance.

*Frank Nouchi*[7]

This is obviously not the usual style of polemics about scientific theories, except when they deeply disturb the conception that man has of his nature and of the world around him, as was the case for Galileo or for Darwin, or when they hide some perverse misuse of science aimed at ideological domination, as is unfortunately sometimes the case in our civilised societies. In some of the quotations above, the latter interpretation is clearly suggested: some authors, like Chomsky, the famous linguist, did not hesitate to accuse Skinner of Nazism, by resorting to unambiguous metaphors.

European critics often discard Skinner's contribution as a typical product of American society, which does not fit in the context of European culture, or that should be looked at with suspicion in order to avoid contamination. These quotations from Moscovici and Vonèche illustrate this somewhat contemptuous judgement. Those critics do not answer embarrassing objections to their ethnocentric appraisal of Skinner's work. They tend to ignore the fact that, like it or not, things which originate in the USA eventually invade Europe sooner or later—as with popular soft drinks, computers, or indeed the student revolution that received the 1968 date only because of a persistent European illusion of being at the start of everything important. They do not give their reasons for accepting sympathetically other American productions, such as humanistic or cognitivist theories, to remain within the field of psychology. (One explanation, as given by Vonèche, is to point to the European origins of those acceptable approaches, pointing to Piaget as the originator of American cognitivism! This explanation proceeds from the same Eurocentrism denounced above.) Above all, they do not explain why attacks against Skinner were far more numerous and violent in his home country than anywhere else, nor why personalities as different as Noam Chomsky and Spiro Agnew (the former a brilliant linguist and a famous active libertarian; the second a rather conservative Vice-President of the USA, who did not finish his term because of a financial scandal) joined in fighting against the Harvard psychologist, though resorting, of course, to quite opposite arguments.

When a man is attacked from many different horizons, by people usually opposed to each other, it is likely that he has disturbed all of them, possibly because he is saying important things that nobody wants to hear. His adversaries then resort to a common strategy: they overshadow his work. If the work is written, they convey a misrepresentation of it, or they themselves fail to read it correctly. Second-hand treatment makes for a generalisation of the distortion. Trusting prominent critics, people neglect to read the work first-hand, and unfounded arguments are reproduced and amplified. This mechanism has been at work with respect to Skinner's writings and ideas throughout his career, as we shall see. The main example, and undoubtedly the most decisive one, has been Chomsky's critique (1959) of Skinner's book *Verbal behavior* (1957).

But many other cases can be pointed out, notably in two important publications devoted, in the 1980s, to Skinner's contribution. One is a special issue of the highly praised journal *The Behavioral and Brain Sciences*[8] entitled *Canonical papers of B. F. Skinner*, in which more than 100 authors were invited to write "open peer commentaries" on Skinner's reprinted selected papers. The second is a book edited by S. Modgil and C. Modgil under the title *B. F. Skinner: Consensus and controversy* (1987). About two dozen authors argue for or against a number of aspects of Skinner's view. Both publications—besides acknowledging the place that Skinner still holds on the scientific stage—abound in misrepresentations and errors of interpretation, even under the pen of otherwise serious authors.

At this point, one might ask the question: How is it that Skinner has been so frequently misunderstood and misrepresented? The authors of a recent essay have a simple and straightforward answer: the reason is that his message was neither clear nor consistent.[9] In other words, when readers misunderstand a scientific author, one can only conclude that the text is not clear, and only the author can be blamed for it. Readers' judgements are to be trusted. We are aware, however, of the various sources of bias that can bring readers, even of scientific material, to misinterpret what they have under their eyes. Readers are prone to perceive and read what they want to see. They do not easily give up stereotypes, and they occasionally go as far, in defending their own point of view, as to build straw men which replace the author they are actually reading. We shall see in Chapter 10 how Chomsky's criticisms, for example, illustrate these mechanisms, to a point that might pass intellectual honesty. But persistent misreadings surprisingly also focus on the most basic, almost classical and unequivocal aspects of Skinner's theory. For example, many psychologists have continued to characterise Skinner's theory as typical *stimulus-response* (S-R) psychology in spite of his perfectly clear statements to the contrary.[10] Skinner's style is especially elegant and unambiguous, and although several lines of evolution in his thinking can be traced throughout his writings (the contrary would indeed appear unusual in such a long career),[11] he has also made a point of re-stating his main ideas in several contexts, and at various levels of sophistication, for audiences with different backgrounds. Skinner cannot be blamed for obscurity, and we should look in other directions to account for misinterpretations.

If we want to know Skinner's ideas, we must go back to his writings rather than rely upon distorted or oversimplified second-hand accounts. This is also the only appropriate way if we want to elucidate the ties between "philosophical" (or "ideological") writings (those most widely read by non-specialists) and scientific writings (often misread by specialists themselves). Before dealing in some depth with what I consider to be the central issues in Skinner's theory and in the debates around it, let us take a general look at Skinner's work and point to some landmarks of his life and some features of his character.

## SKINNER'S WORK: AN OVERVIEW

The first scientific papers by Skinner were published in the early 1930s. He never stopped writing from then until the day before he died, and his now closed bibliography amounts to more than 200 titles, including a dozen books.

His contributions, however, have not been only in words. It should not be overlooked (as sometimes happens) that he has provided the psychological laboratory with a new and exceptionally effective technique that is now part of the tools used by many researchers, whatever their theoretical inclination, not only in the experimental study of behaviour proper, but in various fields where behaviour is important at some stage of inquiry, such as neurophysiology or psychopharmacology.

While contributing many empirical facts, Skinner has clarified, if not always solved, a number of problems in which experimental and theoretical psychology was sinking about 50 years ago. He has been seminal in the development of new applications, such as behaviour therapy and behaviour modification—now a well-accepted approach to helping people with psychological problems or suffering various handicaps—and programmed instruction (though their debt to Skinner is rarely acknowledged by those who apply his ideas today to computer-assisted learning).

Skinner's theoretical endeavour has mainly consisted in elaborating further the concept of psychology as the science of behaviour, originally formulated by Watson early in this century. He has enriched and refined *behaviourism*, by adding to the initial definition many qualifications derived from knowledge accumulated over time and from his critical reflection, expressed in a less passionate style than Watson's. But he has rigorously followed the basic principles of behaviourism more than any other psychologist after Watson, making that point clear by labelling himself a *radical* behaviourist. We shall elaborate on that point later.

Finally, Skinner has been bold enough to apply to human affairs at large the conclusions of his scientific analysis of animal behaviour. He has questioned the traditional view of human nature and man's relation to his physical and social environment. In his Utopian novel *Walden Two* and in several papers and books—of which *Beyond freedom and dignity* is the main one—he has denounced our unwillingness to deal with matters of human behaviour by resorting to the scientific approach which we feel is appropriate, and indeed effective, in technological or medical matters. This part of his work is certainly responsible for irritating many of his readers.

## BEHAVIOURISM: A SHORT REMINDER

Behaviourism is a school of thought that originated early this century. Its birth is usually identified with J. B. Watson's famous paper "Psychology as the behaviorist views it" (1913). But, as is often the case, the idea was in the air. It had been explicitly stated in an historical lecture by the French psychologist H. Piéron in 1908.[12] And it had been practised for some years by scientists like Pavlov.

The core of the behaviourist's position is that the subject matter of psychology is *behaviour*—which can be observed from outside, as are the phenomena studied in natural sciences—rather than mental states subjectively apprehended by the subject himself. This was essentially a methodological change. Up to then, scientific psychology, a young field of science little more than half a century old, still relied on introspection as the main source of data in spite of successful efforts to develop experimental rigour and control, and in spite of its use of measurement and quantification. Although this was no major obstacle to progress in some domains, such as basic psychophysics or the study of elementary motor reactions in human adults, it proved to be quite unsatisfying when dealing with more complex phenomena, such as thought and problem-solving, or with subjects who could not report on their internal life, or, even more simply, could not understand verbal instructions to do so, as is the case with animals, pathologically disabled persons, or individuals speaking another language.

At another level, though closely related to the methodological aspect, behaviourism had important epistemological implications. It put psychology in the realm of natural sciences,[13] dispensing with the old dualist distinction between Mind and Matter. The issue here is not between materialism and spiritualism or idealism, but whether psychology has more chance to progress by working with the hypothesis that its subject matter is amenable to the same approach as other aspects of the world, and more specifically of the living world.

Behaviourism, once formulated clearly by Watson, spread very quickly. It pervaded not only American psychology but European psychology as well. Most textbooks would, from then on and until recently, start with a definition of psychology as the *science of behaviour*. There seemed to be a sort of consensus on that point. This does not mean, however, that behaviourism eliminated other schools of thought. On the European continent, Gestalt psychology developed at the same time in Germany; in Geneva, Piaget started his monumental work about 10 years after Watson's manifesto, while the study of animal behaviour in the wild emerged as modern ethology in the 1930s, mainly under the influence of Konrad Lorenz. These approaches were not necessarily opposed to the behaviourist position, but they put the emphasis on other aspects.

French psychology offers a peculiar and interesting case with regard to behaviourism. As mentioned earlier, Piéron can be considered, historically, as the founder of behaviourism, if the date of the first formulation is to be taken as a criterion. He did not really start the movement, though his own work has undoubtedly been quite in line with the behaviourist position. One explanation might be that he was not assertive enough, compared with Watson. One could also argue that France was not ripe for that revolution, or that it was in some sense already beyond it: Pierre Janet, whose influence extended over several decades, had in fact developed a psychology of "conduct" that, in many respects, foreshadowed some tenets of Skinner's radical behaviourism. But on the other hand, French psychologists, with few exceptions, were never very receptive to radical behaviourism, and turned with enthusiasm to cognitivism when it emerged in the 1960s.

Behaviourism took shape mainly in the United States, where, following the impetus given by Watson, a handful of second-generation behaviourists—the so-called "neo-behaviourists"—developed their own versions of a science of behaviour during the second quarter of the century. One of the best known, and possibly the most influential, was Hull, who is still today taken as the main reference when behaviourist theses are discussed. He did not contribute any major methodological novelty, or any important empirical discovery. He was fascinated by formalisations, and engaged in building an ambitious hypothetico-deductive system of behaviour. One of the most severe critics of his book *Principles of behavior* (1943) was Skinner (1944), which clearly shows that behaviourism was not a unified church! Looked at from a distance, Hull's endeavour appears rather sterile and premature.

Another prominent figure among neo-behaviourists was Tolman, whose name and work we shall meet again. Tolman is rightly considered to be one of the fathers of modern cognitivism. His main book, significantly entitled *Purposive behavior in animals and men* (1932), dealt with a crucial and difficult problem in scientific psychology: namely the organisation and anticipation of action towards an end. He also discovered that animals interacting freely with their environment in the absence of any biological need, such as hunger or thirst, would eventually learn something about it. As the situation in which he discovered this was the then familiar maze for rats, he suggested that his subjects built a *cognitive map*, obviously an ancestor of the internal representations of cognitive psychology. We shall comment further on that later on.

Skinner, the youngest of these second-generation behaviourists, and different enough from all of them not to be included among neo-behaviourists, took a totally distinct stand. On the one hand, he remained much more strictly attached to the essential tenets of Watson's conception. On the other, he moved away from Watson much more basically than the neo-behaviourists and elaborated his genuine brand of behavioural psychology. As we have seen, he called himself a radical behaviourist. As we shall progress, we shall grasp what this means. At this stage, a few landmarks might be useful to characterise the commonalities between the various brands of behaviourism, and to point to crucial issues about which Skinner developed original views.

For a behaviourist, psychology cannot claim scientific status if it does not take, as its subject matter, events that can be observed with methods in use in other natural sciences. Its task is to identify the variables of which these observable events are a function. This view had many opponents, because it appeared to reduce the realm of psychology to motor acts directly accessible to an observer and to leave out of account the innumerable internal events which each human individual knows to take place inside himself. This is seriously mistaking the basic methodological principle of behaviourism. Behaviourism does not deny the existence of internal events. But on the one hand, it denies the subject's capacity to give a scientific account of them (in that respect, it is close to Freud's or Janet's view); on the other, it denies that internal mental events have an essentially different status from behaviours easily observed from outside. The problem of psychology is to make them accessible for analysis—a problem encountered by any science—and to treat them as behaviour proper, rather than as the inferred and unverifiable sources of behaviour.

*Antimentalism*, a central theme in Skinner's thinking, is not a denial of mental events, but a refusal to resort to them as explanatory entities. A classical example will help in understanding the arguments for that position. Common sense tends to attribute an act to some causal internal source, often conceived of as a need or drive. It sounds fairly correct to invoke hunger when an animal or a human being is eating or searching for food. It is tempting to extend the same explanation when someone is engaging in aggressive action, attributed to some aggression drive; when someone imitates another person, because of a need for imitation; or when a few individuals get together, because of their common need for affiliation. We are left with the task of explaining the need and soon discover that we have only placed the problem a bit further back. Scientific psychology was plagued with such "explanatory fictions" by the time Skinner started his reflection on mentalism, and developed his concept of reinforcement (which testifies that behaviourism was never quite as dominant as is often said). As he emphasised, the objection is not that these things are mental, but that they stop all further attempt to explain. Reading current psychological literature shows that the problem is still with us. Its resurgence in scientific psychology is linked with the rise of cognitivism, and there is no doubt that the status of mental events in psychological descriptions and explanations must be examined now in a far more subtle way than was the case 40 years ago. It is clear, however, that Skinner's attitude towards cognitivism is rooted in his traditional view of mentalism. We shall have to deal with that issue in some detail later, since it is, indeed, one of the central epistemological problems psychologists have to face.

Another much debated point about behaviourism is *environmentalism*. Behaviour would be said to find its explanation in the action of the environment upon the passive organism. It is true that behaviourists have shown systematic interest in the role of the environment. This should cause no surprise since, after all, psychology is concerned with the relation between an organism and its surroundings. It seems difficult to think of psychologists who would not, in some way or another, try to understand that interaction. However, they have various views on that matter. Some of them insist on innate endowment, that defines beforehand what part the environment will play in an organism's history; they see it as merely revealing pre-wired potentialities. This was the position taken by Lorenz, at least in his early work on animal behaviour. Others emphasise the organisation of the individual, i.e. the structure of the individual's intelligence, personality, unconscious, mind, and so forth, with no explicit reference to the environment. Structuralist schools of thought, which were so successful in human and social sciences in the 1960s, pertain to that category, as did a number of classical approaches in psychology much earlier. Others, like Piaget, look at the subject acting upon the environment, eventually failing to master it, then getting some feedback from it that enables him to correct his action, in a sort of dialectic interchange. This is typically the interactionist view.

Still others give the main role to the environment. It is conceived of as mechanically provoking the reactions of the organism, that is activated from outside, as a puppet with no genetic memory, no structure, no will. This view is supposedly typical of so-called *stimulus-response* (S-R) psychologies, which in turn are often identified with behaviourism. I shall not discuss here the question whether pure stimulus-response psychologies have ever been proposed. What is clear is that Skinnerian behaviourism is *not* a stimulus-response psychology. His conception with regard to the role of the environment is unequivocally different, and is a central tenet of his theory, as we shall see in Chapter 3.

# NOTES

1. Quoted from *Le jeune lion dort avec ses dents*, Paris, 1974. Translation is mine. The author is a French journalist.
2. Quoted from a review of the French translation of *Beyond freedom and dignity* published under the title *Are we but rats?* in the French weekly magazine *Le Nouvel Observateur*, 5 February 1973. Moscovici is a prominent French social psychologist. Translation is mine.
3. Quoted from an address of the then Vice-President of the United States in Chicago, published in *Psychology Today*, January 1972.
4. Quoted from "Psychology and ideology", the opening paper of the first issue of the journal *Cognition*, 1972, *1*, 1–46, under the name of the famous American linguist.
5. Quoted from S. Modgil and C. Modgil (Eds), 1987, p.72. The author is professor at the University of Geneva.
6. Quoted from an obituary published in *The Guardian*, 28 August 1990, under the title "Fanatical guru of behaviourism". The author is a distinguished British professor of psychology.
7. Quoted from an obituary published in the reputable French daily paper *Le Monde*, 21 August 1990. Translation is mine.
8. 7, 4, 1984 ; see also Catania and Harnad, 1988.
9. R. W. Proctor and D. J. Weeks, *The goal of B. F. Skinner and behavior analysis*, New York, Heidelberg: Springer, 1990.
10. See, among other texts on that particular issue, the introductory chapter of *Contingencies of reinforcement*, 1969, and Chapter 3 in this book.
11. Skinner himself was aware of his own evolution, and of imperfections in formulating some of the problems he had been dealing with. He has commented on several occasions on his early work. An especially enlightening case is the paper entitled "The behavior of organisms at 50" (Skinner, 1989, Chapter 12).
12. Piéron, H. 1908.
13. As opposed, after the dichotomy suggested by Dilthey, to the sciences of the mind, or *Geistwissenschaften*. The debate is not extinct in contemporary psychology and more generally in contemporary philosophy of science. The issue at stake is whether a frontier should be traced beyond which different tools of investigation should be used (for example hermeneutics rather than heuristics), and, if this is the case, at which point such a frontier should be drawn. Should the realm of human sciences encompass individual human

behaviour, or only social life and culture? Another view is that each level of complexity requires appropriate methodological tools, but not basically different epistemological concepts.

# 2 Sketch for a Portrait

## BIOGRAPHICAL LANDMARKS

Scientific works have an existence of their own, independent of the scientists who produced them. They are, as Popper would put it, part of *World 3*: that is, the set of all those cultural objects created by humans throughout history that are now part of our social environment. The intrinsic quality of a scientific contribution has nothing to do with the feelings of the scientist, or with the events of his personal life. The biography of great creators is valuable material for historians of science and arts, or for psychologists interested in the creative process. It is usually not useful in appraising the work itself. In exposing Skinner's work and in clarifying some current mistakes about it, we should not, normally, need to refer to the man.

I shall, however, provide a few biographical landmarks, for two reasons. The first relates to our habits and taste: in spite of the preceding remarks, everyone likes to know about the man or woman behind a piece of work, be it a novel, a painting or an equation. The media have largely encouraged that trend in their own way of popularising science, and I shall not go against it, forcing my reader to intellectual austerity and unsatisfied curiosity.

The second reason has to do with a peculiar situation already alluded to. Skinner has been attacked on many sides. Part of the attacks have been against various aspects of his ideas or writings, and are, as such, in the tradition of fair intellectual debate, however violent it can be on some occasions. But part of the attacks have been *ad hominem*; and more often than not they have been mixed with arguments about ideas. It is therefore necessary to disentangle slanderous rumours from sound controversy. A brief sketch of the character and life of B. F. Skinner will suffice.

Little was known of Skinner's life, except to close friends and relatives, until the publication of his autobiography, issued in three volumes from 1976 (when he was 70) to 1983 (a short autobiographical paper appeared in 1970 as an opening chapter of a *Festschrift* volume (Dews, 1970)). In the first volume of the trilogy, *Particulars of my life* (1976), Skinner tells the story of his childhood and adolescence, until his admission to Harvard, which was the starting-point of his career as a psychologist. The story would not be very different for thousands of other children who grew up in the first quarter of the twentieth century in any small town in the eastern part of the USA. In a way, it tells us more about provincial life in those days than about an exceptional individual destiny: Skinner's young days were not exceptional. His father was a lawyer, which gave him some status in the small railroad town of Susquehanna, in Pennsylvania State, though not quite up to his ambition. His mother, as all middle-class women in those days, took care of the house and family. She was handsome, clever, and a good Presbyterian. Fred had a brother, younger by two years, who died at the age of 16.

The young Fred liked school. A first and lasting passion took possession of him, under the influence of a cultured teacher: reading. At the age of 14, he was puzzled by the debates about the real identity of William Shakespeare, and read Bacon, whose work would later influence his scientific thinking. He was a "normal" boy, with more interests in books than in sport. He liked building and designing things, from sleds and model airplanes to a perpetual motion machine—which, he confesses, did not really work!

Fred entered Hamilton College at the usual age, where he did not find the stimulating intellectual context he had expected. Most students were not really involved in what they studied, and Skinner resented having to do uninteresting things, like attending the chapel service. Except for his enjoyable and profitable contacts with the Dean's family, where he served as a tutor to one of the children and where he came across interesting books, music and visitors, college life did not appeal to him. He reacted by playing hoaxes, and eventually got involved in student anti-establishment revolt, of a much milder and local, purely literary, style than the campus revolutions 40 years later ! He tells of a hoax he played with a friend at the beginning of one of his college years. They had posters printed and spread around announcing a lecture, on the campus, by Charlie Chaplin, supposedly under the "official" auspices of their professor of composition. The local newspapers gave the event wide publicity, and the whole area was turned upside down. A crowd of potential listeners drove to the campus and a swarm of children gathered at the railway station to welcome the great actor. This was only the first of a series of "nihilistic gestures" that were more directly addressed towards the Faculty and the symbols of the institution.

When Fred left college, he felt like engaging in a literary career. He read Proust, partly in the recently published translation of the first volumes of *A la recherche du temps perdu*, but in French for other volumes. This did not meet his father's wish to see him study law, and possibly join him as partner. However, his father accepted his staying at home, just as a start for his work as a writer. No piece of literature emerged, only A *digest of decisions of the Anthracite Board of Conciliation*, a hack job taken to rescue himself from his literary disaster. He fooled around, spending six months in Greenwich Village, then a summer in Europe. Finally, he turned his back on literary ambitions. He came across modern psychology—Watson, through a paper by Russell—and decided to replace literature with science.

Skinner himself commented with humour on the failure of his literary career:

> I had failed as a writer, because I had had nothing important to say, but I could not accept that explanation. It was literature which must be at fault. A girl I had played tennis with in high school—a devout Catholic who later became a nun—had once quoted Chesterton's remark about a character of Thackeray's: "Thackeray didn't know it but she drank." I generalized the principle to all literature. A writer might portray human behavior accurately, but he did not therefore understand it. I was to remain interested in human behavior, but the literary method had failed me ; I would turn to the scientific. Alf Evers, the artist, had eased the transition. "Science," he once told me, "is the art of the twentieth century." The relevant science appeared to be psychology, though I had only the vaguest idea of what that meant.[1]

Having given up literature, Skinner was later to become one of the best scientific writers of our time. He eventually returned to literary genres in his Utopian novel, his essay *Beyond freedom and dignity* and in a number of non-technical papers.

Skinner entered Harvard for the Fall semester in 1928 at the age of 24. He decided to fill the gaps in his psychological knowledge and to catch up quickly with the graduate students. He worked hard, allowing himself minimum leisure time, devoted mainly to music. He completed his Ph.D in psychology in 1931. His thesis was of a purely theoretical nature: it dealt with the concept of the reflex. It was a first landmark in his reflection on the causation of behaviour.

Skinner had, at that time, already adhered to the behaviourist position, that was not much praised in the Harvard Psychology Department. It was headed by E. G. Boring (whose *History of experimental psychology* became a classic) who remained a firm opponent of Watson's position. But Skinner's intellectual qualities were impressive enough to convince everyone.[2] He was offered the possibility of staying at Harvard, at the laboratory of Crozier, a physiologist, where he had carried out his experiments while a graduate student. He did not leave Harvard until 1936, spending the last three years as a Junior Prize Fellow of the recently created Society of Fellows, "at the time the most generous support a young scholar could ask for"—and certainly the most prestigious.

In 1936, Skinner was offered a teaching position at the University of Minnesota, where he continued his experimental work and further elaborated his theoretical views on what would become his major scientific contribution, i.e. the *operant conditioning* model (as we would say today). He published his first book, *The behavior of organisms*, in 1938. It is still a classic reference for those who study the behaviourist schools of thought or want to understand the elaboration of Skinner's thinking about behaviour.

Leaving out the details of a period that Skinner himself considers as the most rewarding he experienced as a teacher, I shall point only to two features of his Minnesota days. One concerns his private life. In the same year that he moved to Minnesota he married Yvonne Blue, who had studied literature at the University of Chicago. They had two daughters, whom we shall mention later on. The second point has to do with his scientific activities, and is important if we want to understand later developments. Although his experiments were mainly with animals—preferably rats and pigeons—Skinner retained an interest in human behaviour. In fact, as with most experimental psychologists using animals as subjects in the laboratory at that time, he was not primarily concerned with species' specific behaviour but with general laws of behaviour, as general physiologists used rabbits and frogs to draw general physiological laws. But, more specifically, he spent some time on aspects of human behaviour at first sight quite remote from rats' conditioned lever-pressing: literature and verbal behaviour. He occasionally taught a course on the psychology of literature. And he laid the foundations of his later book on *Verbal behavior*.

After a short interlude at Indiana University, as Chairman of the Psychology Department, Skinner returned to Harvard in 1948, where he remained for the rest of his career. At the time of his death, he held the position of Emeritus Edgar Pierce Professor of Psychology, after the name of the Chair he had occupied before his retirement, and still enjoyed an office space at William James Hall.

The Indiana period, otherwise greatly burdened with administrative duties, was marked by a major intellectual event. He wrote the Utopian novel *Walden Two*, published in 1948. The title is reminiscent of Walden pond, near Concord, Massachusetts, where the writer Henry David Thoreau, in the late nineteenth century, had retired for one year, for an experience in what we would today call the ecological way of life. The book describes a small community where people live a harmonious and creative life, void of the useless complications and of the waste of resources typical of modern life. This was Skinner's first large-scale application to human behaviour of the scientific principles he had drawn from his experimental work. But it is in a way more than that. It reflected Skinner's deep concern for the problems of modern man and modern society. That this concern was not only a rational one was clearly shown by the way in which the book was written. While he admitted being a rather slow writer—producing an average of two words per minute in his scientific papers—he wrote *Walden Two* in less than two months, and with great emotion, as a sort of "self-therapy", according to his own words. A "positive" Utopia, in contrast to Huxley's *Brave new world*, the book is crucial for grasping Skinner's thinking, and it is also the piece of work that is the most revealing of his character and personal preoccupations.

# A CONTINUING CONCERN FOR HUMAN AFFAIRS

From then on, writings dealing with human behaviour would accumulate, once more in the scientific vein: in 1953, *Science and human behavior*, followed four years later by *Verbal behavior* (1957) which gave the linguist Chomsky the occasion for his famous critical review. While experiments on animals were being carried out more efficiently than ever with a small group of co-workers and bright graduate students—resulting in the publication of the technical *Schedules of reinforcement* (Ferster & Skinner, 1957)—Skinner engaged in several specific fields of application. One was education, another was behaviour disturbances.

There is nothing surprising in the fact that a psychologist, particularly if he specialises in learning mechanisms, gets interested in education. Thorndike, Thurstone, Piaget and Bruner are only examples from a long list. Skinner's motivation, however, came from a casual visit he made to the classroom of one of his daughters, where he was struck by the absurdity of the situation:

> Here were twenty extremely valuable organisms. Through no fault of her own the teacher was violating almost everything we knew about the learning process. I began to analyze the contingencies of reinforcement which might be useful in teaching school subjects and designed a series of teaching machines which would permit the teacher to provide such contingencies for individual students.[3]

Skinner's analysis of the teaching-learning processes was to have a tremendous influence on educational research and—unfortunately to a lesser extent—educational practices. But it also released violent attacks, more particularly addressed to his project of teaching machines. The word *machine* evoked the threat of mechanised education, and raised the opposition of all those attached to a "humanistic" approach to education. The debate was a passionate one. Opponents failed to understand the points made by Skinner in his criticism of current educational practices and to foresee the development of the new technologies he had envisaged. Teaching machines have changed their name to computer-assisted learning, which nobody complains about, and Skinner's pioneering work is usually not even mentioned in introductions to a now widely accepted and fashionable "technology of teaching".

Skinner's approach to educational problems was typical of his style in dealing with human problems in general. He started with a critical analysis of traditional conceptions and practices, in the light of scientific concepts, and he then defined the main lines of a suitable application of the latter to the field concerned. Altogether, he tested his proposals himself in his own teaching : he designed a programmed course, implemented it mechanically, using a record turntable, and made an experimental application of it with his undergraduates at Harvard, correcting the program as many times as needed as a function of results, to finally publish it in the form of a programmed textbook (Holland & Skinner, 1961).

Skinner collected his papers on education up to 1968 in a book, *The technology of teaching*. But he never lost interest in educational matters in later years, as testified by the place devoted to them in his recent writings.[4]

At about the same time as Skinner engaged in the field of education, some of his students were venturing into applications to mental patients. As with education, this was not the first attempt to apply the principles of learning to abnormal behaviour. Watson himself had been a pioneer in the field, and Pavlov had shown permanent concern for psychopathology. More recently, members of the Yale school had put much energy into trying to cross-fertilise dynamic psychology and learning theory, leading Dollard and Miller[5] to undertake a translation of the processes observed in psychotherapy in terms of learning mechanisms. In some way, what was soon to be called *behaviour therapy* already had a history.[6] But Skinner and his followers gave it a decisive impetus, providing it with a renewed formulation of learning principles, with a wealth of empirical findings, suggesting explanatory models for pathological behaviours and strategies for modifying them. They also put emphasis on methodological rigour in transferring the experimental approach to the clinical situation.

The movement developed rapidly, and in many directions, sometimes unexpectedly, as is often the case in the domain of clinical psychology. Skinner, of course, cannot be blamed for errors, excesses, conflicts, breaches of ethical rules and oversimplifications that occasionally occurred in behaviour-modification practices. Nor can he be held responsible for changes in theoretical discourse—an interesting shift from *behavioural* to *cognitivo-behavioural*, then to *cognitive*. He was never concerned with orthodoxy, and he never thought of maintaining the coherence of an official school.

The latter remark might look surprising, since Skinner is often represented as an authoritarian personality, with a wish for power that he could fortunately only exert over rats in his laboratory. All those who have approached him will testify to the contrary. He was a most urbane and tolerant person, in scientific exchange as well as in private conversation. He showed no taste for harsh polemics, and would leave unfair arguments unanswered rather than engage in dispute. As a teacher, he could hardly be less directive than he was. He would never impose his own views, even to those working close to him. He has certainly been widely honoured and respected by his followers, and invited hundreds of times to contribute to their meetings, journals or other undertakings, but he never cared for keeping them under his control, as Freud did, in the most sectarian style, banishing dissidents; as Piaget did—of whom a respectful and admiring colleague once said in his presence and on a most formal academic occasion that "his genius was matched only by the childishness of his character";[7] as Lorenz did, anathematising deviationists of the British and American schools of ethology for their compromises with behaviourists.[8] Skinner was never one of those sacred monsters whose personal charisma is closely mixed with their intellectual influence.

Skinner is also frequently pictured as a narrow-minded scientist, who believed that the world is concentrated in that little part of it he happened to study, who thought that human beings are like pigeons or rats, because he had long ceased to share normal people's interest in human feelings, emotions and creations. This hasty judgement ignores the refined musician, spending hours at his spinnet, the amateur of literature, reading French classics in their original version, the connoisseur of Diderot, Stendhal and Proust, no less aware of the richness of human culture than any of his fellow psychologists professing humanism, and no less interested in his own personal experience. To the prominent French psychologist Paul Fraisse, who visited him shortly before he retired and asked him how he would keep himself busy, he replied: "I shall take care of my inner life." This was no abjuration of behaviourism. It was a way of pointing out that inner life is what it is, whatever the scientific manner used to describe and explain it, just as the rainbow retained all its beauty after Newton had accounted for the breaking up of white light into its colour components, to use Skinner's favourite comparison.

## A CASE HISTORY IN SLANDEROUS DISPARAGING : THE "BABY BOX" STORY

In spite of his gentle personality—or possibly because of it—Skinner has been exposed to personal attacks, to extravagant accusations, to nasty rumours. Of course, the individual was not at stake, but his ideas about education, about psychological treatment, about society were. The story of the "aircrib" illustrates that better than any other example.

In 1943, the Skinners decided to have a second child. After his wife had remarked that she somewhat dreaded the constraints of the first year, Skinner decided to do something to alleviate the burden. He analysed the ways babies were cared for and considered possible simplifications, while improving comfort, social interchange and the mother's satisfaction. The solution was the aircrib, or "baby-tender" as he called it. This was a spacious compartment, mounted on a wheeled table, with a large glass window, temperature and air control, in which the baby could stay naked and comfortable, kept in the presence of the mother wherever she was working in the house. A strip of sheeting covered over a canvas, which served as a mattress; this could be moved to a clean section as needed by simple cranking. The baby, rather than suffering from excessive cover or from being wet, or simply from being awake and alone, could move freely, in an optimally stable atmosphere, and in permanent visual contact with the mother at times when the latter was busy and would not be able to pick the baby up.

The baby-tender was ready to receive Deborah Skinner as she returned from the obstetric clinic. She spent a fairly happy baby life in it, with just a little more attention from a less exhausted mother than usual and grew up quite normally later on. She was healthy and especially resistant to colds. A few months after her birth, a ladies' magazine reported on the device, and it was the start of the public debate about the "baby box". The word had been used in the title of the article, unfortunately, and it led to the confusion with the experimental conditioning chamber, known as the "Skinner box". This confusion was exploited for years by detractors who accused Skinner of having carried out experiments on his own daughter. This story suffices to indicate that such accusation was really besides the point, since Skinner's motivation when building the aircrib was not to build another experiment, but merely to meet the legitimate wish of his wife for easier child care.

A few parents adopted the device for their own child, but it never became really popular. It had a period of renewed success—a moderate one, since only a few hundred units were sold—between 1957 and 1967 when they were produced by a small company. Occasionally, a former "box-raised baby" would be in a Skinner audience and would come up to him with a happy smile at the end of the lecture. Thirty years after Deborah Skinner's pioneering experience, a German psychologist published results on the psychological and physiological benefits of raising babies in a comparable environment, to Skinner's satisfaction.[9] This did not compensate, perhaps, for slanderous rumours that went on for years about the horrible treatment imposed by the Harvard psychologist upon his poor, defenceless daughter, and about the dreadful consequences it had on her. If it had dreadful consequences at all, it was only those of hostile attacks indirectly aimed at her father's ideas. He summarises in the last pages of his autobiography, in a rather euphemistic form, a 40-year story of misdirected attacks and slanderous gossiping:

> Deborah had survived the rumors about her. When a distinguished English critic told Harry Levin that he was sorry to hear that she had committed suicide, Harry replied, "Well, when did she do that? I was swimming with her yesterday." A well-known psychiatrist told Eunice Shriver that the child we "raised in a box" became psychotic; he apologized abjectly when I wrote to ask where he had heard the story. Later it was said that Deborah was suing me. These rumors were sometimes fostered by clinical psychologists who found it useful in criticizing behavior therapy. One night, just as I was falling asleep, the phone rang and a young man said, "Professor Skinner, is it true that you kept one of your children in a cage?" Possibly because of the baby-tender and the rumors about it I had been too solicitous.[10]

Deborah Skinner is now an artist in London, married to a professor of economics, and she was until her father's death in as harmonious relations as one can be. No one would have taken such an interest in her if her father had not been disturbing to many.

# HAS MANKIND A FUTURE?

Skinner's criticisms about education and psychological treatment were only part of a more general problem which had already held his attention in *Science and human behavior* and in *Walden Two*: modern society as a whole is going astray because appropriate solutions to problems are not being applied, although they are sometimes available. About half of his writings in the last 30 years or so were devoted to that issue. He thought it important enough to formulate his views for the layman in *Beyond freedom and dignity* (1971) and kept on alerting his fellow men and women in his most recent papers. His 1987 book *Upon further reflection* opens with a chapter entitled "Why we are not acting to save the world".

Skinner's message is not one that people accept easily. It hurts many established values, many deeply rooted habits. To the threatening problems mankind faces today—the pollution of the biosphere, uncontrolled demographic growth, the increasing discrepancy of wealth between nations, the growing aggressive conduct between and within nations, the wasting of resources, the use of nuclear weapons—Skinner suggests solutions that differ from popular and often-heard ones. He does not appeal to a rejection of science and to a nostalgic return to some idyllic pre-scientific way of life: on the contrary, he urges us to put to work what we know, from scientific sources, about human behaviour, as we have, and rather successfully, put to work our scientific knowledge in physical and medical matters. Nor does he appeal to some sort of spiritual revival, to a crusade of the Mind against the forces of the devil: the main error, and one that hinders any progress towards solutions, is the conception humans have of their own nature, based on an illusory belief in freedom and sovereignty. If men do not give up this illusion and endorse a more realistic view of their place in the universe, mankind could head for disaster. The danger is no less great than if mankind would obstinately refuse to recognise its dependency upon its biological environment, and the consequent necessity to preserve it. In a way, the danger is greater, since our efforts to preserve our biosphere are doomed to failure if we do not start by finding ways to implement them in daily human behaviour.

To those who think Skinner has oversimplified psychology, ignoring his warnings can have no consequences, because taking them seriously could only lead to a worsening of the situation. But who knows? He could be right, and it could be, one day, too late to tell. Sometimes, resistance to Skinner's proposals reminds me of the attitude of the medical profession when Lister insisted that doctors and surgeons should wash their hands carefully before going to their patients and before going from one patient to another, because he thought that was a source of infection. It just sounded too simple, and not worthy of serious physicians' attention. Happily enough, that simple message eventually got through and the practice was adopted.

The issue is too serious to treat with passionate invectives. It cannot be disposed of by accusing Skinner of dehumanising mankind. Maybe he has only put mankind in its right place, after Galileo, Darwin and Freud, and, by doing so, has made a contribution to giving it its true humanity.

## NOTES

1. Skinner, 1970, p.7.
2. This, as later successes in Skinner's academic career, speaks counter to the strange accusation made by Proctor and Weeks (1990) that Skinner was a fake scientist. On the contrary, he appeared so good that intelligent individuals who did not share his views have not objected to appointing him in their department. Boring must certainly be credited for having played that role at Harvard.
3. Skinner, 1970, autobiography, p.16.
4. Each of his last three books of collected papers (Skinner, 1978, 1987, 1989) contains several chapters on educational issues.
5. Dollard, J. and Miller, N. E. (1950).
6. For a history of behaviour therapy, see, among other sources, Kazdin, A. E. (1978) and Schorr, A. (1984).
7. R. Tissot, in his Inaugural Lecture, after having been appointed Professor of Psychology at the University of Geneva (published in *Médecine et Hygiène*, 26 May 1971).
8. See *Evolution and modification of behavior*, 1965. For a discussion of the evolution of Lorenz' thought itself, Chapter 6.
9. Reported in *A matter of consequences*, 1983, p.349, referring to an issue of *Time* in 1973.
10. *A matter of consequences*, 1983, pp.385–386.

# 3 The Skinner Box: A New Microscope for Psychology

## A MAJOR CONTRIBUTION TO LABORATORY TECHNIQUES

Whatever remains of Skinner's theorising and social philosophy, it is likely that experimental psychologists will continue to use the laboratory technique that has come to be called the Skinner box, in spite of the designer's insistence on labelling it "operant conditioning chamber". As this book is not intended for specialists of experimental psychology, we shall not describe in detail the properties of that procedure and the variety of problems it has made accessible. It is, however, essential, if the reader wants to correctly appraise Skinner's place in twentieth-century psychology, that he gets at least an intuitive grasp of what the Skinner box is about, and of the sort of empirical data it is able to provide. Effective observational and experimental procedures are important elements in the progress of any science; the history of natural sciences has been conditioned, among other things, by the progresses made in amplifying the power of the human eye, first by resorting to simple magnifying lenses, eventually improved in the optical mechanism of the microscope, then replaced by the much more powerful electronic microscopy devices. In the past, psychology has had its own series of technical advances, which have sometimes proved more decisive in generating breakthroughs than volumes of theorising. Contemporary cognitive psychology, for instance, makes ample use of the so-called "mental chronometry" technique, which is an application of the reaction time measurement—one of the earliest phenomena to be studied by scientific psychologists in the nineteenth century—already suggested in 1869 by the Dutch psychologist Donders.[1]

Similarly, the Skinner box is not only a piece of equipment designed and widely used for the study of acquired behaviour in animals: it has been exploited to investigate, with unprecedented efficiency, a number of other aspects of behaviour in various contexts, that will now be illustrated by typical examples. A classical issue in the history of science is whether research procedures can be described and appraised independently of the theoretical elaborations that are usually linked to them. There is obviously no all-or-none answer to that question. The microscope can be described for itself, and does not seem too much theory loaded. The Skinner box is undoubtedly more closely related to Skinner's analysis of operant behaviour, and to the general theory he has drawn from it. (Another interesting, though equally difficult issue, in each particular case, is how far the theory has been at the source of the procedure or the procedure has shaped the theory.) We shall not avoid mixing the two levels, the purely technical level and the theoretical one, in describing the procedure, but it is clear, however, that the Skinner box has acquired its own independence as a laboratory technique used by many experimenters around the world with no commitment whatsoever to Skinner's theory.

## THE OPERANT BEHAVIOUR CHAMBER

The Skinner box is basically an extremely simple device. Its simplicity has led to the erroneous conclusion that it can only help study very simple aspects of behaviour. On the contrary, simple devices (as well as simple concepts) in science often seem to give better access to complex realities than complicated ones. The wide use made of mental chronometry, referred to above, in modern cognitive psychology is another case in point.

A typical Skinner box is a chamber, the dimensions of which leave some free space for the animal subject to walk around—its size is therefore adapted to the size of the species used. It is equipped with some response device, technically called a manipulandum: that is to say, some piece of equipment, such as a lever, a plastic key or a chain, that the subject will activate. The rat or the cat will push a lever, the pigeon will peck a key, the monkey will pull a chain, etc. Usually, this simple gesture, or more correctly the movement imparted to the manipulandum, will be converted into an electric signal, easily recorded, and defined in a given experiment as a *response*. In addition to the response device, the Skinner box includes a device that delivers some reinforcing stimulus. The most classical case is a food dispenser, that delivers, under automatic control, a pellet of calibrated food, which can be used as what is called a positive reinforcer; although this would not exactly match an expert's definition of a positive reinforcer, to a lay observer it would appear that a hungry animal would find the food attractive, and that it would work to obtain it.

Here we come to the functional aspect of the Skinner box: that is, the relation between the response and the reinforcer, an aspect which is in fact defining the concept of *operant behaviour*. The principle of any experiment with the Skinner box is that the subject will obtain a reinforcer if, and only if, it has produced a response. It is, by necessity, an active organism, which can rely only upon itself to be rewarded. This is a major point, that is generally overlooked in the layman's use of the word *conditioning*, which has the connotation of constrained behaviour. In his first book, *The behavior of organisms* (1938), Skinner made it clear that he was studying the *spontaneous* behaviour of the organisms. He certainly did not mean that his rats were exhibiting free will, but that they came to the experimental situation with a set of potential behaviours that would eventually be emitted and lead to the production of the particular response required in order to be reinforced.

Skinner was to elaborate further upon the problem of the origins of that set of behaviours, as we shall see. One essential point, however, that cannot be delayed if the basic process of operant conditioning is to be understood, is the way the desired response eventually emerges from the set of "spontaneous" behaviours. In experimental practice, the transition can be observed best in the phase called *shaping* of the operant. Although there are other means to reach the same goal, it is generally convenient for the experimenter to intervene by manually controlling the reinforcement while watching his subject. Unless the subject keeps sleeping or remains prostrate in a corner of the cage—in which case there is no hope of ever obtaining the response—it will move around and produce various bits of its behavioural repertoire. In doing so it will be, at some times, closer to the manipulandum than at other times. The experimenter will make sure that a pellet is delivered precisely at those moments. He will soon observe that the animal will tend to be closer to the lever or key more often. He will progressively restrict the conditions for providing a pellet, up to the point that the final response will be produced quite normally. What has taken place is *selective* reinforcement, by the experimenter, of units of behaviour, among those produced by the subject, that eventually correspond with the particular structure or *topography* of the defined operant. The selection of the appropriate units is clearly possible only because the subject exhibits *variations* in its behaviour. We can already state that a Skinner box is an experimental (therefore admittedly artificially built) space in which behaviour is shaped and maintained by a process of selection among variations. As Skinner puts it, it is control by consequences that can be compared to the process at work in biological evolution. We shall comment on that analogy at length later. At this stage, let us come back to the basic features of the Skinner box.

## CONTINGENCIES AND SCHEDULES

The basic relation between the operant response and the reinforcement has been described above in its simplest form: it was assumed that, once the response had been shaped, it is reinforced each time it is produced. This simple relation can be changed into much more complex ones. These attracted Skinner's attention from the early days, and have been extensively explored further by many of his followers. The expression *contingencies of reinforcement* refers to the various types of relation between response and reinforcement, more precisely implemented in so-called *schedules of reinforcement*. We shall not go into the intricacies of them in depth, but a few examples are needed.

A fixed or an average number of responses can be required before a reinforcer is delivered, and the ratio *Responses per Reinforcer* extended to limits that, in animals, might challenge the cost in physical energy, and in humans occasionally result in ruin. Gambling behaviour can be analysed as resulting from a *Variable Ratio Schedule* in which the individual is rewarded intermittently after a variable number of responses (the stakes), that can be so high that the reinforcer (i.e. gains or return) will never actually be experienced. In other cases, reinforcers are available only after a time interval has elapsed; the interval can be variable, and thus unpredictable, or it can be fixed, making for a periodic patterning of behaviour, that will be described more fully below. Different schedules and contingencies can be in strength simultaneously, involving different motivational systems, or providing for comparisons between different types of cost-benefit arrangements.

Four main classes of contingencies are traditionally distinguished, that are best represented in a two-by-two matrix as follows:

TABLE 3.1
A Two-by-Two Matrix Summarising the Basic Categories of
Contingencies of Reinforcement.

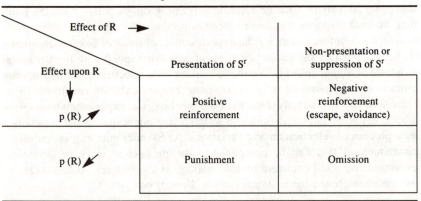

| Effect of R → | Presentation of $S^r$ | Non-presentation or suppression of $S^r$ |
|---|---|---|
| Effect upon R ↓ | | |
| p (R) ↗ | Positive reinforcement | Negative reinforcement (escape, avoidance) |
| p (R) ↙ | Punishment | Omission |

On the horizontal dimension, the consequence of the response R, either the presentation of some stimulus ($S^r$), be it attractive or aversive, or the non-presentation of an (expected) stimulus (or the suppression of a stimulus already present). On the vertical dimension, the effect of the above described relation upon the response, the probability (p) of which may increase or decrease. See text for examples.

It is easy to illustrate each box of the matrix with a concrete example from human daily life. So-called positive reinforcement contingencies have already been explained: they involve the presentation of some event, say food, as a consequence of the response, which results in an increase in the probability of that response being produced: good cooking will encourage us to return to a restaurant. (In daily language, one would probably say that the reinforcing event is attractive, or pleasant, but this is not an essential property in the view of the specialist.) Negative reinforcement refers to contingencies in which the termination or the non-presentation of some event after the response has been emitted results in the increase in probability of the response (such an event would plausibly be qualified as aversive from a subjective point of view). For example, many drivers respect speed limits not because they do not like fast driving, which indeed they do, but because it is a way to avoid being fined. Punishment contingencies involve the presentation of some "aversive" event after a defined response, with the consequence that the response will be produced less often, at least while the contingencies are in strength: occasional harsh fining will reduce fast driving in most drivers. Finally, omissions, or frustrative non-rewards as they have sometimes been called,[2] refers to contingencies in which a previously delivered "attractive" reinforcer is no longer given after the response, resulting in the extinction of the latter: a decline in food quality will reduce our visits to a previously appreciated restaurant. Though apparently technical, these definitions will help in further discussion.

## A STIMULUS-RESPONSE MODEL WITH NO STIMULUS

One important feature of the operant procedure, as designed by Skinner, is the choice of a very simple unit of behaviour, usually a short and well-specified motor act. The corresponding data recorded in a typical experiment are responses distributed in time, with the rate of responding, that is, a measure of the number of responses by units of time, as the favoured expression used in the treatment of results. There is no doubt that the choice of rate was made at the expense of the structure of responses, which Skinner did indeed neglect, with arguments that did not survive some of the criticisms formulated by ethologically inclined experimenters. Later developments have shown that the study of rate and of structure of responding are complementary (see Chapter 6). This must not hide the fact that rate has proved to be a very efficient measure for many purposes, and that many lawful empirical data have been collected and repeatedly confirmed by using the simplified procedure proposed by Skinner.

The reader will have noticed that, up to now, we have not used the word stimulus, which would appear to be an essential ingredient if, as is often claimed, Skinner is indeed a Stimulus-Response psychologist. Indeed, changing from one schedule to another, implying only a different relation between response and reinforcement, without any stimulus being introduced, will generate another, sometimes completely different pattern of response rate. Such a contrast can be observed, in a simple but quite striking case, between a schedule in which reinforcement is delivered after a fixed number of responses and a schedule in which it is available only after a given delay has elapsed: the first schedule generates sustained activity—typically high rate—while the second induces a periodic alternation of pauses and phases of responding reflecting the control by the time variable. Figure 3.1 illustrates the comparison, using the traditional cumulative record popularised by Skinner.

Of course, stimuli of all sorts can be introduced, and made to gain control over responding. However, they do not really trigger behaviour: they only define the occasions upon which responses will be reinforced. Their role will be easily grasped from some of the examples below. These have been selected, out of hundreds of possible illustrations of the use of operant techniques, only to show the variety of problems that have been dealt with, not necessarily by Skinner himself but by researchers in most varied fields.

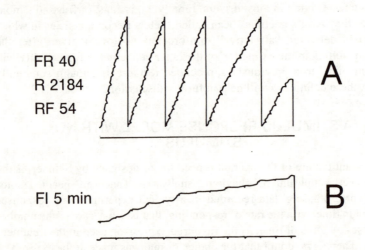

FIG. 3.1.    Two distinctive behavioural patterns under different schedules of reinforcement, without any change in external stimuli. In A, an individual cumulative curve of responses obtained under a Fixed Ratio schedule, in which 40 lever-presses were required for one reinforcement (small amount of food); in B, a curve obtained in a Fixed Interval schedule, with a 5 minutes periodicity between availability of reinforcement. Abscissa: time, i.e. duration of the session, one hour; ordinate: cumulated responses (the pen resets after 500 responses). Oblique deflections on the cumulative record show reinforcements. On the horizontal line at the bottom of B, they indicate availability of reinforcement, which is not delivered until a response is emitted. Cumulative records, made in real time during the experiment, are easy to read: the more responses per time unit (in other words the higher the rate of responses), the steeper the slope; periods with no responses produce flat sections on the curve, as in B after each reinforcement, where regular pauses reveal fine adjustment to the time interval. The subjects were cats.

## DISCRIMINATION: FROM EXTERNAL STIMULUS
## TO INTERNAL STATES

Stimulus control enters the scene when an organism is to tell the difference between two external events, for instance the colours of traffic lights. This is easily achieved by requiring a response to one colour (stop at red) and no response to green (keep moving), or by requiring a different response at each colour. Animals can be trained to make such discriminations just as well as humans. Pavlov had already obtained them using his own procedure, but he never approached the accuracy that has become routine with operant techniques. This is due essentially to the high degree of automatisation that is now the rule: Skinner had developed ingenious electromechanical devices that would ensure completely automatic control of the experiment; the computer has taken over and improved on-line control, including immediate treatment of results, even of a very complex nature. A discrete motor response, such as a key peck, is of course much easier to put under automatic control than is the salivation studied by Pavlov.

Sensory discrimination is the basis for psychophysical studies. Psychophysics is first concerned with determining which part of the physical world an organism is able to perceive—for instance, which acoustic waves produce hearing—by locating the limits, or absolute thresholds under which, and eventually beyond which, there is no "sensation". It is further concerned with the power of resolution within these limits, and to that end so-called differential thresholds are measured. This part of psychology had an early development in the last century, and it has numerous practical applications, for example in diagnosing sensory deficits.

In humans, a psychophysical experiment is classically performed by instructing the subject to signal when he perceives a stimulus, or when he can tell the difference between two close stimuli. It was thought for years that equivalent studies could not be run with animals, because they cannot be given verbal instructions about what the experimenter wants them to do. The great French physiologist Claude Bernard, who was an ardent defender of the experimental method, would admit that it has some limitations, and he gave as an example the obvious impossibility of experimentally approaching the internal world of animals' sensations. Students of behaviour have shown that he was wrong, but it was not until operant procedures were available that data on animal sensation could be collected with the same degree of rigour as in humans.

In the following example, borrowed from Maurissen (1979), absolute thresholds to tactile stimulation have been determined in one monkey, using a sophisticated vibrator as the stimulus source and a refined operant procedure. Just as for air vibrations which produce auditory sensations, the frequency (or number of cycles per second) of mechanical vibrations can be changed, as well as their amplitude. Tactile receptors detect some frequencies better than others: sensitivity is highest, corresponding to lowest thresholds, around 100cps. In Fig. 3.2, results from one experimental monkey, tested twice to check the reliability of the measurement, are shown, together with thresholds obtained, using the same technique, from a human subject. Not only are these results precise and reliable, but they match well with human data, which allows for the use of experimental animals in exploring effects (such as those of toxic agents) that can hardly be studied in humans. The same author describes the alteration of vibration thresholds following administration of a substance that enhances the efficacy of radiotherapy. This indicates a neurotoxic side-effect of the drug.

Psychopharmacologists have gone a step further in exploring the internal world of animals. They have trained animal subjects in discrimination tasks involving presumably different internal states induced by psychotropic drugs. Compounds used to relieve anxiety, depression or other unpleasant psychological conditions should, hopefully, produce changes both in the patient's observable behaviour and in his subjective feelings about himself. Rats were offered a choice between two response levers, each associated with a different drug, or with a drug as opposed to a saline solution—drug(s) and/or saline being injected prior to the experiment. Precautions were taken, as usual, to make sure that the correct choice was not made by chance; this is easily achieved by requiring a number of responses, rather than just one, which shows that the subject is not hitting the correct lever by chance,

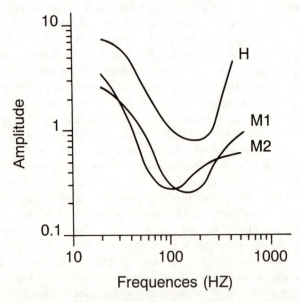

**FIG. 3.2.** Absolute thresholds to tactile vibratory stimulus obtained from one monkey ( M1 & M2; two different measurement sessions) and one human (H). Abscissa: vibration frequency in cycles per second (Hertz); ordinate: amplitude of the vibratory wave, in microns (from peak to peak); both scales in logarithmic units. The operant conditioning method provides results from animals that match those traditionally obtained from humans, with classical psychophysical methods using verbal instructions. (Adapted from Maurissen, 1979.)

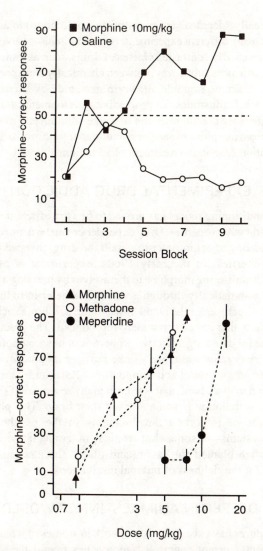

**FIG. 3.3.** Exploring the subjective world of animals. Upper graph: rats were trained to discriminate between their internal state after an injection of morphine and an injection of saline solution. Successive points on the two curves show the percentage of responses (ordinate) on the "correct" lever, that is reinforced when morphine has been injected, throughout a series of 40 sessions (4 per Block, on the abscissa). It can be seen that early in training subjects confounded the two internal states, but they readily learned to discriminate between them.

Bottom graph: generalising to internal states induced by closely related drugs. Rats trained as above to discriminate between morphine and saline were exposed to test with methadone or meperidine, two morphine-like compounds. They generalise their discrimination to these drugs. As can be seen from the dose–response relation, the discrimination is a function of the dose administered.

(Redrawn after Hirschhorn, 1978.)

but that it has really "decided" (as cognitivists would put it) to activate it. It has been shown, by many different experimenters,[3] that animals are able to discriminate not only between clearly contrasted classes of drugs, such as tranquillisers versus stimulants, but, in a more subtle way, between chemically close compounds within the same class. A simple example, drawn from a study by Hirschhorn (1978) is shown in Fig. 3.3. It illustrates the progessive development of a discrimination between a presumably neutral injection of saline solution and morphine, and the generalisation from morphine to another narcotic analgesic, methadone, sometimes used as a transition drug in the treatment of addiction.

## EXPERIMENTAL DRUG ADDICTION

The operant conditioning model has proved to be very efficient in testing drugs for potential addictive properties. Drug dependence can be defined behaviourally as a strong tendency to act in order to obtain the drug, that can be said to have reinforcing properties. In the early 1960s, experimenters offered rats the possibility of administering morphine to themselves by pressing a lever. The drug was delivered automatically through a veinous catheter introduced surgically, so that it would directly enter the blood flow. Figure 3.4 shows such a preparation, and typical results that have been widely reproduced. The practical usefulness of the technique for detecting addictive properties of new compounds is obvious.

Another discovery that was closely linked to operant procedures, in the early 1950s, is called intracerebral self-stimulation.[4] Rats, and later other species, have been shown to work hard, that is to emit many responses if the consequence was an electric stimulation in some areas of their brain. This phenomenon has been the source of important developments in the psychophysiology of motivational systems—a somewhat ironical outcome if we remember that Skinner was often blamed for having substituted the mechanical concept of reinforcement for the richness of internal motivations.

## DEEPER IN ANIMALS' INNER WORLD

Operant procedures have also been put to work in studies of what is called today animal cognition. Current cognitivist approaches favour the study of mental representations and processes. A large part of cognitive research bears on humans, and cognitive psychology probably owes part of its success to its focusing on the human mind. The uniqueness of the human species, however, can never be taken for granted unless animals have been checked for possible equally performing processes. Therefore, animal cognition has attracted many experimenters, fascinated by animals' capacity to build concepts, to manipulate symbolic objects, to solve problems, even of a logical rather than a practical nature, to process mental representations or to learn some rudiments of language. Studies aimed at teaching language to chimpanzees, carried out in the 1960s and

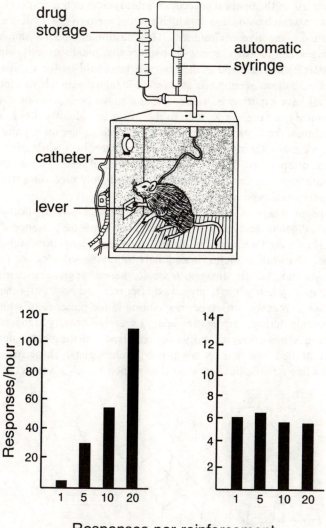

Responses per reinforcement

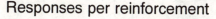

FIG. 3.4. Testing addictive properties of drugs. Top, a drawing showing the device for the study of drug self-administration in animals. Pressing the lever produces, under the defined schedule of reinforcement, a calibrated dose of the drug delivered from an automatic syringe through an intravenous catheter fixed surgically. (After Tirelli, 1987.)

Above, cocaine addiction in one rat. Left: responses emitted in one hour session (ordinate) as a function of the number of responses required for one reinforcement (1mg cocaine per kg of body-weight) under a Fixed Ratio schedule (abscissa). Right: corresponding number of drug infusions per hour. The rat managed to obtain the same total amount of cocaine, adjusting its response output as required by the schedule. (After Pickens and Thompson, 1968.)

1970s, made use of the operant procedure; most typical in this respect has been Rumbaugh's research with Lana, in which a sort of hieroglyphic code was taught in a controlled interactive environment. The question of whether animals have mental images and representations—whatever that means exactly—has long been a matter of debate. And if they have, what could be the similarities or differences with those phenomena as inferred in humans remains an intriguing issue. We all have experienced visual after-effects, a perception of something that is obviously not present as such in the world outside after the fixing of a certain stimulus. For instance, after looking at a red square on a white screen, we perceive a green (complementary colour) square for a while after the red stimulus has disappeared. This is a very simple case of seeing in the absence of a stimulus, though it is dependent upon an immediately preceding stimulation and upon peripheral processes.

This type of image is easily evidenced in animals, as in the following experiment.[5] Pigeons were reinforced for pecking a key in the presence of a green stimulus. They were then tested in the presence of red or yellow stimuli, or in the presence of a white stimulus immediately following red, green or yellow. If pigeons have coloured after-images, as we do, these after-images should occur, in that situation, when white is presented after red, and not in all other cases. This is exactly what was observed: responding in the presence of white-after-red (presumably during a green after-image) was significantly higher.

After-images, however, are hardly to be confused with the mental images that have been studied in depth by cognitive psychologists. These are not just peripheral after-effects, but representations upon which a subject is said to

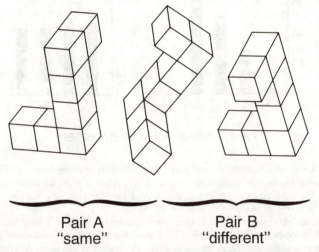

Pair A          Pair B
"same"        "different"

FIG. 3.5.   Samples of stimuli used by Shepard in the study of mental rotation (see Shepard & Cooper, 1982).

operate internally. Shephard is known for his elegant experiments on mental rotation in humans.[6] The principle consists of presenting human subjects with stimuli such as those reproduced in Fig. 3.5 A, and asking them to decide if a comparison stimulus, for instance B or C, is the same presented in a different orientation in space, or whether it is different. Using the classical measure of Reaction Time as an index of mental processes at work, Shephard has shown that the time before deciding varies as a function of the rotation angle, that is to say the size, in degrees of arc, of the modification imposed on A to have it appear as B. This is taken as evidence that human subjects operate on mental representations in much the same way as they do on directly perceived objects.[7] Is this to be considered as a higher cognitive process, specific to humans? Results obtained on pigeons testify to the contrary. In Delius' laboratory, in Germany, pigeons have been submitted to a task similar to Shephard's mental rotation test (Hollard & Delius, 1982); their performance was even better than humans' (Fig. 3.6). This is only one additional example of the efficiency of animal-laboratory procedures designed by Skinner to answer questions raised as to the human specificity of cognitive activities widely explored by contemporary psychology, showing their contribution to important issues of comparative psychology, and therefore of general psychology as well.

# INTERNAL CLOCKS

As a last example, let us enter a field that has progressed tremendously since the development of operant techniques, namely the psychology of time. The adaptation of living organisms to time, and especially to periodic events, has been observed for centuries, but the scientific study of these phenomena, under the label of chronobiology, has been slow to gain recognition. The circadian rhythms of our body are now familiar to us all: many of us have had occasion to experience their disruptions in jet flights or shift-work. The organism's capacity to adjust to time, however, is not limited to the natural synchronisers, such as the alternation of night and day: it is, in fact, exceedingly flexible and extends to whatever temporal regularities may occur in their environment, and to the refined discrimination of the duration of external events as well as of the organism's own activity.

Although it was intuitively known from human experience, this capacity for dealing with time had been little explored, with the exception of a few classical studies on humans of time estimation, which have been contaminated, unfortunately, by the use the subjects inevitably make of chronometric aids— for instance, they cannot help counting silently when estimating the duration in seconds. Animals are presumably free of such technological transfers—though they resort to somewhat comparable tricks of their own, as we now know—and are, therefore, better subjects for studying basic processes in temporal regulations of behaviour.

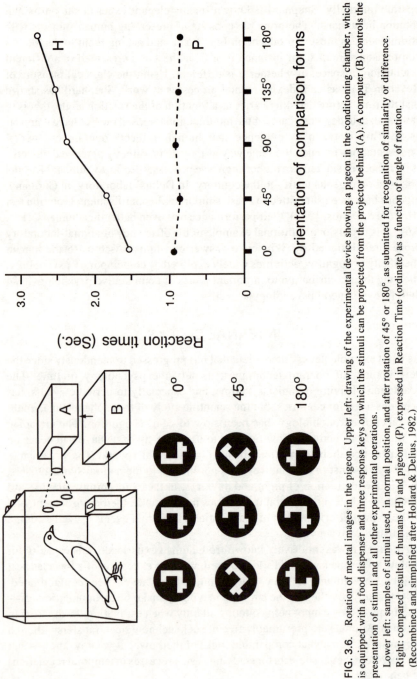

FIG. 3.6. Rotation of mental images in the pigeon. Upper left: drawing of the experimental device showing a pigeon in the conditioning chamber, which is equipped with a food dispenser and three response keys on which the stimuli can be projected from the projector behind (A). A computer (B) controls the presentation of stimuli and all other experimental operations.

Lower left: samples of stimuli used, in normal position, and after rotation of 45° or 180°, as submitted for recognition of similarity or difference.

Right: compared results of humans (H) and pigeons (P), expressed in Reaction Time (ordinate) as a function of angle of rotation. (Recombined and simplified after Hollard & Delius, 1982.)

In spite of some pioneering experiments in Pavlov's laboratory, efficient tools for such study were lacking, unfortunately, until operant procedures were developed, and their automatisation improved. Skinner himself was interested in the effect of one of his schedules of reinforcement, in which food was made available according to a fixed periodicity, as we have described earlier. He described at length, in his first book,[8] how a rat's responding is entrained by the periodic reinforcing event, producing an alternation of pauses and activity periods, which can be seen as a *spontaneous* temporal regulation,[9] spontaneous meaning here that it is not required as a condition for reinforcement. He later described contingencies in which the subject has to pace its responses if it is to be reinforced: in this case, it has, indeed, to estimate a minimum delay implemented, so to speak, in its own motor behaviour. Building on this early work, other experimenters have designed increasingly refined procedures that provide for precise assessment of an animal's capacity for timing its own activity or for estimating the duration of external stimuli. Species have been compared, in search of orderly differences in timing competence. Various response units have been tested in the same species or individual in order to check for the most "species fair" situation with respect to timing competence. Developmental studies have been carried out on very young and old subjects. Mathematical models have been elaborated to account for the peculiarities of the observed performances, and in some cases they have been compared with models applied to biological rhythms. Relations to the latter have been explored, with the basic question in mind: is the internal clock common to biological rhythms and acquired temporal regulations? Humans and animals have been contrasted, leading to the discovery that cognitive development and language bring in new variables that change the properties of temporal regulations. For example, while infants behave very much like animals under periodic contingencies (the previously defined Fixed-Interval schedule), children, after they have acquired language, and adults, exhibit different patterns, presumably based on their implicit interpretation of the situation as either requiring sustained responding (which is wrong, but does not reduce the chances of being rewarded), or being based on correct timing, which humans usually achieve by resorting to some mental counting or other chronometric device.[10]

These are only examples selected from the numerous applications of operant techniques in most various areas of the study of behaviour, as it is practised today not only in psychological laboratories proper, but in multidisciplinary research involving behavioural aspects, together with other dimensions, neurobiological, pharmacological, toxicological and the like. Skinner's ingeniousness in designing a fairly "general purpose" experimental procedure is to be credited for the multifaceted research it has made possible.

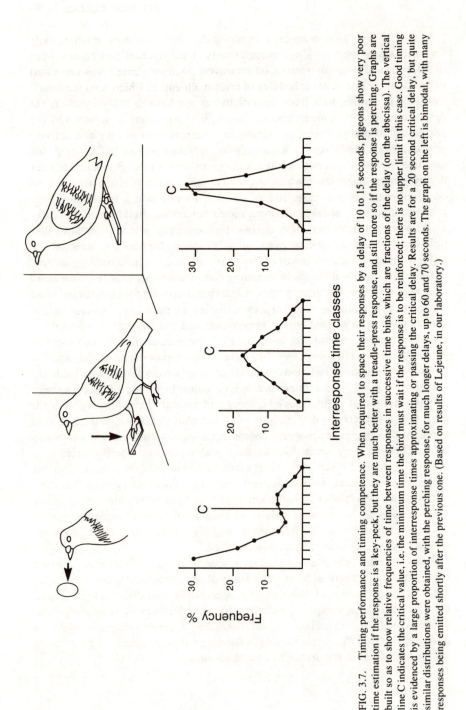

Interresponse time classes

FIG. 3.7. Timing performance and timing competence. When required to space their responses by a delay of 10 to 15 seconds, pigeons show very poor time estimation if the response is a key-peck, but they are much better with a treadle-press response, and still more so if the response is perching. Graphs are built so as to show relative frequencies of time between responses in successive time bins, which are fractions of the delay (on the abscissa). The vertical line C indicates the critical value, i.e. the minimum time the bird must wait if the response is to be reinforced; there is no upper limit in this case. Good timing is evidenced by a large proportion of interresponse times approximating or passing the critical delay. Results are for a 20 second critical delay, but quite similar distributions were obtained, with the perching response, for much longer delays, up to 60 and 70 seconds. The graph on the left is bimodal, with many responses being emitted shortly after the previous one. (Based on results of Lejeune, in our laboratory.)

# NOTES

1. Original publication in Dutch. Translation Donders, 1969.
2. This labelling has been proposed by J. Gray, 1975.
3. See Colpaert and Slangen (1982), Glennon, Järbe and Frankenheim (1991).
4. Olds & Milner, 1954.
5. Williams, 1974.
6. Shephard, R. N. and Cooper, L. A. (1982). *Mental images and their transformations.* Cambridge: the MIT Press.
7. Shephard's results have also been the occasion of a debate between two opposite interpretations, propositional versus iconic, of the mechanisms involved, a debate that need not retain us here.
8. *The behavior of organisms* (1938), Chapter 4, entitled "Periodic reconditioning".
9. We have used the expression *temporal regulations*, in French *régulations temporelles*, from 1962, to name behavioural adjustments to time and duration, be it of external events as in the estimation of the duration of external events, or of a subject's own behaviour, as in the examples given here. For further reading in this area, see Richelle and Lejeune (1980).
10. Many of the issues alluded to here are discussed in Gibbon and Allan (1984), Michon and Jackson (1985), Blackman and Lejeune (1990) and Macar, Pouthas and Friedman (1992).

# SKINNER AND THE EUROPEAN TRADITION: PAVLOV, FREUD, LORENZ AND PIAGET

# 4 Pavlov's Ambiguous Heritage

## AN UNFORTUNATE MISNAMING

The use of the same term *conditioning* to designate the behavioural phenomenon involved in Skinner's procedure and the type of association described earlier by Pavlov, has had unfortunate consequences. In the language of the layman, and sometimes in the psychologist's use, *conditioning* evokes a very simple, mechanistic type of learning, possibly at work in elementary activities of animals, but of little importance in human actions. Moreover, it has a connotation of forced control over behaviour, the organism submitting passively to the will of the experimenter. It is even often felt that conditioning is an artificial phenomenon, born from the perverse manipulation of animals' behaviour by scientists in their laboratory, but with little if any relevance to real life. All this is equally applied to Pavlovian conditioning as well as to the operant conditioning described by Skinner. It is a serious confusion, however, that requires some clarification, since for Skinner operant conditioning was something totally different from Pavlovian conditioning. This is not to say that the connotations of the word, as summarised here, correctly apply to Pavlovian conditioning, but that what Pavlov has studied pertains to a level quite distinct from and far more elementary than what Skinner has analysed.

Pavlov's model is well known from his classical experiment on the salivary reaction in dogs. In the procedure used by Pavlov, salivation was shifted from food, its natural eliciting stimulus—or *unconditioned* stimulus—to the sound of a bell, an initially neutral event with respect to salivation, eventually changed, through association, to the status of *conditioned* stimulus. Pavlov and his co-workers elaborated on that simple event, in many diverse directions: they complicated the experimental situation by introducing and combining inhibitory and excitatory stimuli; they explored the discriminatory capacities of their subjects; they induced disturbances, the so-called experimental neurosis, in the conditioning process by manipulating certain factors; they extended their initial study of associations with external stimuli to the domain of interoception, the sensory information brought to the brain by visceral receptors; they even turned to the level of language and investigated the relations between what they called the Second Signal System and the first one, limited to non-verbal stimuli and common to animals and humans.

This selective enumeration is enough to give an idea of the diversity and complexity of Pavlovian studies of a basic phenomenon which exhibits highly dynamic properties. When looked at carefully, Pavlovian conditioning itself does not appear as elementary or stereotyped, as the popular view would have it. It is also clear that Pavlov provided us with abundant evidence that human organisms do not escape the laws of conditioning. However, the process he described is basically linked to an initial physiological connection: that is, the relation between the unconditioned stimulus and the response that follows—food and salivation, electric shock and leg withdrawal, for example. And when the response is produced by the conditioned stimulus, it remains without any effect, in the sense that the experimenter decides whether or not it will be reinforced: that is to say, whether or not it will be followed by the presentation of the unconditioned stimulus. Hence, perhaps, the idea that conditioning means submitting to some external agent's will or caprice.

These are precisely the points that make for the distinctive features of operant conditioning. If we compare the food delivered as a reinforcer in the operant situation with the Pavlovian unconditioned stimulus, we must note one important difference: it is not linked, before any conditioning takes place, to the operant response. Food does not produce a lever press in rats. And, still more crucial, the agent producing the reinforcer is the subject (by emitting the response), not the experimenter, who is only responsible for having arranged the contingencies. Contrary to the subject of a Pavlovian experiment, the organism in an operant situation is not passive: he plays an essential part in the interaction with the environment.

## SOME HISTORICAL SPECULATIONS

How is it that, given these basic differences, the same term *conditioning* has been used? And why complain about a confusion for which Skinner himself seems to be responsible, having adopted a label that would almost inevitably produce it? These are sound historical questions. Part of the answer can be found in the way American psychology had assimilated Pavlov's work and part in the context of Skinner's early work.

Although not a psychologist himself—he always viewed his own work as the work of a physiologist, studying brain functions, after having studied the functions of the digestive tract—Pavlov was adopted by American behaviourism because he provided a demonstration of the feasibility of an objective study of behavioural events. He did not, however, distract them from their preference for motor learning, a model more relevant to human learning in general than the study of autonomic reactions. This very active field of learning was widely based on studies of instrumental learning, extensively using the popular maze technique. A major theoretical background was provided by the Law of Effect, formulated by Thorndike; the law stated that those behaviours followed by success would tend to be stamped in the repertoire of an organism, while those followed by failure would be stamped out. This anticipated the more concise formulation that behaviour is controlled by its consequences. Skinner, of course, acknowledged the relationship.

When he came across Thorndike's work on cats learning to open the bolt of their "puzzle box", Pavlov assimilated it immediately to his own model of conditioning.[1] As he did not have the unconditioned stimulus at hand, he appealed to a "reflex of freedom", an expression that would be replaced today by the notion of "escape response". He failed to note that the success of the cat was fully in the cat's own action, a characteristic not present in his dogs, and upon which Skinner would later found his distinction between Pavlovian or respondent conditioning and operant conditioning.

Since the concept of instrumental learning had been forged and used already to designate a process different from Pavlov's conditioning, why did Skinner not simply take it over, rather than forging his own term? First, Skinner, as he himself confesses,[2] was very impressed and influenced by Pavlov's book on *Conditioned reflexes* (1927) and initially called the lever press of his rats a *reflex*. Second, the problem he was struggling with had been raised among investigators working along Pavlov's lines by about the same time. Miller and Konorski (1928) had described a type of conditioning somewhat different from the traditional Pavlovian type: a shock produced a leg flexion, which was followed by food; eventually, the leg flexion appeared without any shock. This was the occasion for Skinner to write a seminal paper, where he explicitly stated for the first time the distinction between Pavlovian (called type S) conditioning and *operant* (or type R). Third, he was not satisfied with the research carried out in most American learning laboratories: mazes appeared to him as providing few lawful results in relation to the energy spent, and the theorising seemed to him unfounded.[3] Hence his reluctance to frame his genuine contribution within the context of the typical American learning laboratory of the time.

There might be other explanations, but whatever his reasons, Skinner did forge the expression *operant conditioning*. He used it extensively in his writings so that it became a technical term eventually adopted universally whenever Skinner's technique or the related concept is referred to. It is pointless to speculate about the way his ideas would have been received, had he used another term, that would have marked the contrast with Pavlov's conditioned reflex not by resorting to the same word with a qualification, but by resorting to a totally distinct term or expression. In fact, in many occurrences, in his and others' writings, the term *conditioning* has been dropped, leaving *the operant* in a substantive form. However, this has not changed the popular view associated with the label conditioning.

## OPERANT STEREOTYPY

Such persistence might not be exclusively due to original misnaming. The visitor to a traditional operant laboratory, especially in the first years when the technique was developed, was struck by the apparently compulsive activity of pigeons and rats in their experimental cubicles, often emitting their responses for hours at very high rates. He would quite normally have qualified such behaviour as stereotyped, and assigned it to some constraining factors of the experimental environment, which means, after all, constraints controlled by the powerful experimenter. We can ignore the image of the almighty scientist abusing his subjects: clearly, any experimental work involves the exercise of power over nature for the sake of better understanding, but this power is only perceived and eventually objected to when it is exerted over living organisms, especially in the realm of behaviour. However, the impression of stereotypy was based on objective characteristics of the situation. Skinner's decision, when designing his procedure, had been to use a very simple motor response, easily defined in space and time and therefore easily counted. This provided for a measure of rate of responding, at the expense of the structural complexity that is usually the source of fascination when we observe behaviour, animal or human. A bird building its nest, a spider spinning its web, a sheep mothering her lamb are undoubtedly more attractive than a rat pressing the same lever hundreds of times. That something important had been lost by that choice is obvious, as we shall see when we discuss the relation between Skinner and the ethological tradition (Chapter 6).

But such deliberate limitations are common courses of action in science. They offer the possibility of analysing, in an admittedly simplified context, basic processes which might be masked by the diversity and complexity of things as they present themselves to direct observation. Skinner's working hypothesis was that one basic mechanism might account, at the individual's level, for the emergence and maintenance of behaviour, however complex, exactly as one general process, based on selection among variations, accounts for the emergence of the variety of living forms throughout biological evolution. Whether this hypothesis has been fully confirmed is another story. What is certain is that it has produced important new outcomes.

The choice of rate of a simple response had an important technical consequence, unless what we take as a consequence could have been the source of the choice itself. A simple motor response provided for easy automatic recording, and combined with simple reinforcing events for automatic on-line control of the experiment. Whether this was the consequence or the source of the choice is a question that can be asked when we read the account by Skinner himself of the elaboration of his technique.[4] He tells us how, working on very simple startle reactions using a one-way tunnel, he worked out how to spare himself from handling the rat to put it back to the departure end, walking from one end of the long table to the other. Step by step, he had eventually automated everything and invented an early mechanical version of what was to become the cumulative recorder, which has been used for years in operant laboratories.

Skinner was always concerned with efficiency, and never ceased building ingenious gadgets to better solve practical problems, be it in the laboratory or in daily life. The baby-crib was a case in point, as were various devices he designed in his last years and reported in *Enjoy old age* (1983). The automation of the operant chamber was further facilitated by technological advances: from the crude mechanical devices, Skinner moved to electromechanical relay circuits, which were later replaced by on-line computer controls. The high degree of automation already attained in the 1950s and 1960s was not usual, in those days, in psychological laboratories. The natural tendency, when one has a very efficient tool available, is to use it intensively.

This is what Skinner and his followers did. Encouraged by their equipment, they explored a wide range of contingencies of reinforcement, emphasising environmental control over behaviour. In a process typically based upon the dialectic relation between variation and selection, they paid almost exclusive attention to the selective aspect, at the expense of the "variation" aspect. One consequence was that they studied essentially what was called steady or stable states: that is, behaviour as it is maintained for long periods of time once the organism has acquired it and has adapted to the controlling contingencies. The phase of learning proper was neglected, which is where the variation in behaviour can be observed and analysed, as is strikingly obvious from *shaping*, the initial phase of a conditioning experiment in which the experimenter carefully watches the subject and reinforces it for behaviours progressively approximating the desired response. Variation is, of course, much more difficult to deal with, and it is no wonder that it was overlooked. But the fact that it was neglected contributed to the idea that operant behaviour *is* a type of conditioning, if by this word is meant some sort of stereotyped behaviour strictly constrained by environmental variables. Had Skinner himself and his fellow-experimenters not indulged in the facility of automatised experimentation, and had they at least devoted some time to studying the second, no less important facet of the process, operant behaviour might have appeared to observers in a completely different perspective, closer to problem-solving behaviour, to exploration and creativity than to conditioning; a perspective that is indeed Skinner's own in his later theoretical analysis. In a way, there is a divorce between what was done in most operant laboratories in the 1950s and 1960s and the ideas developed by Skinner from the early 1950s as to the evolutionary analogy applied to operant behaviour (see Chapters 6, 7 and 8).

One possible important source of the frequent misrepresentations of Skinner's contribution and of the criticisms addressed to it could be the fact that it has been appraised on the ground of the experiments of that period, rather than on the reading of his theoretical writings. What appeared as an opportunity to most young experimenters in the field, and what indeed was an opportunity at the technical level, could very well have been a major misfortune for the destiny of Skinner's ideas in the realm of psychology at large.

## VARIABILITY

The operant procedure can be put to work to explore the other, no less important, part of the learning process: that is, behavioural variation. Although very few experimenters engaged in that type of work until the late 1970s, more and more have done so in the recent past.[5] A typical experimental situation can be illustrated as follows. The general idea is to provide for a demonstration of behavioural variability. Suppose you live in a modern city perfectly designed after a grid pattern of streets, as represented in Fig. 4.1. You live at the corner of block A1 and work in an office in D4—the letters identify the streets along the South–North

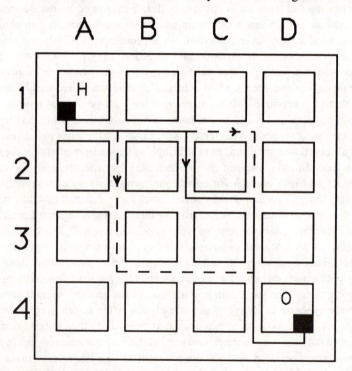

FIG. 4.1.   Daily walk to your office: fixed or flexible?

axis, the figures along the East–West axis. You can walk many different ways (in fact 20, if we exclude detours that would make the walk longer). Let us suppose that they are all strictly equivalent, that no street is more attractive than another. Will you walk the same way day after day, or change occasionally? If changing provides some final advantage, will you switch from routine to variety?

That simple situation is easily transposed to a laboratory set-up for animal or human subjects. A maze directly simulating the city configuration could be used. A transposition in an operant chamber, however, would be a simpler solution, and would provide for easier cross-species comparisons, including human subjects. To that end, the topographic pattern is transferred from the real locomotor space to the visual space, as shown in Fig. 4.2. On one of the walls of the cage the subject is presented with a matrix of electric bulbs (4 × 4, for example). Two response levers or response keys are located on another wall, together with the food dispenser. At the beginning of a trial, the upper left bulb is on. A trial is completed and reinforced when the bottom right bulb is on. Only one bulb is on at a time. By pressing the left lever, the subject moves the lit bulb one step from top to bottom; by operating the right lever, he moves it one step from left to right. A total of six responses, three on each lever, in any order, will successfully bring the trial to an end. Will the subject always use the same sequence of responses, following the same path in the visual maze? If so, under which conditions will it exhibit variability in its choice? Could it be reinforced for being variable, that is to say, for producing sequences different from the previous one, or from the previous ones? Such questions have been addressed in a number of experiments on animals and humans. (In order to maintain the motivation of human subjects, the situation has been implemented on video screen and given adequate animation.)

It has been shown, among other things, that after exhibiting a certain level of variability, subjects will eventually stick to one path, presumably the most economical way of adapting to the situation. If reinforced only intermittently, rather than upon each response sequence, they will become more variable, as is also the case when the reinforcement is discontinued in so-called experimental extinction. Variability increases if it is made the condition for reinforcement, and in developmental studies in humans, it can be observed that variability, appraised as described above, increases with age. Typical results are illustrated in Fig. 4.3. These are only examples of what can be done to explore rigorously the neglected aspect of the learning process. We shall recall these simple experiments later, when dealing with problem-solving and creativity in humans (Chapter 11).

## ONE OR TWO TYPES OF CONDITIONING: SOME FURTHER WARNINGS

The above account suggests that operant conditioning was misnamed, and that it could have been more appropriately presented as a basic model of coping with environmental conditions, a model of active problem-solving. Some specialists

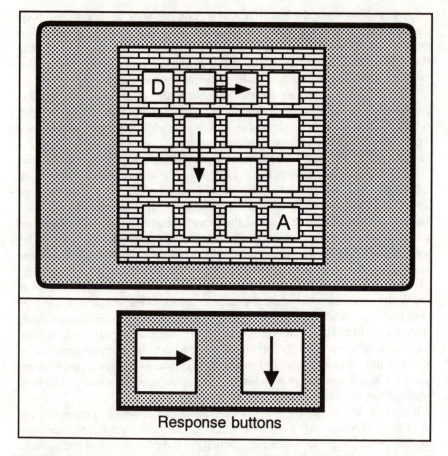

**FIG. 4.2.**   The visual matrix adapted for exploring behavioural variability in humans. The matrix is displayed on a TV screen, and represents a bank building, with a bag of dollars visible in the upper left window D. To complete a successful trial, the subject has to bring the bag to the bottom right window A, from which a security guard will take it to a safe. This can be achieved by pushing the left button and the right button in any order, with a resulting shift of one window rightwards or downwards respectively. There are twenty possible equivalent sequences of three left and three right responses. Any extra step out of the matrix ends the trial, a robber taking the money away. The whole scene is of course animated, and subjects love it!

will strongly object to that interpretation. They would argue that both types of conditioning, respondent and operant (type S and type R in Skinner's early labelling; Type I and Type II, after a later established use among specialists of learning; Pavlovian and Skinnerian, if one prefers proper names), are traditionally treated under the same heading in scientific psychology handbooks devoted to learning processes. They would further argue that both types have many things

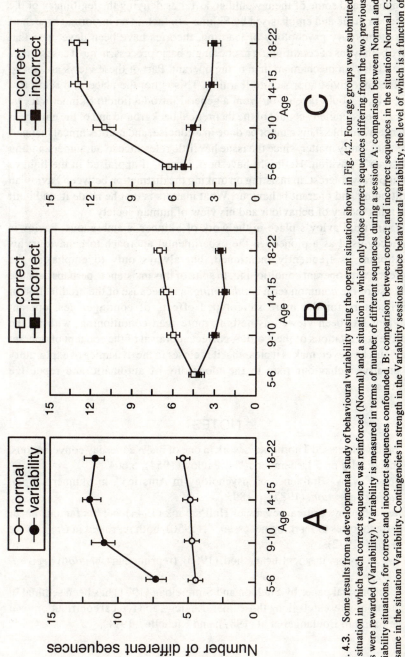

FIG. 4.3.   Some results from a developmental study of behavioural variability using the operant situation shown in Fig. 4.2. Four age groups were submitted to a situation in which each correct sequence was reinforced (Normal) and a situation in which only those correct sequences differing from the two previous ones were rewarded (Variability). Variability is measured in terms of number of different sequences during a session. A: comparison between Normal and Variability situations, for correct and incorrect sequences confounded. B: comparison between correct and incorrect sequences in the situation Normal. C: the same in the situation Variability. Contingencies in strength in the Variability sessions induce behavioural variability, the level of which is a function of age. (Results drawn from an unpublished Doctoral Thesis by B. Boulanger, Liège, 1990.)

in common, and some of them would go as far as denying the legitimacy of the distinction made and emphasised by Skinner. In fact, in an important branch of the contemporary psychology of learning, theories have been developed that reduce both types of conditioning to one single basic process, in most cases closer to the Pavlovian mechanism than to the operant. Part of these views are linked with the cognitivist approach to learning. This is not the place to discuss that issue, which would take us far from a general introduction to Skinner's ideas, and require a detailed account of the theoretical background and of the empirical evidence available. This cannot be done in a concise, and non-technical manner. It does not really matter, since the issue has little relevance to our understanding of Skinner's position. He might have been wrong, if appraised in the light of contemporary interest, in insisting on making the distinction between Pavlovian conditioning and operant behaviour. What matters is that he made it, and built upon it his theory of behaviour and his view of human society.

To sum up, Pavlov's place in the work of Skinner is ambiguous. Pavlov is duly recognised as a pioneer in the experimental approach to behaviour; his conditioning is frequently mentioned, but always only to emphasise the difference with operant conditioning. In spite of this insistence, perhaps because of the use of the common term *conditioning*, and because of the predilection of experimenters for the more stereotyped effects of contingencies, operant behaviour has been viewed as nothing more than conditioning, with all the negative connotations of the word. A correct appraisal of the concept of operant behaviour, however, makes it clear that it is closer to the dynamics of exploratory and creative behaviour than to the monotony of automatic and repetitive reactions.

## NOTES

1. Pavlov discussed Thorndike's work in one of his Wednesday conversations, specifically on 5 December 1934. Pavlov (1954), p.604.
2. See "Pavlov's influence on psychology in America", in Skinner's *Upon further reflection*, (1987), p.189.
3. See Skinner's critical review of Hull's book (1944) and his famous paper "Are theories of learning necessary?" (1950), both reprinted in *Cumulative record* (1972).
4. A case history in scientific method, (1956), (reprinted in *Cumulative record*, 1972).
5. A theoretical paper by Staddon and Simmelhag (1971) has been seminal in promoting research along those lines. Reviews and typical contributions can be found in Boulanger et al.(1987), and Richelle, (1991).

# 5 Freud in Skinner's Writings

## UNEXPECTED FIGURES

Skinner's position toward Freud and psychoanalysis is of particular interest for several reasons. First, he is known as one of the influential figures in the field of behaviour therapy, an alternative to Freudian approaches to psychological disturbances, based on theories as to their nature and their origin radically different from Freud's views, and on practices diametrically opposed in almost every aspect. Second, the position of Skinner within the behaviourist school of thought, with respect to the psychoanalytic movement, is distinct from that of other behaviourists of his time. Hull, the most prominent of them, and his colleagues at Yale University, had actively engaged in efforts to integrate Freudian analysis and learning theory. Regular meetings of the Yale group took place in the 1930s and 1940s; members of the group would eventually submit themselves to psychoanalysis, some of them travelling to Europe to that end.

These efforts were reflected in a number of publications of historical significance.[1] Skinner was not a member of that group—his age is not a sufficient explanation—nor of any other group. He carried out his early work in isolation with respect to the neo-behaviouristic school dominated by Hull, and he wrote a very negative critical review of the latter's book *Principles of behavior*.[2] Finally, until he turned to extrapolations to human behaviour, starting with *Walden Two* and continuing with *Science and human behavior*, he had been concentrating exclusively on animal research, and was little prepared, or inclined, at first sight, to draw on Freud's ideas. It is all the more surprising that he has done it more than from anyone else.

55

Some statistics are relevant here. We shall ignore those books and journal papers devoted exclusively to experimental research on animals or related highly technical or theoretical matters. We shall retain for consideration those books and papers (usually re-issued in book form as collected papers) dealing with human behaviour. We can practically ignore what Skinner published between 1930 and 1953, the year when *Science and human behavior* appeared. Starting with that major volume, we shall then be provided with an ample production of texts on various aspects of human psychology, including *Verbal behavior*, *Contingencies of reinforcement, Beyond freedom and dignity*, and three volumes of an *Autobiography*. Relying upon the index, when available, we might like to count the number of times Freud's name appears—adding, as appropriate, the number of entries on *psychoanalysis*. Before turning to figures, however, a word of warning is advisable: Skinner is one of those scientific authors who quotes and refers very little. Therefore, figures must be compared to those referring to other names.

It appears that Freud is by far the most referred to author in Skinner's writings. In *Science and human behavior*, he is given no fewer than 15 index entries, against four for Thorndike, three for Darwin and Pavlov, two for Descartes or Galton, and just one for many others, including Carl Rogers, William James and B. F. Skinner himself! In *Verbal behavior*, Freud is first again, with 18 entries, with Shakespeare only second to him with 16, and other favourites such as T. S. Eliot, A. Trollope or B. Russell ranging between five and ten. We find the same picture in *Contingencies of reinforcement*, where Freud appears 17 times, while Darwin and Watson are referred to six times, followed by Lorenz, James, Pavlov, Rousseau and Marx, each being quoted five times, and many others—from Chomsky to Cervantes and from Bacon to Neisser—having lower scores. Freud is still the winner in the third volume of Skinner's autobiography, *A matter of consequences* (1983) (the first two lack an index), and he keeps an honourable, if not always first, position in the more recent volumes of collected papers—the topics of which are less likely to evoke Freud's work.

## A TRIBUTE TO THE DETERMINIST

So much for figures. Does the relative frequency of references to Freud not simply reveal Skinner's stubborn opposition to psychoanalysis? Is it anything more than further evidence of the inescapable importance of Freud's theory even for those who claim to dispense with it? A look at the tone and content of passages referring to Freud gives an unexpected answer to these questions. Let us summarise the general features, and then examine more closely a few passages as illustrations.

Skinner makes a distinct evaluation of different aspects of Freud's contribution. He credits him for having convincingly shown that causes of human behaviour are usually not accessible to an individual's consciousness, and consequently that introspective reports provide no safe basis for a science of behaviour. He also credits him for his emphasis, in accounting for current conduct, on past-life experiences and events, often responsible for emotional associations and far more important than the belief in rational self-control. Moreover, he acknowledges the quality of Freud's observations on a limited number of individual patients (Skinner, as with Pavlov, Piaget, Lorenz and a few other creative psychologists, was never interested in accumulating statistics on group results), and his talent in unveiling relations between events observed in otherwise distant contexts (as in making rapprochements between historical or mythical relations, daily-life experiences and pathological symptoms).

On the other hand, Skinner objected strongly to the use of internal constructs, especially mental apparatus, as providing way-stations between the variables originally at work and the observed behaviour or symptom. To him, Freud was, in that admittedly most important aspect of his work (and undoubtedly increasingly important as he got older) working counter to his own scientific ambition. He thus contributed largely to the resurgence of mentalism, which Skinner always considered as the main obstacle to a truly scientific psychology. Though it never suffered any compromise on this essential point, Skinner's opposition was always expressed in a cool, gentle style—which he used indeed in discussing any concepts differing from his own, in contrast with the aggressive tone adopted towards him by many of his opponents: Chomsky was an extreme case in his mixing *ad hominem* arguments with scientific matters.[3]

These different evaluations of various aspects of Freud's work were stated in a concise way in a paper entitled "A critique of psychoanalytic concepts and theory" (1954).[4] It is crucial reading for those who want to learn about Skinner's attitude toward Freud. It is, for the most part, devoted to the critical discussion of Freud's mental apparatus. But before engaging in that discussion, Skinner briefly states what psychology owes to the father of psychoanalysis. A few sentences of this opening paragraph are worth quoting.

> Freud greatly reduced the sphere of accident and caprice in our considerations of human conduct. His achievement in this respect appears all the more impressive when we recall that he was never able to appeal to the quantitative proofs characteristic of other sciences. He carried the day with sheer persuasion—with the massing of instances and the delineation of surprising parallels and analogies among seemingly diverse materials.[5]

Skinner not only admires Freud's penetrating insights and imaginative rapprochements. He even absolves him, in a discussion on mind and brain, for indulging in speculative exercises, because Freud was convinced that the neurological substrates of mental dynamics and mental entities would eventually be discovered.[6]

Skinner repeatedly pointed to the failure of psychology in providing a consistent theory of human conduct that could be used by other social sciences and make the formulation in one field translatable into and compatible with formulations in other fields. He notes that:

> The student whose behavior is the concern of the educational specialist bears little resemblance to Economic Man. Man the Political Animal is not a promising patient in psychotherapy. Yet it is the same man who is being studied in all these fields, and it ought to be possible to talk about him in the same way. *Psychoanalysis has come closest to supplying a common formulation*, but it arose as a form of therapy and some touch of psychopathology survives when it is applied to everyday life. In spite of many claims to the contrary, it has not contributed a workable theory which is generally useful.[7]

In spite of the final reservations, which naturally lead to suggesting that the experimental analysis of behaviour is a serious candidate to that end, it is, to say the least, amazing that psychoanalysis is presented as *coming closest* to a unified theory of man. It would seem that in Skinner's eyes no other psychologist, including Watson, had "come closer" than Freud to such a consistent theory. None had been, indeed, closer to the behaviourist view that conscious processes are not the key to laws of behaviour. In an important paper, "Behaviorism at fifty" (1963), Skinner once more credited Freud for discarding consciousness and introspection as efficient tools for accessing to mental processes. While stigmatising Freud for having:

> devised, and never abandoned faith in, one of the most elaborate mental apparatuses of all time. He nevertheless contributed to the behavioristic argument by showing that mental activity did not, at least, *require* consciousness.[8]

In a comment on the issue of the unconscious, he correctly points to the fact that the real problem is not the unconscious, but the emergence of consciousness, "all behavior being basically unconscious".[9] He goes on to remind us that Freud's unconscious is not simply a stage before awareness, but the product of social and moral punishment, a process of repression that Skinner re-phrases in terms of contingencies of (social and verbal) reinforcement in the cultural community. This is only one example of a frequent transcription.

## REPHRASING FREUDIAN MECHANISMS

A large part of the references to Freud, especially in *Science and human behavior* and in *Verbal behavior*, are concerned with the reformulation of Freudian concepts or mechanisms in the terms of the experimental analysis of behaviour. This is in line with the tradition of the Yale group, though there is no evidence that Skinner ever noticed the similarities of approach. None of the members of the Institute of Human Relations is cited, and it seems plausible that Skinner simply ignored their work. At any rate, he did not feel his own theoretical attempts to be akin to Hull's constructs, as his critique of Hull's book[10] and other comments clearly testify. This exercise is based on the assumption that the observations made by Freud were basically correct, though his theoretical interpretations of them might be wrong. It applies especially well to those processes known as defence mechanisms, such as displacement, reaction formation, rationalisation, and the like. Skinner insists on the convergence between his own analysis of punishment and the Freudian concept of repression. He always viewed punishment as a rather poor way to control behaviour because it does not permanently reduce a tendency to respond, which is "in agreement with Freud's discovery of the surviving activity of what he called repressed wishes".[11] The effects of punishment on verbal behaviour, resulting in disguised speech, displacement, slips of the tongue and mishearing, witticisms and the like, are almost systematically discussed with reference to Freud's penetrating observations. Skinner notes the convergence between Freud's analysis of symbols and his own account of metaphor as an especially important device in verbal behaviour.[12] He appeals to Freud again when discussing the use of symbols in dreams, and searching for variables, in the subject's recent or past experience, that are responsible for particular symbols:

> The attempt to do so is often called the interpretation of dreams. Freud could demonstrate certain plausible relations between dream and variables in the life of the individual. *The present analysis is in essential agreement with his interpretation.*[13]

As an amateur of literary production (he was especially fond of reading classic French, as well as English, authors in their original text), Skinner often appealed to it, not only to illustrate his point, but to provide insightful descriptions and interpretations of human conduct in the numerous cases where a scientific account was still lacking. This has been the occasion for other positive references to Freud's work. He credits Freud, for example, for having initiated one of the two movements which, in Western culture, have developed a propensity for self-description, the other being the literary movement of self-analysis culminating with Proust.[14] He has been especially interested in the relationship between literary work and the psychology of the reader, a relationship much less emphasised traditionally than the more obvious links between a piece of literature and the psychology of its author. He credits Freud again for having perceived that important relationship long before others: "It was not so commonly recognized before Freud that the relation between a literary work and the *reader* is partly of the same sort [as the relation between a literary work and the writer]".[15]

## MENTAL APPARATUS

These examples will suffice to show the place of Freud in Skinner's work, and the generally positive way in which the contributions of the founder of psychoanalysis are recognised. This is not to say, as I have pointed out earlier, that Skinner agrees with Freud on everything. Major points of disagreement concern mental entities. Skinner's objections to Freud's mental apparatus have been elaborated at length in those parts of his writings in which he sets the bases for behaviour therapy. It is clear that their conceptions of mental disorders and of the strategies most effective to cure them are radically opposed. However, fundamental as it may be, the opposition does not bear upon certain features of behaviour therapy as they have eventually developed in some of the multifarious brands of modern psychological practices. For example, exclusive focus on non-verbal behaviour, neglect of past individual history, and the use of aversive controls, have nothing to do with Skinner's inspiration.[16]

One might ask, at this point: why is it that Skinner did not provoke the sort of interactive confrontation that had been typical of the Yale group? Why did he not induce psychoanalysts to pursue with him and his followers the sort of dialogue that had proved so constructive around Hull? This point of history would require thorough investigation in individual characters, sociological variables and evolution of the fields concerned. I have not carried out such an investigation, and can only venture a few suggestions.

Although Skinner agreed, on a number of occasions, to participate in debates with psychodynamists[17] or psychotherapists of various schools, he was certainly more motivated to bring together people working along his own lines than to spend time reconciling people sharing other views. Curiously enough, he was not at all a school leader, as Freud or Piaget were—which implies some sense of exclusiveness and some intolerance to deviations, and a strong will to establish a permanent core of devotees around oneself. The "Skinnerian school" that eventually emerged was not so much his own product as it was the product of his students and followers, who took him as their revered leader. This self-asserting movement, that had both a basic research and an applied facet, cut itself off from dialogue with other psychologists by taking a number of steps resulting in isolation (founding strictly focused new journals, starting a separate division at the American Psychological Association, organising specialised meetings, etc.). Looked at from the outside, the so-called experimental analysis of the behaviour movement appeared as a closed group, whose members had the reputation of taking little care for interacting with other psychologists. This possibly unintended complicity between Skinner and the Skinnerians might, unfortunately, have dissuaded others from engaging in interactions with Skinner himself, or in directly examining his writings on relevant issues. Part of the seminal potential of his work might have been lost in this way. It would not be the first time in history, and in intellectual history, that disciples obstruct a master's message.

It is fair to note, on the other hand, that psychoanalysis evolved in a way that did not generally favour scientific confrontation. Not only did it break down into a number of schools that were more or less hostile to each other—a sign of obvious difficulty in reaching agreement on objective criteria of scientific validity—but psychoanalytical discourses in many cases became more and more esoteric, discouraging the uninitiated from looking for possible convergences with other descriptions and interpretations.[18] In many cases, psychoanalysts have openly given up Freud's early ambition to account for human conduct in scientific terms. There is little wonder, then, that scientific psychologists who, like Skinner, pay tribute to Freud's work, find any echo at all.

## COGNITIVISMS, MIND AND THE MENTAL APPARATUS

In the view of many, this short survey on Freud in Skinner's writings will appear to have but historical interest, since contemporary psychology is often said to build on the ruins, rather than the foundations, of behaviourism. Even if one concedes its part in psychologists' inclination to dramatise the history of their own field, and to experience scientific progresses as revolutions rather than evolutions, behaviourism is admittedly no longer the dominant -*ism* on the contemporary scene. It has been supplanted by cognitivism, to the point that many psychologists have become cognitive scientists, leaving psychology to the past or to unscientific practitioners.

In so far as behaviourism has been rejected on the grounds of scientific errings, and replaced by an approach supposedly more appropriate to the understanding of the human mind, it is important to ask what is the position of cognitivism toward psychoanalysis. This is not an easy task, because, no more than behaviourism in its time, cognitivism does not cover a unified conception. If we want to characterise it, we are faced with differences which make it necessary to talk about many *cognitivisms* rather than cognitivism. A wide range of cognitive approaches have flourished in the field of therapy, often emerging, somewhat paradoxically, from the behaviour therapies themselves, but these cognitivisms can hardly be taken as tough scientific psychology. Cognitivism in the realm of basic research does not offer a unitary picture either.

I have attempted elsewhere to put order into a somewhat confusing situation by distinguishing four main facets, ingredients or brands in current cognitivisms,[19] and I shall review them in detail in Chapter 9. But it is appropriate to summarise the classification in the present context. The first kind of cognitivism appears to have taken over the tradition of scientific psychology, with improvements in methods that now give access to heretofore unaccessible phenomena, and changes of emphasis due to the stimulation from the computer metaphor and model. The second has much deeper epistemological implications, since it redefines the subject matter of psychology as being the mind, or representations, or some other internal entity or entities, rather than behaviour, as it used to be agreed upon for almost one hundred years. The third is insisting on the control exerted by upper, i.e. cognitive processes over the lower layers of psychological organisation, such as emotions. The last points to the clear-cut distinction often made, and reflected in the training of psychologists and in their practice, between the realm of cognition, which would deserve interest from the part of those engaged in basic research, and the domain of emotion and affect, that would be the daily diet for those working in the practice of helping people. For the sake of conciseness, I have labelled these four varieties *methodological*, *epistemological*, *ethical* and *institutional* cognitivisms. Methodological cognitivism does not concern us here, but the other three kinds call for some remarks in relation to Freud's approach.

By shifting the subject matter of psychology from behaviour to internal entities, epistemological cognitivism has relegated behaviour to the status of a by-product of internal agents, with little interest in its own right, at most a useful indicator of mind and cognitive processes until direct methods will be discovered to analyse them. This is perfectly compatible with Freud's construct. The mental or psychic apparatus has exactly the same basic properties: it is not directly observable, but it can be inferred and its mechanisms can be conjectured by looking at external events—symptoms having the same status in Freud's theory as behaviours in the conception of some epistemological cognitivists.[20] There is no doubt that, in that respect, cognitivism is much closer to psychoanalysis than behaviourism.

## COGNITION OR LIBIDO

Appealing to mental processes or apparatus also means reinstating the internal subject as the source or cause of his conduct. While the Freudian mental apparatus is filled with impulses, affects, desires, symbols of an emotional origin and tensions or conflicts of all sorts, the internal man of epistemological cognitivism is more of an expert in problem-solving. With one additional step to ethical cognitivism, it is the rational man that is rehabilitated, with the power of reason controlling affect, the power of will imposing decision, the power of consciousness dominating the unconscious, the magic of knowing solving the distress of feelings or the intricacies of passions. Top-down causation, a self-gratifying formula borrowed from neurobiology, appropriately moves the pendulum back in the direction of rationality, after the excess of Freudian monsters and MacLean's reptile brain. Correction for overstatement is part of the scientific endeavour, but it remains to assess how adequate to reality, or how illusory, the new picture of Man is. To a large extent, cognitivist approaches to psychotherapy, resorting to conscious changes in perception of the world and in knowledge of what really goes on, might reveal naïve confidence in the power of logic in human affairs.

I want to point out here the paradoxical situation of cognitivism with respect to Freud's tradition. On the one hand, it converges with it in giving priority to the internal apparatus; on the other, it diverges strongly by favouring a view of man as a rational being that Freud had largely contributed to demolishing. Thus, we might not be much better off on the way toward a synthesis than was the case with behaviourism. It remains to be decided whether that particular aspect of modern psychology, i.e. the return to Mind, rather than behaviour, as its subject matter, will survive as a crucial step forward in building a consistent theory of man, or will reveal but an accident in paradigms. As to the coming back of rationality, unfortunately there are no signs that humans are free from bottom-up causation. Freud's message about civilisation and its discontent, echoed by Skinner's pessimistic analysis of current social practices (see Chapters 14 and 15) are still advisable reading.

# NOTES

1. Among others, J. Dollard, L. W. Doob, N. E. Miller and R. R. Sears, *Frustration and aggression* (1939), and J. Dollard and N. E. Miller, *Personality and psychotherapy: An analysis in terms of learning, thinking and culture* (1950).
2. Skinner, 1944.
3. Historians of psychology in the second half of our century cannot overlook, besides his unquestioned influence in the field of linguistics and psycholinguistics, the part played by Chomsky in shaping the sociological map of cognitive psychology. In this respect, his written attacks on Skinner (Chomsky, 1959; 1972) are illustrative of a *mélange de genres* quite alien to rational exchanges of ideas among scientists. For a critical appraisal of the famous 1959 review, see Richelle (1972, or in English, 1976). See Chapter 10 for further developments on this issue.
4. Published in *Scientific Monthly*, November 1954; reprinted in *Cumulative record*, 1972, pp.239–248.
5. Quoted from *Cumulative record*, 3rd edition, p.239; reprint of the 1954 *Scientific Monthly* original publication.
6. "Freud was free to speculate with great abandon because, as a strict determinist, he believed that a physiological substrate would eventually be discovered." *Contingencies of reinforcement*, Chapter 9, "The Inside Story", p.280.
7. Italics are mine. Quoted from *Contingencies of reinforcement*, p.97, a reprint of a 1966 paper.
8. Quoted from *Contingencies of reinforcement*, p.225.
9. From a note—on Awareness—to the reprint of "Behaviorism at Fifty" in *Contingencies of reinforcement*, p.246. On Skinner's view of consciousness, see Richelle (1974).

10. See Skinner, (1944).
11. *Science and human behavior*, p.184.
12. See *Verbal behavior*, pp.92-99, and *passim*.
13. Italics are mine. Quoted from *Science and human behavior*, p.293. Reading the full section from which this quotation is drawn makes it clear that distant effects over time did not raise any particular problem in Skinner's view of learning processes, which means that previous history, including the early history of an individual, is crucial in accounting for his present behaviour. If behaviour-therapy practices have sometimes been blamed for ignoring the individual's history, it cannot be attributed to Skinner's account.
14. See *Verbal behavior*, pp.386–388.
15. Quoted from *Verbal behavior*, p.273. It is worth noting that this relationship was not given much attention among literary experts, until the so-called *reception theory* school which originated in Konstanz in the 1960s.
16. For a discussion of these issues, see Richelle, 1982, 1990.
17. For instance, he was confronted by F. Alexander in a meeting on *Integrating the approaches to mental disease*, the proceedings of which were edited by H. D. Kruse in 1957. See *Cumulative record*, Chapter 16.
18. The hermetic character of some psychoanalytical writings would deserve study from the point of view of intelligibility. A possible strategy would consist in having selected texts translated into different languages, of various degrees of linguistic distance from the original, and translated back in the original language. The operation could be repeated several times. The exercise could also involve different translators working on the same texts. The hypothesis would predict different final outcomes for Freud, Lacan, Watson, Piaget, Skinner, etc.
19. For a more detailed presentation of the point alluded to in this paragraph, see Richelle, 1986, 1987. For a balanced view of the history of the cognitivist movement, Gardner (1985) is a readable source. Gardner hardly mentions Freud in substantial contexts, which indicates that Freud's interest in a mental apparatus is not seen as a foreshadowing of the current interest in the Mind. Gardner simply states at the beginning of his account that scientific psychologists did not really know what to do with Freud's speculations and turned to other directions in search of the mysteries of the human Mind.
20. Even of those dealing with animal behaviour, as for example Dickinson (1980).

# 6 Skinner and the Ethological Tradition

## OF RATS AND MEN

Most of the empirical work carried out by Skinner has been on animals, and in so far as it has provided us with lawful results, it can be seen as a contribution to the study of animal behaviour, even by those who are not ready to accept his extrapolation to humans. But research on animals in the laboratory is often rejected as irrelevant by students of animal behaviour in the tradition of ethology, on the grounds that experimental situations put artificial constraints on animal subjects, preventing the expression of their real, natural repertoire, observable only in the field, that is to say in their normal environment, or ecological niche. If Skinner's research is refused any validity outside the animal laboratory at the level of human psychology, and altogether any validity as a contribution to the study of animals precisely because it has been done in the laboratory, what is left of his experimental work?

The question cannot be answered without putting Skinner's work in its historical context, which means, in this case, the evolution of the relations between American laboratory psychology and the ethological tradition, mainly of European origin. We should first remember that the use of animals in the behaviour laboratory, as was common in the first half of the twentieth century, was not aimed essentially at studying a species' behaviour for itself: rats were not used because of any special interest in the way rats behave. They were used as a tool, or as a model, as we would put it today, to draw laws generally applicable to any species, although humans are of course the major interest of psychologists. Their frame of reference was general, rather than comparative psychology. This was not strongly questioned, since physiology had adopted the

65

same strategy. Awareness of species' differences was not lacking: comparative psychology, as comparative physiology, existed as well. But comparative psychology in the American tradition was essentially limited to the experimental laboratory approach, and anyhow, it was not the preoccupation of learning psychologists, from Thorndike to Tolman, or from Hull to Skinner.

Comparing the data he obtained with his new procedure with those collected in maze studies, Skinner thought he had gained in generalisability, hence in validity in extending them to humans. No real equivalent of a maze had been designed for humans, while the patterns in the rate of responding under various schedules of reinforcement proved to be strikingly similar across species, including humans. The number and variety of species were quite limited, as compared with zoological diversity: rats, pigeons and monkeys remained the main references. But Skinner could claim, on experimental evidence, that these behaved in the same way, and that humans did too, by juxtaposing the cumulative records of individual subjects pertaining to those various species, and asking "which is which?".

The concept of cross-species generality was somewhat linked, and unfortunately so, with the notion of the arbitrariness of the operant response. Skinner insisted that the operant reponse is arbitrary by contrast with the permanent, physiologically established relation between the unconditioned stimulus and the unconditioned response of Pavlovian conditioning, a prerequisite to the formation of a conditioned reflex. This led to the idea, possibly to some extent in Skinner himself, that any response can serve as an operant, that all responses one might think of are equivalent, and consequently—if interspecies differences are, for that matter, negligible—that the laws of operant behaviour transcend species-specific singularities.

Moreover, in spite of many diverging points with other learning psychologists, Skinner remained essentially in the tradition of the study of acquired behaviour, as it had been established in the USA in the first half of the century. The emphasis was on learning mechanisms with no reference to development, nor to inborn genetic endowment. The learning processes were studied in and for themselves, as the result of environmental variables introduced at any moment of an organism's life. This does not mean that learning psychologists were naïve enough to think that organisms are born without any genetic constraints, but that learning processes could be isolated from their influence and appraised, so to speak, in a pure state.

## ETHOLOGY: ANOTHER LOOK AT ANIMALS

No position could have been more alien to the conception defended by the ethological tradition, grounded in the patient work of animal observers, which found its scientific credentials in the 1930s and 1940s in Europe, especially through the empirical and theoretical work of Konrad Lorenz. Here animal behaviour was studied for itself, in its own right; species-specific behaviour was given main attention; and taking over the old fascination for instincts in animals, phylogenetically established activities were given priority over individual learning. The richness of the natural behavioural repertoire matched the morphological diversity of living species, and it could only be observed where it normally occurred: that is to say in the field, in the ecological system where a species had evolved and is actually living, not in the reductionist situation of the laboratory. As a rule, behavioural processes could only be understood through a developmental analysis in the growing organism.

Ethologists, for years, had few interactions with laboratory psychologists. Usually they were members of a distinct scientific community, trained as zoologists, in biology departments, not as psychologists. They studied behaviour as part of biology, and, following Lorenz, they thought of their science as the biology of behaviour, rather than as psychological work proper. With few exceptions, they were practically ignored by psychologists working with animals in the laboratory. And reciprocally, ethologists rarely came across the latters' work. They did not publish in the same journals, they did not attend the same scientific meetings, they did not read each others' writings.

Interactions did not occur until the 1950s or 1960s, when some attempts were made, especially in the British school, with Thorpe and others, to merge the comparative laboratory psychology contribution and the ethological approach. This movement was not widely accepted; it was vehemently criticised by Lorenz (1965), who pronounced a sort of excommunication of those who were contaminating the ethological orthodoxy with heretic elements from the behaviouristic schools of thought. Behaviourism was later one of his targets in a non-technical essay on *The eight capital sins of civilisation* (1973). Things have changed since then, and Lorenz himself must be credited for having modified his view after examining more closely the learning issue. Although he never gave up his insistence upon genetically determined, species-specific behaviour (a stand that ethologists of the next generation would eventually abandon for more qualified positions as to the factors shaping the phenotype), and although he had long held the paradoxical view that learning itself is inherited (in the sense that what an organism learns is exactly what is allowed by its specific genetic endowment), he came later to a much more sophisticated position, recognising the importance of Skinner's operant process, and developing the notion of more or less open (or closed) programmes for learning in the various species. His master synthesis, entitled *The fundamentals of ethology* (1981), includes an analysis of the place of learning that is very different compared to the views expressed in his early work.

It should be noted that ethology gained an increasingly wide audience among the human sciences as well as in biological circles, especially in psychology and psychiatry. This influence was obviously much earlier in Europe than in the USA,[1] and eventually pervaded specific fields, such as child psychology. The Nobel

Prize, awarded in 1972 to Lorenz and two other European ethologists, put their work on the public stage, and phenomena such as imprinting or the bee dance entered the lay culture.

## THE MISBEHAVIOUR OF ORGANISMS

American psychologists of the behaviourist tradition, including Skinner, were slow to pay attention to species-specific peculiarities. They finally did so under the influence of two factors: one external, the other internal to their field.

The external factor was the growing influence of ethological literature, and objections by ethologists about the study of animals in the laboratory, one aspect of the evolution just described. At the same time—and this was the internal factor— laboratory experimenters came across the species-specific repertoire in their experiments aimed at drawing general laws, independent of species' differences.

In the operant laboratory, the crucial event seems to have been the description made by the Brelands of the uncontrollable intrusion of specific behaviour during conditioning experiments, a phenomenon they labelled "instinctive drift". The Brelands had undertaken the conditioning of animals of various domestic and wild species to be shown as attractions in fairs and entertainment parks. They were first fairly successful, and indeed pioneers, in diversifying the range of species submitted to operant techniques. In order to make the show last, and thus satisfy the paying public more surely, they arranged contingencies in space and time in a somewhat different style as compared with the usual laboratory set-up. For instance, they trained pigs and racoons to fetch coins in one corner of a spacious territory and bring them to the opposite corner where they had to put them in a sort of piggy-bank; after the animals had stored a number of coins, they received food. Animals did learn without any difficulty, but after having performed the sequence nicely for some time, they began to engage in undesirable behaviour, at least from the viewpoint of the trainers. Pigs would stop on their way, bury the coin in the sand, and take it out with their snout; racoons would spend a lot of time handling the coin, with their well-known washing-like movements. This was at first amusing, but eventually it became time-consuming and would make the whole show appear very imperfect to the spectator. Commercially, it was a disaster. The Brelands, however, perceived the scientific interest of the phenomenon and made a systematic study of it. They reported their observations in one article,[2] with the evocative title *The misbehavior of organisms*, an ironical allusion to Skinner's first book. Their main interpretation was that behaviours from the natural repertoire of the species emerged in the conditioning situation, and eventually took such extension that the learned activities, initially shaped and maintained consistently, would appear erratic. This phenomenon they called *instinctive drift*.

The reason why this had not been observed before can be explained by the fact that laboratory situations do not usually provide the temporal and spatial conditions that favour the pervasive production of natural behaviours, and also by the very simple fact that experimenters did not usually directly observe what was going on in the experimental cage. They used to rely upon their automatic equipment, the advantages of which can appear, in this context, to be counterproductive. They were happy and proud to show how automation had freed them from the permanent watching of their subjects, allowing them the freedom to read or write while the cumulative recorders unrolled their subjects' activity (meaning, of course, the activity they had decided to put under experimental control, i.e. the operant response). They did not care for other types of activity that could also have occurred. They thought there were none, or that, if there were any, they were not interesting.

In the years that followed the Brelands' observations, but often quite independently, a number of experimenters described what the animals did during an experimental session, beside the operant response. They could be seen in the somewhat paradoxical situation of running automatised experiments with sophisticated equipment ,while peeping into their experimental cage and noting, in a naturalistic way, as field ethologists would do, any bit of whatever behaviour their subject produced. A whole sub-field of study came to existence within the field of animal learning, devoted to what came to be called the *biological constraints on* (or *boundaries of,* or *limitations to*) *learning*, or, looking more at the positive side, *predispositions* or *preparedness to learning*. It took into account, in explaining learned performances, the species' characteristics that favour or impede the learning of a given combination of responses. Responses as simple, and as common and well-established in the operant laboratory, such as the pigeon's key-peck, were shown to cover units of motor behaviour of very different types—such as extremely short ones, hardly amenable to operant control by the reinforcement, and longer ones that can be submitted to control by contingencies. The same key-peck was shown to be inappropriate when one wants to appraise the species' capacity to estimate time, for example, because of its involvement, with hardly modifiable properties, in food-searching and food consumption (pigeons cannot wait more than 12 or 15 seconds if they are required to signal the end of the estimated minimal delay by pecking a key, but, as shown in Fig. 3.7, they can control delays of one minute or more if they are allowed to respond by jumping on a perch).[3] It was also shown to resist any training as an avoidance response to an impending shock, presumably because the natural reaction of the bird to an electric shock consists of tossing its head back, a movement exactly opposite to the one involved in key-pecking.

This new area of study has brought important changes in the field of animal learning, both outside and within the Skinnerian orientation. The concept of the arbitrariness of the response, in its extended (and as we have noted above, erroneous) sense, has given place to acceptance that species-specific characters must be taken into account when defining a response, or a stimulus, for experimental purposes. The emphasis has been put again upon the structure of

reasons, or for food). Hence the development of appropriate morphological tools, such as teeth and claws. In so far as current aggression in mankind can be traced back to those times, it is clear that what was then an advantage for survival has turned into a dangerous tendency that could lead the species to self-destruction when served, as it is now, by tools that multiply by thousands the power of individual defensive or offensive pieces of anatomy.

Aggression also illustrates another point repeatedly emphasised by Skinner. It has, admittedly, its phylogenic history—which Lorenz had attempted to recreate in a brilliant, if not fully unquestionable way.[10] It has also, especially in humans, an individual and sociocultural history, that can be significant in explaining occurrences of aggressive behaviour. Skinner has warned that sources of behaviour should not be reduced to the phylogenic factor without convincing evidence that other factors are indeed negligible, which is rarely the case, especially in humans. The recent or present environmental causes responsible for aggressive acts in humans are so many and so familiar that they need not be documented here. There is no reason to displace the problem by appealing to some ancestral instinctive aggressivity, that would absolutely need to express itself in one way or another (this was Lorenz' view, which can only lead to vague proposals for channelling it into peaceful harmless activities, like sport, the ethological version of Freud's sublimation). This is an easy way to escape from the identification of other, more accessible causes, and the responsibility to change them. Anyhow, whatever the importance of phylogenic determinants of current aggressive behaviours, there is no reason to believe that they have to occur, that their manifestation cannot be changed.

Simple examples in animals show that aggression is not just an inevitable output of some internal aggressivity. Pigeons trained to peck a key to avoid an electric shock will eventually attack another pigeon placed in the cage during the experimental session. This is possibly a simple, primitive case of attribution. It matters little here whether their attacks can be traced to their species history or have a more local origin; what really counts is that they occur under that particular set of contingencies. The same will not be observed if the bird is rewarded with food on a schedule that leaves little opportunity for intrusive behaviour of any sort.

To sum up, Skinner did not deny the evolutionary origin of many aspects of behaviour, nor did he deny species-specific differences derived from evolutionary history. Such denial would have been paradoxical from a scientist who proposed to extend the model of biological evolution to individual learning and to cultural history. He insisted, however, that we take all three levels into account when explaining human conduct (the first two when explaining animal behaviour), and he rightly claimed that the first level, the level of biological evolution, is no more "natural" than the other two. This is the balanced attitude that many have taken after him, inside and outside ethology or psychology, on later occasions, when that recurrent issue has been revived again, as in the debate on sociobiology.

# NOTES

1. As an example, ethology was among the obligatory assignments of all psychology students at my university (Liège, Belgium) from 1961. See also M. Richelle and J. C. Ruwet (1972).
2. K. Breland and M. Breland, 1961. See also their book, 1966.
3. See Richelle and Lejeune, 1980; 1984.
4. Besides the numerous papers and books devoted to the biological constraints on learning (classical references are Hinde & Stevenson-Hinde, 1973, Seligman & Hager, 1972), there is now a choice of both introductory or specialised books on animal behaviour that elegantly combine the two traditions (see, among others, Lea, S. E. G., *Instinct, environment and behaviour*, London: Methuen (1984)). To be complete, the parallel evolution within ethology must be mentioned: researchers in ethology have paid increasing attention to the flexibility of species-specific behaviour, especially when appraised in details throughout development, which means that what is prepared by the genetic endowment of the species is modulated by the individual's interactions with its environment.
5. The paper was reissued with additional notes in *Contingencies of reinforcement* (1969) and printed once more among the "canonical papers" submitted to peer commentaries in *The Behavioral and Brain Sciences* in 1984. Although some of the comments were very critical, or pointed to some of the flaws alluded to in the text, most commentators, especially within the field of ethology, though not agreeing completely with Skinner, did recognise the significance of the paper both in helping the understanding of his position and in promoting the dialogue between ethologists and laboratory-learning psychologists.
6. The issue of the role of behaviour in biological evolution has been central in the reflection not only of a number of ethologists, but also of great psychologists. Piaget devoted to it one of his last books, *Le comportement, moteur de l'évolution* (1976), which he calls "a small and foolhardy work". Piaget had for long taken inspiration in the views of the biologist Waddington, which Skinner does not seem to have been familiar with, as can be inferred from the rare allusions to his work.
7. Skinner and Morse (1957).
8. See Chapter 3, p.30.
9. Skinner and Morse, 1957, in Skinner (1972), p.538.
10. Lorenz, 1966.

# 7 Piaget and Skinner: Constructivism and Behaviourism

## RECIPROCAL IGNORANCE

Piaget, like Skinner, was one of the prominent figures of mid-twentieth-century psychology. Their scientific production covered roughly the same period, from the 1930s to the 1980s. Piaget, eight years older than Skinner died in 1981, nine years before him. In contrast to the work of many psychologists from European non-English speaking countries, admittedly of more modest stature, Piaget's work made its way to the United States of America, and an important part of his writings were translated into English. (Incidentally, this was not a condition for Skinner to read them, since he read French quite fluently, as has already been said.)

In spite of these favourable circumstances, the two giants of psychological science blissfully ignored each other.[1] When one of them, on rare occasions, alluded to the work of the other, it was always over-simplified caricature. Perhaps we should accept this as an unavoidable bias in great theorists; it might be part of their asserting the originality of their own system, which could be made more salient by contrasting it with earlier or rival theories misrepresented for the sake of argument. Perhaps this is the price to pay for theorists to reach highly consistent formulations of their own thoughts, which might in turn be a factor in their stimulating other scientists in their field. The price might be estimated a bit high, when it maintains and perpetuates oppositions when recognition of convergences would be more fruitful.

There is no doubt that, around 1950, both Piaget's and Skinner's theories were among the most, if not *the* most, influential in psychology. They evolved in very different traditions, which might explain why they progressed along parallel lines for half a century, with no or minimal encounter. Mentions of Piaget in Skinner's work are scarce, and always simplify the case. The same is true of the master of constructivism towards the last, and the most distinctive, of American neo-behaviourists. Such reciprocal ignorance is surprising if one recognises, behind obvious differences in discourse, the concern for similar issues on both sides, and the close, though unexpected, relationship between the manner in which they both stated some crucial questions at the end of their career, for future researchers to elaborate further.

Piaget never acknowledged the specificity of Skinner among behaviourists. On one occasion, in one of his last books, there is an indication that he was aware of it, but he mentions it only to put Skinner in his place, that is, in the indiscriminated team of behaviourists. To Piaget, they are essentially Stimulus-Response empiricists, against whom he fought obstinately throughout his long career. He blames them for looking for the origin of behaviour exclusively in the environment. He accuses them of exalting the stimulus, as, on the opposite wing, he accuses neo-Darwinists for the converse error, the exaltation of endogenous factors. When Piaget discusses the behaviourist tenets, he usually refers to Hull or to Watson. Although he sometimes warns his reader that he is dealing with *classical* behaviourism, he never thinks it necessary to consider other, more recent forms. This means ignoring the fact that Skinner, while rightly seen in many respects as the most Watsonian among Watson's heirs, proposed on many important issues conceptions completely distinct from his behaviourist fellows, including Watson himself. Some of them have been criticised more harshly by Skinner than by outsiders to behaviourism. For instance, Skinner repeatedly underlined that thinking cannot be reduced to sub-vocal speech, a thesis of Watson's often referred to by Piaget as the best of behaviourism's contribution to the study of intelligent behaviour. Skinner's destructive review of Hull's famous book, *Principles of behavior* seems to have been totally ignored by Piaget.[2]

The following quotation is only one out of the many texts of Piaget discussing the behaviourist view, but it is exceptional in the sense that it ends with one of the rare allusions to Skinner. It could be the only occasion on which Piaget revealed that he was aware of the distinction to be made between Skinner and classical behaviourists:

> In so far as the subject acquires some knowledge, be it the "know-how" characteristic of sensorimotor learning or higher forms of understanding, it always implies that he has succeeded in recording some observables in the objects around him, the external world being in a sense the only possible source of cognitive progress: to any external stimulus thus there corresponds a response of the subject, although defined by Hull in terms of "functional copy" of the external situation. In other words, the environment is the one that holds full power, and is, so to speak, active, in a very positive way, while the subject remains passive in the role of mere receptor. Even when Skinner's pigeons press a key, this inchoate action upon the environment results in nothing more than discovering its properties to then submit to its variations as external reinforcers of various values.[3]

On his part, Skinner, in the many writings in which he ventures to interpret complex human behaviour in the light of concepts arrived at in the study of animal learning, never looks closely at Piaget's position. If he mentions it at all, it is only to discard it, as pertaining to mentalistic conceptions, responsible not only for the slow progression of psychological sciences at large, but for the incapacity of our societies to adopt a view of man that would eventually help to solve their problems.

One of the rare allusions to Piaget occurs, significantly enough, in a paragraph entitled *Structuralism*. Piaget is presented as a typical case of developmental structuralism, in which changes occurring in ontogeny are described as a sequence of stages corresponding to some internal evolution: "what grows is said to be something in the mind, as with Piaget".[4] The main flaw of Piaget's theory is, therefore, its mentalism. Skinner seems to ignore the nuances brought by Piaget in his critical analysis of the notion of structure, which had been the theme of a small book published in the middle of the structuralism vogue in Paris, without doubt the most entertaining and witty of Piaget's works.[5] More important, Skinner similarly overlooks the core of Piaget's constructivism, a lifelong attempt to account for one important part of what the word *mind* refers to by studying its natural history throughout development.

Perhaps such mutual ignorance is only one example, be it the most striking one, of a paradox in modern psychology, that is the separation of the fields of learning and cognitive development. To any naïve observer, it would seem sound that these two fields would merge naturally. It would seem that whoever is concerned with learning processes should take some interest in development, since the developing phases are usually, in most organisms, especially rich in new acquisitions, and hence offer the most appropriate conditions to study them. Conversely, it would seem that, whenever one refuses to conceive of development as the simple unrolling of some pre-formed innate programme, one should normally be led to appeal to processes of behavioural modification resulting from the interaction of the organism with its environment, which are the subject matter of any psychology of learning. Far from being the rule, such convergence has been slow to emerge, and, even now, it remains completely overlooked by many. Attention for so-called developmental constraints on learning, such as the critical or favourable periods first described in relation to the phenomenon of imprinting, was exceptional among specialists of animal learning until the 1970s, while the developmentalists of the Geneva school showed little systematic concern for the place of learning mechanisms in cognitive development until about the same time. Efforts at mutual integration have taken place in the field of animal behaviour, but more often than not, development and learning are still juxtaposed, when they are not opposed: a situation particularly damaging when it comes to training practitioners in areas of application, such as education, in which, for all practical purposes, the two aspects cannot reasonably be kept apart.[6]

## CONVERGENCES

If it could not have been expected that Piaget and Skinner would have explored their complementarities, it is up to their followers to do so. The task is by no means alien to the intuitions of both men. In spite of his rather rigid, early view of learning psychology in the behaviouristic tradition, Piaget finally opened the door and, in his own group, encouraged experimental studies on the effects of various types of learning.[7] Skinner, on his part, seems to have been aware of the need for a synthesis when he wrote, as a conclusion to a short commentary on structuralist theories of development: "It remains for us to supplement developmentalism in behavioural science with an analysis of the selective action of the environment."[8]

Both Piaget and Skinner have approached the subject matter of psychology as belonging to the wider field of biological sciences, although neither of them appealed to physiological methods proper. This is, admittedly, a rather general point of convergence, but it is nonetheless an important one: modern psychology has not yet reached unanimity as to its links to biological sciences on the one hand and to social sciences on the other. One view consists in assuming continuity between the basic adaptive processes in living material and sociohistorical processes, as encountered in the human species. This is not reductionism, in the sense that it is not denying that new structures and new processes emerge, for instance with the unprecedented development in humans of symbolic functions and natural language, a prerequisite for the transmission of acquired behaviour and knowledge, and therefore for cultural history. But it is refusal of a clear-cut qualitative distinction that would oppose the human species to the rest of the living world, and apply to it, as many humanistic psychologies or philosophies still do, basically different conceptual tools and empirical procedures.

Piaget's entire work is focused on the idea that there is continuity between the most elementary forms of living systems and the most complex products of human intelligence. His abundant empirical contribution is wholly aimed at demonstrating such continuity. And several of his theoretical writings, such as *Biology and knowledge*,[9] are devoted to an explicit elaboration of the same theme. The biological roots of central notions such as assimilation-accommodation, equilibration-disequilibration, have been repeatedly stated by Piaget.

In a similar way, Skinner has defined behaviourism not as a theory of psychology, but as a philosophy of science that links psychology definitely to biological sciences. He has underlined, with increased insistence as time went on, the analogy between the process of operant conditioning and the processes at work in biological evolution, a central theme that will detain us further.

As most biologically oriented psychologists, Piaget and Skinner equally moved beyond the old debate on innate versus acquired, on heredity versus learning, which was revived in a peculiarly passionate manner not long ago, in the context of human intelligence. From the very beginning, Piaget had argued against nativist theories, and he repeated his arguments on several occasions, when such views appeared again, be it in the field of ethology, linguistics or anthropology.

Skinner's views in this respect are less familiar, because he is usually considered as an extreme environmentalist: he takes the organism as a *tabula rasa*, which will passively receive the prints of the environment. This misinterpretation overlooks the numerous texts in which Skinner has made his position clear. Referring to Watson's famous passage in which the father of behaviourism claims that, given a dozen healthy babies and his own specified world to bring them up, he guarantees to take any one at random and train him to become any type of specialist, Skinner reminds us that these lines, often quoted as denial of any inherited component, appear in a chapter devoted to "how man is equipped to behave at birth", and that they should be read in their original context. He emphasised, as an obvious fact, that new behaviour cannot be acquired throughout an individual's life if there are no minimal units, which cannot originate but in phylogeny:

> Some phylogenic contingencies must be effective before ontogenic contingencies can operate. The relatively undifferentiated behavior from which operants are selected is presumably a phylogenic product; a large undifferentiated repertoire may have been selected because it made ontogenic contingencies effective.[10]

But he strongly objected to those views which, in order to explain highly complex forms of behaviour, such as logical thought or natural language, appeal to some pre-formed innate device, that would only have to get into action.[11] Like Piaget, he wondered how individual behaviour can find its place in evolution and account for the progressive emergence of organisms whose complex actions cannot be assigned to the miracle of a single mutation. His attempts at explaining the origin of some species-specific behaviours—briefly alluded to in Chapter 6— unorthodox as they might seem to the neo-Darwinian biologist, were motivated, indeed, by the same concern as Piaget's obstinate efforts to articulate the history of a species and the individual experience of its members by resorting to the phenomenon of phenocopy.[12]

These are rapprochements of a rather general nature. There are, however, deeper convergences, mainly on two major points. One is what can be called the primacy of action; the other is related to the evolutionary analogy and the place of variations in building up new behaviours.

## IN THE BEGINNING WAS ACTION!

Common to Piaget's and to Skinner's theories is the concept that the emphasis, when studying behaviour, should not be on the stimulus, nor should it be upon the mind, but upon action. In this respect, both theories could, in an equally

relevant way, be introduced by quoting Faust's famous words when he thought
about the very origin of things :

> It is written: In the beginning was the Word.
> Here I am stuck at once. Who will help me on?
> I am unable to grant the Word such merit,
> I must translate it differently
> If I am truly illumined by the spirit.
> It is written: In the beginning was the Mind.
> But why should my pen scour
> So quickly ahead? Consider that first line well.
> Is it the Mind that effects and creates all things?
> It *should* read: In the beginning was the Power.
> Yet, even as I am changing what I have writ,
> Something warns me not to abide by it.
> The spirit prompts me, I see in a flash what I need,
> And write: In the beginning was the Deed![13]

In fact, Faust's final intuition has been paraphrased in modern psychological
jargon and applied to Piaget: "In the beginning was the response". Piaget, as is
well known, has traced the origin of logical and abstract thought in actions
exhibited from the earliest stages of development, and progressively coordinated
and internalised.[14] Goethe was clearly foreshadowing genetic epistemology. But
he was also anticipating Skinner's radical behaviourism. For, in spite of a
persistent misinterpretation, one of the most distinctive features of Skinner's
theory is, as we have already seen, that it has definitely turned its back to the
Stimulus-Response view that had characterised some brands of behaviourism.
The S-R formula was replaced by the central notion of the selective action of
the environment. Piaget's sentence, as quoted earlier, that "to any external
stimulus corresponds a response of the subject", if it does correctly describe
classical types of behaviourism, does not apply to Skinner's. In the first chapter
of his book *Contingencies of reinforcement*, Skinner states his position in an
unequivocal manner, which makes it all the more surprising that he has been
persistently depicted as an S-R psychologist. After discarding the traditional view
of the environment as a simple stage or setting in which behaviour takes place,
without any real interaction, he denounces the insufficiencies of the conception
that gives the environment a releasing or triggering role. In a section significantly
sub-titled "Beyond stimulus and response", he makes it clear that:

> No account of the interchange between organism and environment is complete until
> it includes the action of the environment upon the organism *after* a response has
> been made.[15]

Two points are crucial in that sentence: first, behaviour is an interactive process—
there is an *interchange* between the organism and the environment—and, second,

the environment is important because of its action *after a response has been made*, that is, because of its selective action. Obviously, some behaviour must take place first, if the environment has to exert its selective action at all. Thus, contrary to Piaget's description of the behaviourist position, the environment is by no means, in Skinner's theory, the "unique source" of behaviour. As typically exemplified in the operant-conditioning chamber, we start with action: action upon the environment, that will in turn shape action by a process of selection. As Faust's statement goes, in the beginning was behaviour! Or, after Skinner's early definition of his own enterprise, *spontaneous* behaviour.

Once this parallel between Piaget and Skinner as to the primacy of action has been admitted, one might object to deeper convergencies by arguing that there is little in common between Piaget's ambitious project, aimed at accounting for the highest forms of intellectual activities, and Skinner's scope, limited to elementary motor responses in animals. If it is true that Skinner's empirical work did not substantially contribute to our understanding of cognitive functions, he did, nonetheless, extend his general conception of behavioural interchange far beyond the simple, acquired motor responses in rats and pigeons. He extended it to perception, which he views as action rather than as a process of copy recording, echoing Piaget's preference for the wording *perceptual activities* instead of *perception*. And still more significantly for our purpose, he extended it to intellectual (cognitive would be more fashionable, of course) behaviour and knowledge, as captured in the following, truly Piagetian statement: *Our knowledge is action.*[16]

Explication of his epistemological view can be found in many places in Skinner's writings. The text that follows is especially illustrative of his opposition to empiricism, since it was a spontaneous reply to Franz Alexander in a symposium where the famous psychoanalyst had been defending a theory of knowledge along the lines of classical British empiricism:

> The notion that knowledge consists of sense impressions and concepts derived from the sense impressions was, of course, the view of British empiricism and is still held by many people. *But others, including myself, believe that it is incapable of representing human knowledge adequately.* Even a simple idea is not, as Locke supposed, an assemblage of sensory materials in response to stimulation. To suppose that physical knowledge exists in the mind of a physicist as psychic or mental material—as the way he looks at the world—*seems to me quite absurd.* At no time is a physical theory a psychic event in the sense of an image or sensation.

> To say that physics always gets back to sense impressions is simply to say that the organism is in contact with the environment only through its sense organs—a very obvious axiom. But the organism does more than soak up the environment. It reacts with respect to the environment, and throughout its lifetime it learns more and more varied ways of reacting. *An alternative conception of knowledge, which many of us hold, is that knowledge is action rather than sensing, and that a formulation of knowledge should be in terms of behavior.*[17]

Although I do not wish to indulge in multiplying quotations, I cannot resist a final rapprochement :

Operant behavior is essentially the exercise of a power: it has an effect on the environment.[18]

The organism acts upon the environment, rather than being simply submitted to it. As to the highest levels, where behaviour plays a non-negligible role, this role is by no means limited to compensate for alterations or aggressions from the environment: it may consist, on the contrary, in conquering actions aimed at extending the environment.[19]

Which is which? Only the British spelling of the word *behaviour*, and maybe comparative conciseness, suggests Skinner as author of the first quotation, unless one is biased by the idea that Skinner was possessed by a thirst for power, and cannot read the word *power* under his pen without giving it ideological connotations, which it does not convey more than the "conquering actions" ("les conduites conquérantes") of the Piagetian subject.

# THE EVOLUTIONARY ANALOGY I

These similarities, although usually overlooked, especially by Piaget and Skinner themselves, provide the basis for an integrative theory of development and learning that is further supported by their sharing the use of the evolutionary analogy in accounting for the ontogeny of behaviour. If we appraise both theories in terms of their value for further research, we cannot help emphasising the perspectives opened by the discussion of the role of variations in behaviour, on the part of the master of constructivism as well as of the master of radical behaviourism. In both, the theme of behavioural variations was increasingly central in their respective last writings. It is indeed the core of the book, *Adaptation vitale et psychologie de l'intelligence*, to which I have referred several times. More important than his arguments concerning the phenomenon of phenocopy proper, which to biologists might sound rather poorly founded, Piaget's discussion of evolution in plants is a pretext to deal with an issue that has been faced in the study of behaviour, in traditions as different as his own and behaviourism. The problem of the origin and role of behavioural variations is linked, in Piaget, with his concepts of equilibration-disequilibration. Without entering the intricacies of his theoretical elaborations, suffice it to say that, for Piaget, development can be described as a succession of equilibrium states. He was left with the question: how is it that the organism does not remain in the first state of equilibrium it can enjoy? Why does it eventually fall into disequilibrium, just to start all over again towards another equilibrium, at some higher level? To state that the environment offers some resistance to maintaining the equilibrium does not explain anything, if the organism is not endowed with some "sensitivity" to environmental challenges, which is best implemented in terms of variations. As Piaget states, in a very classical biological style, "there is always, in succession, variation and selection". Such variability cannot be accounted for by the environment:

> The environment plays a fundamental role at all levels *(that is in biological evolution of species as well as in cognitive development)*, but as object of conquest, and not as shaping causation, which is to be looked for, again at all levels, in endogenous activities of the organism and of the subject, both of which would remain conservative and unable to innovate . . . in the absence of the many problems raised by the environment or the external world, but which can react to them by trials and explorations of all sorts, from the elementary level of mutations to the higher level of scientific theories.[20]

This text, though it appears in Piaget's arguments in reply to the behaviouristic error, is, in substance, very close to Skinner's view, except in its affirming the endogenous character of variability. Skinner would be less assertive on that point, and would suggest, rather, that variations originate either in the phylogenic or in the ontogenic history, which means in any case in an interaction with the environment. It is easy to speculate about how Piaget could have drawn from Skinner's analysis of operant behaviour, in terms of selective process, to complete with a heretofore missing link his own ambitious theory based on the continuity of the same processes at all levels of evolution. If his theory holds, one would expect it to encompass the level of learning, which is precisely what Skinner did contend. His is essentially a synthetic theory extending the evolutionary principles to individual behaviour. We shall see in more detail in Chapter 8 how Skinner elaborated on that theme.

At this point, it is worth noting that contemporary psychologists, generally unaware in the past of the convergence between Piaget and Skinner on such a major issue, now seem to recognise it. One case in point is Mehler, who in a recent book[21] discusses his own view of "specific selectionism" by contrasting it with three types of "general selectionism": namely Piaget's, Changeux' and Skinner's. Mehler's reference to Skinner is especially significant, since he was among those psychologists who, some years ago, heralded the death of radical behaviourism.[22] The importance of Skinner, as one of the psychologists who, together with Piaget, resorted to the explanatory power of the evolutionary model, is now duly recognised.

## NOTES

1. As this chapter does not focus on life anecdotal events, but on the written contributions of the two giants of twentieth-century psychology, I have not attempted to establish when and where Piaget and Skinner had the

opportunity to meet. Skinner reports in his autobiography (*A matter of consequences*, p. 213) his visit, upon invitation, to the University of Geneva in 1962. He lectured in French, and was introduced by Piaget himself, who refused to speak English, which he understood perfectly.

2. Review of Hull's *Principles of behavior*, *American Journal of Psychology*, 1944, *57*, 276-281. The paper has been reprinted in *Cumulative Record*, 1959.

3. *Adaption vitale et psychologie de l'intelligence*, 1974, p.28 (translation mine).

4. *About behaviorism*, p.67

5. *Le structuralisme*, Paris, Presses Universitaires de France, 1968.

6. For a discussion on these issues see Richelle, 1986; 1991.

7. Part of this work was published in Inhelder, Sinclair and Bovet, 1974. For a critical appraisal of their approach, see Richelle, 1976c.

8. *About behaviorism*, p.75 (quoted from the paperback edition, Vintage Books, 1976).

9. First published in French, 1967, translated into English, 1971.

10. *Contingencies of reinforcement*, p.205. Reprinted from Skinner, 1966.

11. See Chapter 10.

12. The issue has been dealt with many times by Piaget, but it has been elaborated in depth, and with unusual freedom with respect to "official" biology, in *Adaptation vitale et psychologie de l'intelligence—Sélection organique et phénocopie*, 1974. The book has once again produced accusations of Lamarckism.

13. Goethe, *Faust I*.

14. This remains a radical difference between Piaget and the cognitivist school of thought, that has equally overlooked the roots of cognitive operations in action and their resulting eventually in action. Examined further in Chapter 9.

15. *Contingencies of reinforcement*, p.5.

16. *About behaviorism*, p.154 (see note 8 above).

17. *Cumulative record*, p.255. This text records comments made by Skinner on Alexander's contribution to a conference on "Integrating the approaches to mental disease", that took place in 1956, in which Skinner delivered a short paper on "Psychology in the understanding of mental disease". Italics are mine.

18. *About behaviorism*, p.154 (see note 8 above).

19. *Adaptation vitale et psychologie de l'intelligence*, p.28.

20. *Adaptation vitale et psychologie de l'intelligence*, p.73 ; translation, and emphasis on text in parentheses are mine.

21. Mehler, J. and Dupoux, E., 1990.

22. Mehler, J., 1969. See Chapter 10.

# III TOUCHSTONES OF RADICAL BEHAVIOURISM: BRAIN, COGNITION, LANGUAGE AND CREATIVITY

# 8 Skinner and Biology

## FOUR BAD MARKS IN THE BIOLOGY EXAM?

Skinner's position with respect to biology has been the source of major misunderstandings, in spite of perfectly clear statements on his part. The most widespread misinterpretations can be summarised as follows:

1. Skinner has neglected, or, worse, denied, that important things take place inside the organism, and especially in the brain.
2. His extreme environmentalism has blinded him to the role of heredity in determining behaviour, and led him to leave out of his theory the contributions of modern genetics and psychogenetics to our understanding of the living organisms; viewed from a biological point of view, therefore, his theory is obsolete.
3. His claim that laws of learning are universals has led him to overlook species-specific characteristics, which cannot escape a biologically minded observer aware of interspecies differences, no less visible at the behavioural than at the morphological level.
4. His late resorting to the evolutionary model to explain acquired behaviour is at best superficial metaphorising, and is not enough to put him in the dignified company of modern biologists.

These often-heard criticisms seem at odds with the central tenet of Skinner's position, that his radical behaviouristic approach to psychology is essentially a way to insert the field within the realm of natural sciences, and more specifically of biological sciences. Was he so naïve, or so mistaken, as to assert such crucial identification while elaborating views alien to modern biological thought? Again, fair reading of his writings does not lead to that conclusion. The criticisms mentioned here are clearly distorted representations of his thought, and they often reflect unsophisticated biological thinking on the part of the critics more than on the part of their target.

We can already dispose with criticisms 2 and 3, which have been answered in Chapter 7. We shall now give attention to points 1 and 4.

## SHALL WE DISPENSE WITH BRAIN OR MIND, OR BOTH?

Skinner's position has often been epitomised as "black-box psychology". The expression implicitly conveys two very different kinds of criticism. One refers to the neglect of the neural substrate and correlate of behaviour, and more generally the neglect of the biological aspects of behaviour. The other refers to the dismissal of any inferred, internal entity, or variable, in psychological description and explanation. Both criticisms have a long history in psychology, going back to early behaviourism, but they have been revived in relation to Skinner's version of radical behaviourism, and in the context of current trends in neurosciences on the one hand, and of the development of modern cognitivism on the other.

It could be argued that these are one single criticism, rather than two. Admittedly, in some of its aspects, the cognitivist approach to psychology has been developing in a very close relationship with brain sciences. However, as we shall see, some cognitivists are making the claim that their science—call it psychology, or the science of information processing, or whatever you like—is clearly distinct from brain science, that it is autonomous in using its own methods and concepts, not reducible to those of neurophysiology or neurochemistry. So it seems appropriate to comment separately on each of these criticisms. The first has to do with Skinner's position with regard to psychophysiology, and, as already mentioned, with biology in general. The second has to do with the problem of mentalism. In the first case, the problem we are facing is a fairly classical problem of delineating frontiers between fields of science, of defining their specific methodological features and of specifying the substantial relations, if any, between them. In the second case, we are confronted with a persistent and most difficult epistemological question, that has pervaded psychology from its early days to the present time, and which is nothing less than the question of the subject matter of psychology, and of the ways it should be dealt with.

Brain sciences have been developing in so fascinating a way during the last decades that Skinner's refusal to look into the black box now appears obsolete. Why should one stay at the surface of things, when tools are available which allow us to look in depth at what is going on inside the head? Why should we deprive ourselves of the possibility that is offered right now to understand the mechanisms underlying behaviour, there where they take place, in the brain?

Some neuroscientists, confident in their power, more or less explicitly suggest that brain sciences can be substituted for psychology, and that the study of behaviour, in particular, was but one step in the history of the search for the mystery of the mind. This is, essentially, the stand taken by Changeux, among others, in his famous book *The neuronal Man* (1983). Cerebral recording, and the most recent and promising forms of cerebral imagery, are supposed to give us direct access to mental elements, percepts and concepts, which compose the mind and initiate behaviour.

No one today would seriously think of disputing the fact that the brain has something to do with behaviour, and indeed probably no one ever did, and certainly not Skinner. What he has advocated is the need for a study of behaviour in its own right, which is quite different from saying that the study of the brain is of no interest. On the contrary, his repeated argument has been that, if our knowledge of brain functioning is to develop, it needs, among other prerequisites conditions, adequate methods for the study of behaviour. If we understand the reasons for this methodological position, we shall also understand how it is that laboratory techniques designed by Skinner were eventually so widely accepted in various fields of the neurosciences. For it might, at first sight, seem paradoxical that operant conditioning, invented as it was by a "black-box psychologist", is now in great favour among neuroscientists of all descriptions, be they neurophysiologists, neuropharmacologists, neuroendocrinologists, neurotoxicologists, to name but a few, as was pointed out in Chapter 3.

The alleged black-box approach had classically been attributed to Skinner's naïveté in biological matters. It should be recalled that one of his very first papers, and part of his doctoral thesis at Harvard, was an exclusively theoretical piece of work, entitled "The concept of the reflex in the description of behavior" (1931). By appealing to the history of main discoveries in physiology, from Glisson and Swammerdam to Sherrington, through Robert Whytt, Marshall Hall and Magnus, he discussed at length the notion of reflex and its bearing on the study of the relations between identifiable events which could be substituted for those forces or entities that, under various names, had been called up to account for an organism's actions. In that early paper, he outlined the main ideas that he would elaborate and to some extent reformulate later in his first and influential book, *The behavior of organisms* (1938). For Skinner, in 1931, the concept of reflex as it was traditionally used by physiologists, was obviously inappropriate to describe the sort of material which psychologists are interested in, i.e. behaviour. The simple relation between a stimulus and a response is clearly inadequate to account for behaviour. This relation is modulated by a number of variables, the study of which is more crucial in an analysis of behaviour than the stimulus-response link proper. Skinner had not yet quite reached the notion of the *operant*, nor the essential relationship in an analysis of behaviour between *response* and *reinforcement*, rather than between *stimulus* and *response*. But he was certainly on the way.

As a graduate student and a young fellow at Harvard, Skinner learned physiology and neurophysiology first-hand from teachers like Crozier, Forbes and Davis. When he later wrote on the "flight from the laboratory",[1] pointing to the brain-drain taking many experimental psychologists to neurophysiological work, he certainly did not underestimate the progress made in the study of the nervous system, nor did he ignore its contribution to our understanding of behaviour. However, he advocated the need for a study of behaviour in its own right, and warned psychologists not to leave their field and turn to physiology. The objection was not that physiology is not interesting—in fact, it was exceedingly interesting, to the point that many first-rate experimenters left psychology to fall under its seduction, a seduction based on its technological sophistication, its degree of development or its academic respectability. Skinner does not question their contribution to science; he only regrets that they were lost to psychology:

> We cannot dispute the importance of their contributions; we can only imagine with regret what they might have done instead.[2]

"What they might have done instead", in Skinner's mind, is to contribute to a consistent description of the relations observed at the behavioural level. If psychology is to develop as a science, and to take its place in the set of life-sciences, it has to provide clear and reproducible facts, to build theoretical concepts on its own ground, rather than escape the difficulties of an analysis of behaviour by borrowing facts and concepts from another discipline. This was the message of the paper mentioned earlier in which Skinner denounced the "flight from the laboratory", in various forms, one of which was the flight to the *physiological inner man*. This was not ignorance of, nor attack against, physiology. Skinner's claim was that psychologists should work at their own levels of analysis, i.e. behaviour, not for the sake of preserving an autonomous psychological science or of organising psychological meetings, but, more importantly, because behaviour is one essential aspect of living organisms, and because, therefore, other sciences engaged in the study of living organisms, such as neurophysiology, neurochemistry and neuropharmacology, cannot progress unless descriptions of behaviour compare in rigour and refinement with descriptions of events at their respective level of analysis. How can we understand the functioning of the visual nervous apparatus, from the retina to the cortical structures in projection and associative areas, if we lack thorough knowledge of the stimulations to which the organisms reacts through its visual receptors, and of how its visual perception is organised at the behavioural level? If the neurophysiology of vision has been developing so efficiently it is not only because of the progress in describing anatomically and physiologically the nervous pathways and centres involved, but also because clear behavioural descriptions were available in the work of psychophysicists and specialists of perception in psychology. And part of the recent progress in the field is undoubtedly due to the fact that animal-behavioural studies have reached an unprecedented degree of refinement, thanks to operant techniques. Many other examples could be found in the field of learning and memory, or in the field of neuropharmacology: tremendous progress in recording, stimulating or lesioning methods, or in tracing neurotransmitters and drugs in the nervous system are only part of the story. Another part is to be found in laboratory-behavioural analyses, which made it possible rigorously to describe and measure the course of individual learning in controlled situations, or to show the effects of drugs on animal behaviour, to detect paradoxical effects or addictive properties, or to demonstrate an organism's capacity to discriminate between different internal states induced by different drugs.

It is no wonder, then, that the procedures designed by a psychologist who took the methodological stand to "ignore what is going on in the black box" have been so widely adopted in various fields of the neurosciences. By working obstinately on his own ground, he has managed to forge a most effective tool for making explicit to the student of the brain some of the things he has to explain when dealing with the functions of that astonishing package of neurons. And if neuroscientists are still so frequently indulging in verbal speculations when talking about consciousness, thought, intention, and the like, it is only because, in those matters, psychologists are still babbling, and are still far from being able to offer their neuroscientist friends more than traditional philosophical or common-sense accounts.

Skinner has repeatedly expressed and commented on his position concerning the relationship between psychology and physiology. There is a wide choice of possible quotations that would equally well present his point. The following passage contains the main aspects of his view:

This does not mean, of course, that the organism is conceived of as actually empty, or that continuity between input and output will not eventually be established. The genetic development of the organism and the complex interchanges between organism and the environment are the subject matters of appropriate disciplines. Some day we shall know, for example, what happens when a stimulus impinges upon the surface of an organism, and what happens inside the organism after that, in a series of stages the last of which is the point at which the organism acts upon the environment and possibly changes it. . . . . But all these inner events will be accounted for with techniques of observation and measurement appropriate to the physiology of the various parts of the organism, and the account will be expressed in terms appropriate to that subject matter. It would be a remarkable coincidence if the concepts used to refer inferentially to inner events were to find a place in that account. The task of physiology is not to find hungers, fears, habits, instincts, personalities, psychic energy, or acts of willing, attending, repressing, and so on. Nor is that task to find entities or processes of which all this could be said to be other aspects. Its task is to account for the causal relations between input and output which are the special concern of a science of behavior. Physiology should be left free to do this in its own way. Just to the extent that current conceptual systems fail to represent the relationships between terminal events correctly, they misrepresent the task of these other disciplines. A comprehensive set of causal relations stated with the greatest possible precision is the best contribution which we, as students of behavior, can make in the co-operative venture of giving a full account of the organism as a biological system.[3]

The arguments for keeping the universe of discourse of behavioural sciences apart from the universe of neurophysiology—or brain sciences in general—are sound enough at the methodological level. There is, however, at least one category of scientists who are not ready to submit to that idea: these are psychophysiologists, who, by definition, are working at both levels, physiological and behavioural, simultaneously. They had already been doing quite good work by the time Skinner campaigned against the flight to the physiological inner man, and they were to continue their work with increasing success. Skinner never objected to their pluridisciplinary, integrative approach. He was aware of the place of such enterprises in the history of science:

> It is difficult to attack this theory [*i.e. pseudophysiologising theory, to be discussed in the next section*] without seeming to criticise the physiological psychologist, but no criticism is involved. There are many precedents in the history of science for borderline disciplines. To integrate the facts of two sciences is an interesting and profitable endeavor.[4]

At the epistemological level, it is also a most desirable achievement. But, again, an integrative science requires an equal degree of experimental control and of conceptual clarity in the various fields it aims to integrate.

Where are we today, more than a quarter of a century after Skinner wrote his apologetic papers in defence of a science of behaviour, as distinct from physiology? No doubt, the "borderline" sciences have made tremendous progress, as Skinner himself recognises in a response to a commentary pointing to the change in the situation; progress partly due, as he also emphasises, to the quality of behavioural techniques now available.[5] The time might be ripe for a true integrative science of brain *and* behaviour to emerge, and current enthusiasm in the neurosciences, revived interest in the old Matter and Mind (Brain and Mind/Brain and Behaviour) problem certainly points in that direction. That is not to say that psychologists should give up their methodological specificity. This might still remain for some time the most appropriate way for them to contribute to an integrated neuroscience.

Curiously enough, the plea for a specific psychological science, as distinct from neurophysiology, has been made, more recently, not by old-fashioned behaviourists, but by some cognitivists. In his influential theory of visual perception, the late David Marr has clearly distinguished three levels of analysis—computational, representational and the level of implementation—and argued for the view that a cognitive science has to deal with them in that order, beginning with the most abstract and general level, and ending with neurophysiological implementation. Marr, who was also an expert in neurophysiology (well-known for his work on the cerebellum), is certainly not more suspect than Skinner to have ignored physiology from within. But, for admittedly quite different reasons, he came to the similar conclusion that if physiology is to elucidate the functioning of the brain, it needs a clear description of what is going on at the psychological level. The difference—and indeed an important one that will detain us further in the next chapter—is in what is meant by "psychological". While for Skinner, it is essentially what is taking place when an organism is interacting with its environment, for Marr it refers mainly to mental events and processes taking place in the head of the subject. In its extreme form, this so-called "functionalist" position,[6] as advocated by Johnson-Laird among others, states that an account of "computational" requirements is not exposed to change according to what could eventually result from a neurobiological description.

If behaviours are viewed as mere indices of internal processes, useful for making inferences about these processes but of no interest in themselves, the status of psychology—defined as the science of internal mental processes—in relation to neurobiology raises, once more, difficult and crucial issues. We are yet again confronted with the old philosophical problem of the substance of mind, and epistemological cognitivism might breed the overt or covert return to dualism, and sometimes to spiritualism (see Eccles, 1979; Popper & Eccles, 1977). Whether this will be viewed, in the long run, as the right answer cannot be decided now, but, for the time being, psychologists should be clear about the way they relate mental processes to neural processes. The extreme functionalist position maintains that the psychological, essentially inferential, description can be carried out with no consideration for neural constraints as specified by neurosciences. These are vowed to decode the hardware level of implementation so that it fits the cognitive account. Psychology is given independent status, as it had earlier in its much-criticised "black box" approach, but with the major difference that mental processes and neural matter occupy the same physical space, which was not the case for behaviour and brain "black box" activity. Functionalism preserves autonomy for psychology, but cuts it from the tremendous progress accomplished in neurosciences, depriving it of the new insights they provide in many psychological questions. Those who no longer care for behaviour, although they do not go so far as to adhere to extreme functionalism, expose themselves to leaving the place to neurobiologists as these will progress on their own ground: if percepts and concepts can be evidenced from brain-imagery techniques, why should one insist on using indirect psychological methods? This was in fact the sort of anxiety-producing question some psychologists had to face after reading Changeux's book *The neuronal man* when it was published in 1983. Along the lines of what we have discussed about action in a previous chapter, I contend that psychology will play its part in the wide field of neurosciences if it keeps, as its genuine task, the study of behaviour and inferred mental states on the same continuum of interaction with the environment.

## THE EVOLUTIONARY ANALOGY II

We have already discussed, on several occasions in the preceding chapters,[7] the bearing of the evolutionary model in Skinner's theory. We already know that it has been applied to the process of operant conditioning, seen as analogous to the process of selection upon variation at work in biological evolution. We have alluded to convergencies on this point with Lorenz and with Piaget. The importance of the issue in understanding Skinner's position is such that it calls for further elucidation and additional comments.

Skinner elaborated on the place of the evolutionary analogy in his view of behaviour in a number of important papers published in the last 15 years of his career. His concern with this model, however, began much earlier. It is usually dated from his 1966 paper in reply to Lorenz' attack against the behaviourist approach to animal behaviour. This might lead to the erroneous conclusion that his interest in the variation-selection model emerged from the stimulation of the controversy about Lorenz' thesis. In fact, he had already appealed to Darwin's mode of explanation much earlier, and quite significantly, in *Science and human behavior*, in 1953. From then on, he kept on invoking it, with two very different though equally important purposes.

On the one hand, Darwinism provided him, as it did biology, with an alternative to finalism, and consequently with a decisive argument against mentalism. By resorting to mental entities as the source of behaviour, mentalism gives a central place, in explaining animal or human action, to concepts such as goal or purpose, intention, will, desire, and so on. A similar concept had been resorted to before in biology to explain the adaptation of living organisms. Within the widely adopted framework of evolution theory, adaptive functions were no longer seen as goal-seeking mechanisms, but as by-products of a past history of selective pressures. Skinner credits Thorndike for having grasped the significance of Darwin's model in accounting for purposeful individual behaviour, for having made it:

> possible to include the effects of action without using concepts like purpose, intention, expectancy or utility

and continuing:

> Thorndike's solution was probably suggested by Darwin's treatment of phylogenic purposes. Before Darwin, the purpose of a well-developed eye might have been said to be to permit the organism to see better. The principle of natural selection moved "seeing better" from the future into the past.[8]

In this context, the evolutionary analogy appears as an inspiring precedent, borrowed from another field of science, that helps quite efficiently in solving an old and admittedly difficult problem in a totally new way. One might object that this was but an analogy, and that, as all analogies, it can be misleading. Opponents to Skinner's view (moving from inner causes in the present to selective action in the past) have argued that, whatever the fate of teleological thinking in biology, humans keep manifesting their will and intentions, as is conspicuous from their verbal statements of future actions. The debate has been revived in contemporary psychology by various cognitivist thinkers, both psychologists and philosophers, many of whom take for granted that humans act in such a way as to implement preceding intentions and goals. The status of these is left without any critical analysis. Skinner's account might have been oversimplifying, although he himself was aware of the complexities brought about by the use of language and the ensuing possibility of talking about future events and actions. But giving intentions a sort of axiomatic status, not calling for any explanation, does not solve the problem. We know from many different theoretical approaches in psychology, psychoanalysis not the least, that overt intentions have their own antecedents, to which they are not necessarily unambiguously related, and that nor are they straightforwardly related to the actions that follow.

In a somewhat different context, Skinner has resorted to the evolutionary analogy, already pointed out, as a key explanatory model for operant behaviour. The process at work in shaping and maintaining acquired behaviour (at least of the operant kind) would parallel the process that accounts for biological evolution: namely, natural selection. The evolutionary analogy offers a powerful tool that allows us to understand how new living forms emerged through biological history, without giving up the causal approach that characterises a scientific account. It is tempting to transfer it to explain individually acquired behaviour. Skinner's endeavour, to a large extent, has been aimed at elaborating a theory of behaviour based on the evolutionary model. While acknowledging the seminal contribution made by Thorndike, when he formulated the law of effect, Skinner pushed the idea much further by using it as the key concept for all acquired behaviour that cannot be reduced to Pavlovian associative mechanisms. Operant behaviours are not triggered as reflexes nor as complex motor sequences such as the so-called Fixed Action Patterns described by ethologists. They are emitted, for some reason, before they can be followed by reinforcement. They are, in a way, spontaneous, to use again the qualification made by Skinner himself in *The behavior of organisms*. The selective action of the environment cannot take place unless it has first been produced. The following lines from *Science and human behavior* unequivocally convey the strength of the concept in Skinner's theory as early as 1953:

> In both operant conditioning and the evolutionary selection of behavioral characteristics, consequences alter future probability. Reflexes and other innate

patterns of behavior evolve because they increase the chances of survival of the *species*. Operants grow strong because they are followed by important consequences in the life of the *individual*.[9]

The paragraph continues with comments on purpose, relevant to the earlier discussion in this chapter:

> Both processes raise the question of purpose for the same reason, and in both the appeal to a final cause may be rejected in the same way.

The theme has grown more and more important in Skinner's writings, especially since the 1966 paper in *Science* already mentioned. He has appealed to the evolutionary analogy to explain the production of novelty and creative behaviour, such as works of art.[10] And several of the most important papers he published in his last ten years were fully or partly devoted to it.[11] In one of these papers, "Selection by consequences", Skinner develops the view that the same process, i.e. selection upon variation, accounts for changes observed at all three levels of life; the level of species or biological evolution proper, the level of individual learning (others would talk of individual information-gaining processes) and the level of culture or social practices. The three levels are traditionally dealt with by different scientific disciplines, biology, psychology and cultural anthropology respectively. There is no question that there are important qualitative differences between the three levels, and that the unique mechanism appealed to is operating in each case on distinct material: gene pools are not the same as motor actions, and the latter cannot be confounded with cultural traits. The common process needs some qualifications at each level, which make for the specificity of the three fields of science concerned. However, the basic process first proposed at the level of biological evolution has been borrowed as an explanatory model at the other two levels.

   The question arises: is there more in that transfer than mere analogy, possibly useful as a didactic tool, but with no substance beyond that? It can be argued that qualifications needed at the behavioural and cultural levels are so numerous and so important as to make the analogy almost meaningless.[12] It may be true that the empirical evidence available at the behavioural and cultural levels is far scarcer than at the biological one, but this is not, in itself, an argument against the potential fecundity of the hypothesis, viewed as substantive rather than analogical. It must be remembered that Darwinism remained a theory poorly supported by convincing empirical evidence, although quite attractive to many, until it eventually merged with genetics. There is no rule or principle that would lead us to discard the substantial use of the evolutionary analogy outside the domain of species evolution to which it was initially and successfully applied. A number of scientists, belonging to various fields and with diverse theoretical inclinations, have assumed substantial continuity in basic mechanisms from biological evolution to individual growth or learning, to cultural evolution at large or in one specific aspect, such as the history of scientific thought. A few typical illustrations, selected among the most prominent representatives of that trend, will be presented here briefly, putting Skinner in good company (and reciprocally) and showing that he has been, in this aspect of his work, neither naïve, nor fanciful, nor isolated. By underlining how he shared the evolutionary analogy with many others, we shall perceive his particular point of view as altogether less original and as reflecting an intuition that apparently emerged independently in different fields and in different minds. Such convergences denote one of the most encouraging features in the making of science: that merging of core ideas as imposed by the problems faced, in spite of otherwise divergent preoccupations. Obviously, all those who have resorted to the evolutionary analogy in their own field of research or in their own theoretical frame have been living in the context of modern science, impregnated as it is by the success of Darwin's seminal ideas. But they have not generally borrowed from each other. On the contrary, they have generally worked in mutual ignorance, as already pointed out for Piaget and Skinner.

Piaget is, among psychologists,[13] the one who has given most weight in his monumental work to the evolutionary analogy, and who has taken it most seriously, most literally. We have already (Chapter 7) discussed his constructivist theory, comparing it with Skinner's position. We have seen that one of its main components is the notion of a fundamental continuity from elementary forms of biological processes to the highest achievements of the human mind as exemplified in logic and science. Piaget can be seen as the most "evolutionary minded" of twentieth-century psychologists, with Skinner next in line.

The evolutionary explanation was also inherent in Lorenz' ethology, as would be expected from a biologist whose first concern, as pointed out in Chapter 6, was accounting for the diversity of species-specific behaviour and relating it to other aspects (morphological) of evolution. We shall not comment on his work further, but he undoubtedly has his place in the present context.

Moving to another field, the history of science and epistemology, one cannot avoid mentioning Karl Popper as one of the most famous thinkers of our times who resorted extensively to the evolutionary analogy taken substantially. One of his major books, *Objective knowledge*, first published in 1972, has the sub-title "An evolutionary approach".[14] The theme is, indeed, pervasive in his writings. And it is no surprise that a biologist, the Nobel Prize winner Jacques Monod, was invited to write an introduction to a French edition of the classic *The logic of scientific discovery*. He rightly pointed out:

Conjecture and refutation play in the development of knowledge the same logical role (as sources of information) as mutation and selection, respectively, in the evolution of the living world. And if natural selection has, in the living world, been able to build the mammals' eye or the brain of Homo sapiens, why would selection of ideas not have been able, in its own realm, to build the Darwinian theory or Einstein's theory?[15]

Monod was only echoing the numerous statements made by Popper, expressing his evolutionary conception of scientific development. Especially relevant to our argument is Popper's characterisation of the growth of knowledge as a special case of learning:

> The growth of knowledge—or the *learning process* [italics mine]—is not a repetitive or a cumulative process but one of error-elimination. It is Darwinian selection, rather than Lamarckian instruction.[16]
>
> All this may be expressed by saying that the growth of our knowledge is the result of a process closely resembling what Darwin called "Natural selection"; that is the natural selection of hypotheses: our knowledge consists, at every moment, of those hypotheses which have shown their (comparative) fitness by surviving so far in their struggle for existence; a comparative struggle which eliminates those hypotheses which are unfit.[17]

Popper goes on to frame this view of the evolution of scientific knowledge in the general view of the development of knowledge—or learning—in living systems, in a formula that Skinner would have approved:

> This interpretation may be applied to animal knowledge, pre-scientific knowledge, and to scientific knowledge.

He further insists, again in a way to which Piaget and Skinner would have subscribed, on the status of the analogy:

> This statement of the situation is meant to describe how knowledge really grows.
> It is not meant metaphorically, though of course it makes use of metaphors . . .
> From the amoeba to Einstein, the growth of knowledge is always the same.[18]

The author could not have come closer to Skinner's own phrasing. However, he has not recognised the similarity, having exclusively focused his attention on Skinner's sociophilosophical writings, especially his Utopia, which he attacked vigorously. Skinner, on his part, does not seem to have been aware of Popper's pervasive use of the evolutionary analogy. This is but another case of reciprocal ignorance on the part of two great intellectuals.[19]

Neurobiology is another field where major recent theoretical advances are centred on the principle of selection over variations. Changeux has resorted to the evolutionary model to account for the formation of synaptic networks in neural development, in his theory of "selective stabilisation". Extending his interests to the functioning of the brain as the organ involved in cognitive processes and behaviour, he has proposed a dynamic approach to cognition after the same model, labelled "generalised Darwinism".

A similar stand has been taken by Edelman, whose book *Neural Darwinism: The theory of neuronal group selection* (1987) not only presents the author's theory of neuronal epigenetic development strongly anchored in an updated version of selectionism and population thinking, but bridges the gap with behavioural sciences by extending the same theoretical scheme to psychological levels of action, perception, categorisation, memory and learning. This book would deserve special mention in the present context, because it is more than another example of the use of the same kind of explanatory principle in various fields. It is, far more explicitly than in Changeux, an endeavour towards synthesis between those fields. We shall limit ourselves to two short quotations from Edelman's concluding chapter that clearly illustrate the commonalities with other thinkers cited above, sharing with them the evolutionary analogy in the substantial sense, and its corollary, the concept of living beings as generators of diversity, a condition to offer the selective process the material upon which it can operate:

> It is important, for example, to distinguish between evolutionarily determined behavioral responses and those dependent upon individual variation in somatic time[20] within a species. In somatic time, the first view implies instruction—information from the environment fundamentally determines the order of functional connectivity (although not necessarily that of physical connectivity) in the nervous system. The second alternative is selection—groups in pre-existing neuronal repertoires that form populations determined by phylogeny and ontogenetic generators of diversity are selected by stimuli to yield highly individual response patterns.

Edelman proposes a neuronal theory that integrates the developmental dimension and the requirements assigned by the study of behaviour both in ethology and in experimental studies of learning mechanisms (the synthesis suggested earlier between Piaget, Skinner and Lorenz), and, though resisting the temptation to venture into generalisation to cultural evolution, he envisions the reconciling between the lawfulness of nature and the individual creation of novelty:

> If extension to such issues finally turned out to be feasible, then it would not be surprising if, to some extent, every perception were considered to be an act of creation and every memory an act of imagination. The individualistic flavor and the extraordinary richness of selective repertoires suggest that, in each brain, epigenetic elements play major and unpredictable roles. Categorical genetic determinism has no place in such systems; neither has instructionist empiricism. Instead, genetic and developmental factors interact to yield systems of remarkable complexity capable of an equally remarkable degree of freedom. The constraints placed on this freedom by chronology and by the limits of repertoires, while definite, do not seem as impressive as the unending ability of somatic selective systems such as the brain to confront novelty, to generalize upon it, and to adapt in unforeseen fashions.[21]

Edelman makes abundant and appropriate references to students of behaviour, and especially of learning, from Thorndike to Macintosh, from Pavlov to

Rescorla. He quite relevantly refers to Staddon (1983), one of the students of behaviour of the post-Skinnerian generation who has developed a theory of learning elegantly aimed at integrating the evolutionary model at both levels of species-specific behaviour and of individually learned behaviour.[22] He has also come across Skinner's own brand of selectionism, and credits him for having insisted on the control by consequences. But he denies him a real understanding of what a selectionist explanation is about. He blames him for being only an instructionist, contending that learning is essentially the printing in of environmental information on the organism.

We know that this is not a fair picture of Skinner's position, although it has been retained by many others, including Piaget. Perhaps one explanation for this particular distortion of Skinner's thinking is to be found in the fact that he has failed to provide empirical support for his theoretical treatment of the variation-selection issue, or, more precisely, to put to experimental test one half of the process, i.e. variation. To the question, "Did the analogy inspire an empirical programme?", Plotkin plainly answered, "No",[23] meaning that neither Skinner himself, nor his followers, had undertaken to validate the analogy at the behavioural level by investigating the sources and the nature of behavioural variation.

It is true that, with the few exceptions alluded to in Chapter 4, little experimental research has been devoted to that important aspect of the learning mechanism, in spite of the place it has been given in Skinner's theoretical writings. The work carried out in Skinner's laboratory, as well as that done by other behaviour analysts, has been almost exclusively focused on the selective action of the environment. Contingencies of reinforcement have been explored in all directions, and attention has been mainly centred on steady states, to the detriment of the acquisition process itself, presumably more appropriate an object of study for those who are interested in the variation process.

How can such disregard be explained? First, one must admit that not all the implications of the evolutionary analogy as a model for operant behaviour were fully appraised by Skinner himself until the late 1950s (if we suppose that he matured the theme from his early formulations in 1953 until his 1966 paper stimulated by Lorenz' publication). This is also the time when he almost completely abandoned practical experimental work to turn to theoretical writings. His important contributions to the laboratory from the early 1930s until the publication of *Schedules of reinforcement* (Ferster & Skinner, 1957) had shown little concern for behavioural variation. There is little doubt that there has been a fascination, in Skinner and in his disciples, for the lawful effects of contingencies of reinforcement, linked to a fascination for the productive side of the highly automatised techniques put to work in the operant laboratory. It is also fair to note that the study of variation, looked at in its own right, is not an easy one. It is difficult to disentangle variation as an intrinsic property of the behaving organism, and variation as the by-product of poor experimental control.

Psychologists who, from the early days of their science had to struggle to establish their scientific respectability, have never been eager to expose themselves to blame for lack of rigour, and one cannot be sure that rigorous empirical studies on variations in the operant could have been possible before computer technology entered the laboratory. That it is now possible has been demonstrated by a number of experiments, some of which have been discussed in Chapter 4. If we consider that some 25 years have passed since "The phylogeny and ontogeny of behavior", we can wonder why this crucial issue in behaviour theory has not given rise to more experimental tests than it has, and we can understand that some misunderstanding has survived on that particular point among Skinner's critics, even those who were quite sympathetic to his views.

## NOTES

1. *Cumulative Record*, (1972), pp.314–330
2. *Cumulative Record*, (1972), p.326
3. *Cumulative Record*, p.269–270. Reprinted from Gildea (1956).
4. Ibid., p.303. Reprinted from *Current trends in psychology* (Dennis et al., 1947).
5. See Author's Response to Open Peer Commentary on "Methods and theory in the experimental analysis of behavior", *The Behavioral and Brain Sciences*, 1984, 7, 541–546.
6. The term *functionalism* has been used to qualify various theoretical and methodological positions throughout the history of psychology, with meanings differing from the one it has in the present context, and in contemporary cognitive sciences. Appropriate dictionaries will serve to clarify the various meanings.
7. See especially Chapters 4, 6, and 7.
8. Quoted from Skinner (1963) as reprinted in *Contingencies of reinforcement* (1969b), p.106.
9. *Science and human behavior*, p.90.
10. See especially two papers (reprinted as Chapters 22 and 23 in *Cumulative record*, 1972) that are pleasant reading, besides containing important remarks on the issue at stake here.
11. See especially 1981, 1984b.
12. This is the position taken, among others, by Plotkin, 1987.
13. For details on other users of the evolutionary analogy in psychology, see Plotkin (1982), Plotkin and Odling-Smee (1981). Van Parijs (1981) has discussed in some depth the evolutionary paradigm in the social sciences.
14. The book includes some papers written earlier. Quotations made in the present chapter are from the 1979 revised edition.
15. From Monod, in Popper, 1978, p.4. Monod's introduction is dated 1971, and appeared in the 1973 edition. Translation is mine.

16. *Objective knowledge*, p.144.
17. Ibidem, p.261
18. Ibidem, p.261
19. Popper's declared repugnance for Skinner's socio-political ideas is not enough to explain the fact that he did not refer to other aspects of his scientific work, and more specifically to his borrowing from evolutionary theory in a way much akin to his own. He kept Piaget in comparable neglect: neither in *Objective knowledge*, nor in his important contribution to the book with John Eccles, *The self and its brain* (Popper & Eccles, 1977), can we find the slightest allusion to the work of the Genevan evolutionary epistemologist, whose major writings were available to anyone in English.
20. The expression "somatic time" refers to the lifetime of an individual organism. In Skinner's term, it could be replaced by "onotgeny".
21. Edelman, 1987, p.329
22. Edelman quoted Staddon, 1983. He could also have referred to Staddon and Simmelhag, 1971.
23. See Plotkin, 1987.

# 9 From Mentalism to Cognitivism

## MENTAL LIFE AND BEHAVIOURISM

To contemporary psychologists, of whom the majority define themselves as cognitivists, or at least as specialists of cognitive sciences, Skinner's obstinate antimentalism appears as his major flaw, if not his capital sin. To them, it definitely leaves him behind, alien to the current advances of psychology, which has turned again to the study of Mind. The issue cannot possibly be clarified without putting Skinner's antimentalism in its original context, nor without diagnosing what cognitivism is about and what its internal problems are today. It is of special importance because Skinner spent a considerable part of his writing activity in the last 20 years repeating his basic position and refining his arguments against the cognitivist tenets.

Skinner's antimentalism must be understood in the framework of behaviourism, and in relation to his own brand of *radical* behaviourism. As is well known, the behaviourist revolution was essentially aimed at escaping from the blind-alley in which scientific psychology found itself by the turn of the century. In spite of its respect for methodological rigour, psychology continued to rely on introspection as a major source of information, or as a major channel for collecting data, concerning mental states or mental life. The approach had proved to be unsatisfactory on many grounds. Among others, the reliability of self-reports in pointing to real determinants of conduct had been seriously questioned by psychoanalysis; psychologists of the Würzburg school had failed in their attempts to elucidate thought processes by resorting to introspective method; students of animal behaviour were not helped by progress in human scientific psychology, while experimental work on animals in physiology proved more and more fruitful in drawing general laws, and in dealing, in a second step, with the human body.

When Watson proclaimed psychology to be the science of behaviour, he was crystallising ideas that had already been expressed in a less assertive style by others (especially by Piéron in France),[1] or that had been put to work elegantly, though with little epistemological elaboration, by Pavlov and his school. It was a second step towards integrating the field in the natural sciences, after the foundation of scientific psychology one half century earlier. Observable events and behaviours were emphasised, and mental states were left aside. Although the new view of psychology spread very quickly, and came to be widely accepted, mentalism did not disappear from the scene, as we have already observed in Chapter 1: mental states, entities or constructs remained flourishing in many areas of psychology, under names such as aptitudes, attitudes, needs, drives, traits and the like. Those psychologists who continued to use these and similar concepts in accounting for human actions were never real behaviourists, even though they would sometimes, if asked, have defined psychology as the science of behaviour. We have already seen that Skinner's antimentalism addressed these abuses of "explanatory fictions", which, to him, had the perverse effect of cutting the way to a real analysis of what goes on, by assigning a causal status to uncontrollable inferred internal states. This has also been his central objection to the psychic apparatus of Freudian theory, although he recognised the quality of Freud's observations and credited him for his deterministic approach to human psychology (see Chapter 5). The contrast between such extreme positions is clear enough, and makes the arguments for antimentalism crystal clear themselves, if still debatable.

A much more subtle issue, and a much more important one with respect to the later rise of cognitivism, has emerged, however, among behaviourists themselves. It has opposed the so-called *methodological* behaviourists to the *radical* behaviourists. They differ mainly in the status they give to mental events or states. Methodological behaviourists admit that mental life is not directly accessible to scientific scrutiny, while assuming, more or less explicitly, that it is what psychologists would really like to understand. So they satisfy themselves with studying observables, being both confident in the success, however limited, of so doing, and resigned to remain for ever, so to speak, at the surface of things.

Radical behaviourism takes a drastically different stand. It contends that mental life is nothing essentially distinct from behaviour, that there is no rationale for distinguishing between observable behaviour and what goes on inside the organism, if it is to be dealt with by psychology at all (we have discussed the problem of the relation between behavioural and neurobiological analysis in Chapter 8). The distinction is only due to pre-scientific, or unscientific, traditional common sense or philosophical interpretations, which are no more relevant to a scientific approach to psychology than the biblical account of creation was to a real understanding of the origins of species. In that perspective, the study of behaviour is viewed as encompassing all that has to be known at the psychological level. It does not leave any place for an impenetrable territory, which for exploration would require tools that are beyond the competence of science, a territory in which could be located some unattainable agents or causes of observed phenomena (which is the methodological behaviourist stand). The meaning of the word *behaviour*, in that context, is not restricted to simple motor actions: it also extends to verbal behaviour, problem-solving and innovation.

One cannot expect that either of these positions would be free of difficulties. Indeed, difficulties exist on both sides, and they plausibly explain to some extent why radical behaviourism has been so strongly rejected by many, and why methodological behaviourism eventually bred cognitivism.

For methodological behaviourists, two positions were possible with respect to the status of mental life. Either it was by essence inaccessible to scientific enquiry, and psychologists would have to satisfy themselves for ever with studying only its overt manifestations in observable behaviour: they were condemned to Platonism, so to speak, doomed to contemplate the image of essences. Or, it could be hoped that the current limitations were only temporary, that progress in the techniques of science would eventually break the frontier and give access to mental life. Although debates around the unpassable limits of scientific knowledge recur throughout the history of all sciences, scientists usually tend to think confidently of their own power, and to leave open the possibility that later they will eventually understand what is closed to them today. As we shall see, cognitivism is partly an evolution of methodological behaviourism that has emerged from progress in experimental procedures giving access to heretofore inaccessible domains; but, in another aspect, it has altogether relegated behaviour at the level of a simple expression of the deeper mental life, finally unveiled.

Radical behaviourism is not without its own problems. Skinner insisted that his objections to mentalism were not so much that the things it refers to are *mental*, but that, more often than not, it destroys the way to real explanation. Skinner recognised that there are such things as internal (if the word mental is to be avoided) events, which pertain to the domain of behaviour. The skin, as he put it, is not that important a frontier. But, if so, we are left with the questions: what is the status of these internal events, and how can they be approached? How shall we trace the limits between what can still be dealt with within a behavioural analysis, and what should be left to physiology—after Skinner's suggestion, on other occasions, that internal processes should be left to those equipped to explore them appropriately? In the simplest case, as in covert speech, it seems fairly easy to account for the process of the internalisation of initially overt behaviour, and even to characterise such "internal behaviour" by resorting to ingenuous procedures, like those used with children by Vygotsky in that particular case. One could extend the same argument to "seeing in the absence of the stimulus seen", or other cases of "perceptual behaviour" with no stimulus present, by looking at perception as action, rather than recording copies to be stored, but such action is clearly not easily accessible to investigation. At some point, psychologists have no other way than to make inferences, and develop procedures that give maximum plausibility to their inferences. There is little doubt that the rise of the concept of "cognitive psychology", and the emergence of a "cognitivist" movement originated in the problem of inferences. But the movement has evolved in so many directions that we must first try to analyse its protean forms, before qualifying Skinner's position.

## COGNITIVISMS: A TENTATIVE FOURFOLD CLASSIFICATION

The rise of cognitivism did not leave Skinner indifferent. He reacted on several grounds, and in very different moods. He has been sometimes pathetic and rhetorical, as in the finale of one of his lectures imitating Zola's style in his famous pamphlet related to the Dreyfus affair;[2] sometimes ironical; sometimes erudite, as in his search for the behavioural origin of cognitive terms and concepts;[3] sometimes disenchanted and resigned, as in his paper "Whatever happened to psychology as the science of behavior?"[4] His very last lecture, delivered a few days before he died, and the manuscript of which he completed the day before he died, was another, particularly firm attack on cognitivism which he did not hesitate to compare to creationism:

> Cognitive science is the creation science of psychology, as it struggles to maintain the position of a mind or self.[5]

Before summarising his arguments, it will be useful to delineate the meaning of the term cognitivism, that has become the magic word of modern psychology. It seems impossible to give one single definition for what appears, under scrutiny, as a common label applied to very distinct things. It is difficult not to come to the conclusion that there are *cognitivisms*, rather than *one* cognitivism. There might be some shifts from one to another, but there are enough differences not to confound them in the same bag. The following classification is admittedly tentative,[6] but it will help in appraising Skinner's criticisms, which do not always address the same type of cognitivism.

It seems appropriate to distinguish four types of cognitivism, characterised by very different emphasis at the methodological or epistemological level, and with very different impacts on the practical and social aspects of psychological sciences. For ease of reference, I shall label these four types *methodological*, *epistemological*, *ethical* and *institutional* cognitivisms, respectively.

*Methodological* cognitivism is perfectly in line with what has preceded it in the tradition of scientific psychology, based as it is on the use of scientific procedures to increase our understanding of a given area of reality. The emphasis on internal processes (information processing, representation, memory organisation and the like) reflects the fact that progress has been made in solving the problem of accessibility, a central problem faced by every science confronted with the limits of observation and the plausibility of inference. New techniques have been designed, or old techniques have been improved, which now make possible the study of phenomena and processes heretofore inaccessible or simply unsuspected (we have seen in Chapter 3 how operant procedures contributed to these progresses). New hypotheses have been formulated, which aim at accounting for properties observed in previously collected data. New theoretical models have been worked out to integrate facts which did not fit into earlier frames. All this has been an *evolution*, rather than a *revolution*; an evolution whose salient phases can easily be identified in the past, including the past of behaviourism. Tolman is generally credited for having stated important issues in accounting for purposive behaviour and for having later, still more clearly anticipating the cognitive approaches, proposed the notion of a cognitive map in his analysis of latent maze-learning in rats. Most neo-behaviourists have been concerned in an explicit way with the processes taking place between the stimulus and the response, and have resorted, with various success, to intervening variables. Skinner has traced the early origin of cognitive psychology, seen as a branch of American scientific psychology grown in the behaviouristic tradition, to the appeal of intervening variables by Tolman. In a review of Laurence Smith's book *Behaviourism and logical positivism* (1987) reprinted in *Recent issues* (Skinner, 1989) as Chapter 10, he comments on Smith attributing Tolman's position to the influence he underwent in Vienna during a sabbatical year (1933–34). He suggests as a plausible alternative or supplementary explanation that Tolman might have thought over Skinner's 1931 paper, that "he had read with excitement and had discussed with his seminar".

Both Tolman and Skinner used similar formulae to account for behaviour causation, except for the status of additional factors—besides stimuli, past history and heredity. Skinner called them simply "third variables" while Tolman called them "intervening variables". Skinner comments: "That may have been the point at which the experimental analysis of behavior parted company from what would become cognitive psychology." Karl Lashley's seminal papers, especially his famous lecture on the serial order of behaviour, have opened the way to the notion of programme for motor action that has revealed one of the most fruitful concepts in later research on psychophysiology and psychology of motor skills.

Hebb's theorising about the type of neural organisation required for learning was revealed to be equally as stimulating as Tolman's or Lashley's contributions, and it is still today, possibly beyond cognitivism, a source of inspiration for connectionists. George Miller, Galanter and Pribram, Broadbent, and, soon afterwards, Neisser were treading in the steps of these and other major forerunners when they laid the foundations of so-called *cognitive psychology*. Just like almost all other fields of science, it has benefited widely from the advances of the computer, both as a technical tool for experimenting with unprecedented efficiency (contemporary refined experiments on attentional processes, for example, would not have been feasible before the computer became part of any laboratory equipment), and as a source of explanatory metaphors, suggesting models of the subject's functioning amenable to empirical verification (an extremely important condition if metaphorical models are to be useful at all). Looked at from a distance, discarding for a while the quasi ideological conflicts sometimes opposing cognitivists to behaviourists, current psychological research appears to be building on the past, which means expanding earlier work. This had to be done, if new questions were to emerge and better tools be designed to solve them. Not all those who are today engaged in such research feel obsessed by their affiliation to any school or sect, and they worry little about an undebatable definition of the object of psychology—as many biologists of the past worried little about the essence of life, preferring to look closely into living organisms, and progress step by step toward a better knowledge that would eventually lead to elucidate the concept of life.

*Epistemological* cognitivism, which could be appropriately called *radical cognitivism*, goes one step further—an important step. Rather than adding new objects to those already explored, thanks to new genuine procedures and models, epistemological cognitivism drastically changes the subject-matter of psychology: mental processes are given exclusive attention, and behaviour is relegated to the status of the observable expression of mental activities, possibly still useful— maybe not for a long time—to infer what is going on inside, but with no interest in its own right. While behaviourism could have been accused, at some time, of ignoring mental life and consciousness, reducing them to epiphenomena of behaviour, epistemological cognitivism has completely reversed the perspectives, viewing behaviour as a mere by-product of mental events. An extreme illustration of such radical cognitivism can be found in Dickinson's theory of animal learning,[7] where the author states that "behavioural changes are only of interest as indices that learning has taken place and as pointers to the nature of the internal representations set up by the experience".[8] The latter, under terms like representation, mental processes, etc., are the real subject-matter of psychology. Behaviours are given consideration only to the extent that, for the time being, inferences must be based on some observable data. Supposing, however, that someone proposed to go straight to mental representations and succeed, we could dispense with behaviour altogether. Epistemological cognitivism has clearly taken the position opposite to methodological behaviourism, especially in its version known as operationalism. The latter recognised that mental life is the important thing, but that only observable behaviours are amenable to scientific analysis. Epistemological cognitivism is more optimistic: it goes unhesitatingly to the study of mental life, using behaviours as long as they will help, with the prediction that we shall eventually dispense with them altogether.

The relationship of epistemological cognitivism with neurobiology raises a number of critical issues, some of which have been dealt with in Chapter 8. If no specifically psychological tools are prescribed *a priori* to study mental representations, one is exposed to abandon psychology for direct neurobiological enquiry, whenever neurobiologists would claim they have direct access to them.[9] This would by no means be a world disaster, only the end of psychological science; but the question should still be asked: can neurobiology progress in the absence of a science of behaviour? Radical cognitivism can only preserve itself from disappearance by asserting the functionalist position, as represented by Johnson-Laird and others, that states the perfect independence of cognitive analysis with respect to the neural level. This means eventually that contradictions could remain unsolved between the cognitive and the neural level. Needless to say, assertions as to the radical break from previous schools of thought are mainly found among epistemological cognitivists.

*Ethical* cognitivism is linked to the rehabilitation of the autonomous control of the psychological agent, of rationality over instinctual pulsions, of free will over unconscious determinants of conduct. It might be a reaction against the Freudian as well as against the Darwinian view of man. All psychological theories which have taken the deterministic hypothesis seriously, and have attempted, as Skinner did, to re-state the concepts of goal, intention, desire, preference or choice, by referring to environmental and historical factors, have come across the fortress of free will, because they were depriving the subject of his autonomy. Ethical cognitivism brings it back to him, be it only by the magic of words. The computer metaphors give renewed respectability to terms like choice, decision, selection, etc. These were usually borrowed from the layman's language by early computer scientists, as quick and easy labels, with no awareness of the problems they raised in psychology; later they were adopted by cognitive psychologists with little awareness of the purely pragmatic reasons for their being present in computer sciences.

Ethical cognitivism has found support in theories recently elaborated in neurobiology and in psychology emphasising top-down (versus bottom-up) causation. This fruitful distinction or bi-directional view of causality, illustrated by a number of convincing descriptions in various fields, had fed new formulations of man's rationality and spirituality, as in Eccles' dualism or Sperry's "non-dualist mentalism".[10] It has been especially appealing to practitioners, and it is no surprise that it has invaded the field of psychotherapy, in which techniques of self-control again seem to be in favour. When looked at carefully, it offers in most respects very little resemblance to methodological and epistemological cognitivisms, the lexical level maintaining illusory, and confusing, unity. Strangely enough, some of the cognitive therapies emerged from the behaviour therapies, as indicated by the hybrid labels of behaviour-cognitive or cognitive-behavioural therapies (see Chapter 12).

Finally, *institutional* cognitivism, in my classification, refers to the explicit or implicit opposition between cognition on the one hand, and emotion, motivation and affect on the other. Emphasis on cognition has often gone together with overlooking or ignoring emotion and motivation. This is not essentially an institutionally based distinction: it goes far deeper than that. But it has important institutional by-products in so far as it establishes a distribution of tasks in academic psychology and a split in curricula which, if I may caricature a little, reserves cognition and mind, with all their current prestige, to experimental and theoretical psychology, leaving emotion and other messy matters to those concerned with people's psychological problems in the fields of application. Many experimental psychologists now tend to think of themselves as *cogni-scientists*, rather than psychologists, and are ready to move to computer sciences' or cognitive sciences' departments to exert their talents. There is no surprise, then, that practitioners, who are, as ever, confronted with people suffering from problems of an essentially emotional and motivational nature, turn away from a basic science that has little to tell them. The recent secession within the American Psychological Association, resulting in the creation of a new society of academics and basic research psychologists, with practitioners making up a large membership of the APA, is in some respects an episode of the cognitive revolution.

## SKINNER AGAINST COGNITIVISMS: J'ACCUSE . . .

Using that admittedly imperfect classification, let us return to Skinner and to his position *vis-à-vis* cognitivism. Although he has not explicitly traced the sort of distinction I have made, it is not difficult to disentangle, among his arguments, those which concern more specifically each type of cognitivism, as characterised earlier.

There are good reasons to think that if cognitivism had been reduced to its methodological brand, Skinner would not have crusaded against it at all. He would have commented on the use of certain mentalistic terms, as he had before, but he would not have identified any new danger for the science of behaviour. Quite in agreement with the description we have made of methodological cognitivism, he notes, in the discussion of peer commentaries to his main papers appearing in reprints:

> Most of what is called cognitive science is work that was carried on in more or less the same way before that magical work was added.[11]

Or, on another occasion, along the same lines:

> There are many cognitive psychologists who are doing fine research.[12]

Furthermore, he acknowledges that important discoveries can take place under various banners, and that you need not be in the privileged club of behaviour analysts to contribute to the progress of behavioural science:

Many of the facts, and even some of the principles, which psychologists have discovered when they may have thought they were discovering something else are useful. We can accept, for example, what psychophysicists tell us about response to stimuli without agreeing that they show a mathematical relation between mental and physical worlds. We can accept many of the facts reported by cognitive psychologists without believing that their subjects were processing information or storing representations or rules.[13]

We can dispose still more quickly of the fourth type of cognitivism, which has not been a matter of concern for Skinner. A clear-cut distinction between cognition and emotion, or cognition and motivation, has been alien to his empirical as well as theoretical work. Although he has elaborated his own way of approaching motivational issues in terms of reinforcing properties, he has always paid much attention to emotional by-products of aversive controls in animals and humans. Moreover, he has repeatedly commented about the place of feelings in a behavioural analysis, showing that the concern for a scientific account by no means alters their subjective importance.[14] He was strongly convinced that basic research on behaviour can have important applications to human society, and he spent much energy in showing in which directions this could be done (see Chapters 14 and 15). The divorce between basic research and practice could only appear to him as a step backwards.

Skinner's objections are mainly addressed to the second and third types of cognitivism, and his attacks are especially strong against epistemological cognitivism. His arguments are well summarised in his statement:

Cognitive psychology is frequently presented as a revolt against behaviorism, but it is not a revolt, it is a retreat.[15]

This retreat is to habits and conceptions that had been abandoned by scientific psychology through a sustained effort to free itself from common sense or philosophical ways of talking about and explaining conduct. Habits at stake are essentially habits in word use; conceptions are about the status of mental events.

Skinner points to the invasion of terms that had been carefully avoided in the past because they were loaded with too many meanings, or contaminated with too loose linguistic uses, to fit a scientific description. He accuses

cognitive scientists of relaxing standards of definition and logical thinking and releasing a flood of speculation characteristic of metaphysics, literature, and daily intercourse, speculation perhaps suitable enough in such arenas but inimical to science.[16]

To him, one of the explanations of the success of cognitive psychology is that it has welcomed again the old ways of talking about human beings, reinstating uncritically the wide use of terms such as intention, belief, mind, representation, and many others. If we look at the current psychological literature, it is difficult not to agree with Skinner that terminology has become less rigid. To pick up only one of the most frequent terms, *representation*, we find that it refers to dozens of different things or concepts, usually left undefined. Skinner contends that in many cases this new style is unnecessary, and that more straightforward behavioural terms would express things more clearly. He has repeatedly rephrased typical statements of cognitive psychologists into his own behaviouristic words, with a result that should appeal to those who do not dislike simplicity.

The concern for words used in psychology has always been central in Skinner's reflection. In one of his major papers, published in 1945, he dealt with the "operational analysis of psychological terms". Unsatisfied with the limitations imposed by operationism on the study of private events, he undertook to explore how verbal reports can be related to internal stimuli and states, and pointed to the role of the verbal community in shaping a subject's description of his or her private world. This paper was important in two respects. First, it made clear that Skinner was taking into account private events, which operationists did not deny but thought impossible to study. Second, it laid the basis for further elaboration of a conception of self-knowledge and consciousness as rooted in the individual's interaction with a verbal community, a view that had been quite independently developed by Vygotsky and by Luria.[17]

One of Skinner's last papers[18] is fully devoted to the lexical exercise of tracing back the etymology of words favoured by cognitivist psychologists. He has no difficulty in showing that in practically every case those terms, or their etymological roots, originally referred to behaviour rather than feelings or states of mind. For example, *perceive* originally meant *capture* (Latin *percapere*), as *comprehend* (the French *comprendre*, understand) meant *seize* or *grasp* (the words are still used in both the physical and metaphorical senses), or *solve*, "to loosen or set free". We must admit that, however interesting, such linguistic inquiry does not really demonstrate that all those terms forged by natural languages do not in fact refer to mental events and states; it only reveals, or better confirms, an old discovery of historical linguistics, that internal events are first labelled and described by words referring to external ones, as abstractions are initially designated by concrete terms, through the pervasive mechanism of metaphor. What Skinner was doing on that occasion is illustrative of his own interpretation of the origins of self-descriptive behaviour and self-consciousness, rather than demonstrative of the irrelevance of cognitive states.[19]

However, the issue is not just one of reinstating verbal rigour in psychologists' discourse. Words used have, in that case, deep implications—which are the core of epistemological cognitivism. We are back again to the crucial alternative: are so-called cognitive processes part of behaviour (are they anything other than behaviour) or do they have a mental status of their own, with behaviour being merely their by-products? Skinner's position, clearly in favour of the first possibility, can be captured in a few major arguments.

1. Cognitive psychology, by resorting abundantly and uncritically to "cognitive" words, attributes to the subject, animal or human, an explicit or implicit knowledge of rules, that are in fact in the organisation of the subject's environment, or, in some senses, in the organisation of behaviour, but not in the subject's head as independent entity to be put to work at will. There are no more reasons to account for discriminative behaviour, or concept classification, or face recognition in terms of "knowledge", than to account for immune reactions. It is fairly obvious that, if there is any order in the universe—which is the basic assumption of science—everything we might like to describe and explain we shall describe and explain by formulating rules, but these need not be attributed to the things described. The physical properties of a bicycle combined with those of the human body strongly determine the organisation of the behaviour of riding a bicycle, but it does not help to insert rules distinct from the riding behaviour itself, or preceding its performance. The issue has been debated with particular respect to the use of language and thought, which we shall consider in some detail in the next two chapters. Although resistant to the cognitivists' abuse of rule knowing and rule applying, Skinner has paid much attention to the status of rules in the sense of verbal instructions that human subjects can receive from others, or can use for themselves, be it in improving motor performance, acquiring adequate behaviour without damage, as in car driving, or in solving problems. Behaviour is then said to be "rule governed", in an explicit way, and in so far as verbal behaviour can be given a higher position in the hierarchy of behaviour organisation, we might like to talk of top-down causation.

2. Cognitive psychology, probably due to the pervasive influence of the computer metaphor, has revived the old copy theory. In short, the copy theory says that when we perceive something, we make a sort of duplicate of the thing perceived, that is stored somehow in our head; when we learn something, memories are similarly stored in appropriate places in our mind, from which we retrieve them as needed, and as we are able. The word *copy* has generally been abandoned, and replaced by more fashionable terms, such as *representation*. Skinner did not wait for the rise of cognitivism to object to the copy theory of perception and memory.[20] He has viewed perception and learning as action, rather than simple recording of the external world. The organism that perceives or memorises is, obviously, a changed organism, but the change does not consist in adding one percept or one memory in some internal storing place.

The primacy of action, not only in acting upon the world but also in catching information from it through sensory channels, is not exclusively Skinner's idea.

It appears to many as a decisive conquest of scientific psychology. It was central in Janet's conceptions, and still more so in Piaget's. As is well known, Piaget traced the ontogenic origins of the most abstract logical reasoning to motor action, and used to talk about *perceptual activities*, rather than perception. Sensory psychophysiology had made it clear that visual or other inputs are, as a rule, not simple recording of physical events readily transduced to internal representation, but active processes guided by refined motor adjustments. The whole functioning of the brain cannot be understood, and its taking and processing of external information does not make any sense, if behavioural output does not eventually follow. Cognitive psychology has so much accustomed us to using the concept of representation uncritically that we easily overlook all its implications. Besides rejecting the view that perceiving, learning, and problem-solving are actions, it implies, as a corollary, that the external world has its inbuilt organisation that determines how its various components will be represented within the mind. In other words, the world outside is given, and the psychological subject is there to collect and treat representations of it. For Skinner, as for many psychologists outside the cognitive school of thought, the organism is changed throughout its interaction with the environment, that is to say the world around has no existence, nor can it be represented, independently of the subject's actions.

It must be underlined that the dominance of representations—or more generally purely mental states—over action, that has marked two decades of cognitivist thought, has been seriously questioned in the recent past from within the cognitivist school. An especially harsh attack against representation has been expressed by F. Varela, whose concern is, explicitly, to give the concept of action prevalence over the concept of representation. He urges the cognitive sciences to return to interactive theories, and proposes the concept of *enaction* in place of representation.[21] Enaction clearly implies that every cognitive process is rooted in active interchanges with the world outside. Varela reinstates the historical (phylogenic, ontogenic, and cultural) dimensions of knowledge—a rehabilitation that is also to some extent inherent in connectionism. In a polar map that shows how various thinkers can be located in relation to traditional cognitivism and to the theory of emergence and action that Varela is advocating, one finds Piaget closest to Varela's ideas, one step removed from more traditional cognitivism as exemplified by Neisser in psychology, Chomsky and Fodor in linguistics and epistemology, and by Hubel and Wiesel in neurobiology. Varela has rediscovered Piaget; he might have thought of rediscovering Skinner.

The point is not to suggest that Varela's and similar views are only resurgences of behaviourism. Current so-called cognitive science obviously addresses different issues, and uses a different language: science does not come back to earlier stages. What is clear, however, is that the recent shift in emphasis from representation to action implies a reintegration of behaviour in its own right, and makes it impossible to view behaviour as merely a potentially dispensable indicator of representations.

Incidentally, it is worth noting in this context the almost complete lack of interest, among cognitive psychologists, in robotics as a possible source of inspiring models. They have generally been exclusively attracted by the models offered by computers as used in the classical task of storing large bunches of information, and applying to them more or less complex logico-mathematical operations. At first sight, robotics, dealing as it does with action upon the world outside, moving in time and space, and adjusting to a real rather than abstract environment, would seem closer to the study of living organisms. With the few exceptions of psychophysiologists specialising in motor skills and similar problems, robotic models have been completely ignored. Whether this was the consequence of the cognitivists putting exclusive emphasis on representation at the expense of action, or of their exclusive fascination for the computer at the expense of robots, is an interesting question. It is related to the traditional problem in the history of science: are theories driven by the (technological) metaphors at hand, or are the metaphoric models selected to fit theories?

3. The copy theory inevitably runs into the trouble of implying some little being—the *homunculus*—who will perceive or recall the copy, which it can only do by making another copy, and so on *ad infinitum*. It requires, at some final point if the process is to stop somewhere, an irreducible agent, who must necessarily escape further analysis. There is some logic in Fodor's appeal to some irreducible central core unamenable to scientific inquiry in his modular picture of mind: it is a consequence of a psychological system based on representations.[22]

Skinner, of course, after a career spent trying to account for behaviour without resorting to an internal agent in command, was not ready to accept its resurrection by cognitivism. His objections are both on the grounds of basic psychological theory (as we have just seen, there is a close, perhaps an inherent, relationship between representations and the appeal to an autonomous agent), and of applications of psychological knowledge to human affairs. They address both epistemological cognitivism and what we have called ethical cognitivism.

For Skinner, the conception of human beings based on free will and autonomy, on their capacity to decide, has proved inefficient in solving the problems of humanity. He has undertaken a behavioural analysis, and a sort of natural and cultural history of those traditional notions, and he has suggested we should shift the focus from them to the conditions that induce individuals and groups to engage in a certain course of action, and to feel themselves as free, self-controlled, happy. By encouraging again the old illusion of the autonomous agent in the human mind, ethical cognitivism has favoured practices of education, psychotherapy, and social control that appeal to internal forces of individuals, while disregarding the contingencies that have shaped, in fact, often surreptitiously, such mental dispositions. Skinner's opposition to it will appear more fully when we deal with his analysis of social issues, education, psychological treatment, and political control (Part IV).

# NOTES

1. See Le Ny, 1985.
2. "Cognitive science and behaviorism", 1985, reprinted 1987.
3. *The origins of cognitive thought*, 1989a, reprinted 1989b.
4. Skinner, 1987a, reprinted 1989b.
5. "Can psychology be a science of Mind?" *American Psychologist*, 1990, *45*, 1206–1210.
6. For a more elaborate discussion of the various types of cognitivism in different contexts, see Richelle, 1986a; 1987b, and Richelle and Fontaine, 1986.
7. The theory is exposed at length in his book *Contemporary animal learning theory* (1980), whose title misleadingly suggests that we hold *the* theory, an obviously over-optimistic or pretentious statement. In order to build that impressively consistent theory, Dickinson had to overlook a number of major dimensions of animal learning: to cite only one example, the contribution of ethology and comparative psychology to contemporary concepts of animal learning is totally omitted (Lorenz' name is even not mentioned; neither are key-words such as biological constraints, species-specific limitations, or phylogenic sources of individual learning). It is interesting to note that the translator of the book into French, G. Richard, himself a competent expert in the field, has been aware of the unfounded pretension of the title, and has changed it to the plural, *L'apprentissage animal, Théories contemporaines* (1984), which unfortunately is no less misleading, since the book is exclusively about one theory, i.e. the author's.
8. Dickinson, 1980, p.21.
9. This reduction, or resorption, from the psychological to the mental, then to the neurobiological was clearly suggested, for example, by Changeux, in his popular book *The neuronal Man* (1983). His famous statement "Man no longer needs Mind. Suffices to him being a neural man" unambiguously discarded cognitive psychology—often defined as the Science of Mind—as of no use, as neurobiology would progress in penetrating the mysteries of the brain directly. Changeux has corrected his views since then, and replied to the accusation of reductionism.
10. Eccles, 1979; Sperry, 1983.
11. *Behavioral and brain sciences*, p.507; Skinner 1984c.
12. *Upon further reflection*, p.119. Reprinted from Skinner 1987b.
13. Quoted from "Whatever happened to psychology at the science of behavior?" (1987). Reprinted in *Recent issues in the analysis of behavior* (1989b), p.63.
14. The issue of feelings has been discussed in many of Skinner's writings. One of his last papers is of special interest, published under the title "The place of feelings in the analysis of behavior" (reprinted as Chapter 1 in *Recent issues*, 1989b). It was written as a reply to another instance of

misinterpretation of the behaviourist position, i.e. that it supposedly denied feelings. The case is ironic, as the classical misunderstanding was conveyed by Johnson-Laird, a well known cognitivist, whose work certainly tells us much less about feelings than Skinner's.

15. *Upon further reflection*, p.120. Reprinted from Skinner 1987b.

16. *Upon further reflection*, p.111. Reprinted from Skinner 1987b.

17. The (paradoxical) social origin of self-consciousness has been emphasised repeatedly by Skinner, especially in *Verbal behavior*, (1957), where he points out that the individual becomes conscious through the progressive development of a verbal community; the same idea was expressed by Luria, who, elaborating on ideas of Vygotsky, viewed the origin of consciousness, the highest form of self-regulated behaviour, as being not in the depth of the organism, but in the complex modalities characterising the interaction between the child and its social environment, and in the acquisition of language; Luria (1969); see Richelle (1974a, 1993).

18. "The origins of cognitive thought", reprinted in *Recent issues in the analysis of behavior*, 1989, Chapter 2.

19. An interesting aspect of the mapping of lexical items to psychological realities is the difference between languages. Words have different histories in different languages, even when closely related, as Indo-european idioms can be. For instance, *Mind* does not have some of the connotations that make *Esprit* difficult to rehabilitate for French psychologists, while it has additional respectability derived from its use in the recent Anglo-saxon *philosophy of Mind*. *Cognition* has practically no past in French, and it would be enlightening to analyse its semantic properties in comparison with *connaissance*, as with *knowledge*.

20. See, among other sources, *Behaviorism at fifty*, 1963b, and the notes added in the reprinting as Chapter 8 in *Contingencies of reinforcement*, 1969b. Admittedly, the term *representation* refers to entities more sophisticated than *copy*, and in some of its technical uses it might have little to do with the latter. But in most cases it raises basically the same problems.

21. See Varela, 1989.

22. See especially J.A. Fodor, *The modularity of mind* (1983, 1986, 6th edn.), and more specifically parts IV, on central systems, and V, containing general conclusions. After having stated in humorous terms "Fodor's First Law of the Nonexistence of Cognitive Science", i.e. "the more global a cognitive process is, the less anybody understands it. *Very* global processes, like analogical reasoning, aren't understood at all", he insists, in the final section of his influential and controversial book, that (p.127) "if central processes have the sort of properties that I have ascribed to them, then they are bad candidates for scientific study". And further (p.128): "If, as I have supposed, the central cognitive processes are nonmodular, that is very bad news for cognitive science".

# 10 The Language Issue

## EARLY INTEREST IN LANGUAGE

For those who see Skinner essentially as a rat psychologist, a chapter on language might seem a bit out of place here. On the contrary, it is a central issue, not only if one wishes to describe Skinner's thinking correctly, but also in order to understand the origin of the most widespread misinterpretations of it, and to capture the peculiarities of the attitudes towards behaviourism that have evolved among psychologists in the last 30 years or so. In discussing Skinner's contribution to the study of verbal behaviour, it has become impossible to avoid reference to Chomsky, for the reason that most people know Skinner's ideas only second-hand through the destructive criticisms expressed by the famous linguist. Some historical details will be useful here in order to make the case clear.

In 1957, Skinner published a heavy book entitled *Verbal behavior*. We shall comment later on its content. Suffice it to point out, at this stage, that this was by no means the product of some recent interest in a field for which Skinner would have been little prepared, nor was it really unexpected material for those who knew what he had been working on for many years. In fact, from the very early days of his career, Skinner had been puzzled by the specific problems raised by verbal behaviour in humans, including their unique creative verbal productions in poetry and literary prose. While busy at experimenting on animals, he kept thinking over the issue, and eventually selected it as the topic of the William James lectures he was invited to deliver at Harvard in 1947. An early confidential version of what was to become the book *Verbal behavior* was circulated at that time. It was used and referred to by George Miller in his seminal book *Language and communication*, published in 1951—a foundation work indeed in giving new

**119**

impetus to the then stagnant psychology of language as well as in conveying information theory to psychologists in the clearest style.

## CHOMSKY'S INTERFERENCE

Soon after Skinner's book was published, Chomsky, then a young linguist possibly known in linguistic circles for his work on *Syntactic structures* (1957), but totally unknown to psychologists, wrote an unusually long critical review, published in *Language*, a journal of linguistics (Chomsky, 1959). Quite unexpectedly, these 30 dense pages had several important consequences.

First, Chomsky suddenly became a star figure among psychologists, who went to his work of the most technical kind in formal linguistics as a source of inspiration. Although he also published two highly technical chapters in the *Handbook of mathematical psychology*,[1] co-authoring with G. Miller—definitely an exceptional discoverer of new ideas and talents—there can be no doubt that such tough, little-read material could not possibly explain his fast growing popularity in psychology departments.

Second, Chomsky managed to persuade his readers that they could dispense with reading Skinner's book. The 30 pages of his review were less, after all, than the 600 pages of *Verbal behavior*, and they were written in the typically assertive style that characterises him, giving his statements an appearance of irrefutable truth. That Chomsky's judgement was taken up by most distinguished psycholinguists is exemplified by the following statement, from Sinclair-De Zwart: "As for Skinner's (1957) interpretations, based on such notions as *response strength* and *schedule of reinforcement*, Chomsky (1959) has definitively demonstrated the meaninglessness of these notions when applied to verbal behaviour".[2] It is no rare thing that critics completely overshadow the work they have been commenting on: some literary or philosophical masterpieces have had to be drawn back from such oblivion. The result was that the questions raised by Skinner, which are crucial issues in the psychology of language, though possibly not in linguistics, were totally overlooked for more than a decade, as long as Chomsky's formalistic views dominated the field. Although Chomsky has to be credited for his stimulating role, it is difficult to appraise to what extent, and for how long, his influence has impeded psychologists studying verbal behaviour from addressing the genuinely psychological questions. Had they read Skinner's contribution they might have spared themselves some wanderings in deep structures.

Third, Chomsky's review was destructive not only of Skinner's view on verbal behaviour, but of behaviourism as a whole. This was stated, among others, by Mehler, on the publication of the French translation of the then already famous review: "In fact," says Mehler, "the decay of behaviourism seems linked with the rise of modern psycholinguistics".[3] To some extent, this sounds like wishful thinking: to a neutral observer, behaviourism is far from extinct if we take as signs of vitality the numerous and successful uses of its methods, the extensive and diversified range of its applications, and after all, the persistence of quite a number of traditional indices of scientific activity, such as journals, societies, and meetings, all of which involve people.[4] It is true, however, that Chomsky has played an important role in the rise of cognitivism, and especially in reinstating the respectable status of mental states, as we shall see when analysing his criticisms more closely.

Give the threefold importance of Chomsky's criticisms, and in spite of the fact that psycholinguists have freed themselves from Chomsky's influence for some years, it is worth summarising the main points of his attack on Skinner. They can be classified roughly in two categories. On one hand, Chomsky objects to Skinner extrapolating: from animal behaviour, supposedly of a simplistic nature, to language, a highly complex and specifically human activity; from the laboratory, where he has forged his concepts, to real life, where those concepts do not account for the richness of human conduct, especially in its linguistic forms; from narrow determinism, possibly applicable to simple animal data, to a field marked by unpredictability, productivity, and individual creativity, which escape traditional causal analysis. These are classical criticisms of the experimental, scientific approach to human activity.

On the other hand, he argues against the behaviouristic position, as inadequate to account for language, and in doing so he points to characteristics of behaviourism that might describe some other brands of behaviourisms, but certainly not Skinner's position. For example, Chomsky argues at length about the Stimulus-Response model, obviously not one of Skinner's tenets, and about drive reduction, a concept completely absent from Skinner's analysis. In making such confusions between Skinner's and others' views, and being otherwise exclusively inclined to a purely formal account of language, it is no wonder that Chomsky failed to grasp the type of functional approach to verbal behaviour that Skinner had advocated; an approach along lines totally different from preceding attempts within the American scientific psychology tradition.

When scrutinised with some critical care, Chomsky's text raises some embarrassing questions, given that the author is, presumably, an exceptionally intelligent person. Did he read the whole book, as one would expect from a reviewer writing such a long comment? If the answer is yes, how could he possibly misrepresent and distort many of Skinner's ideas to such an extent? How could he discuss at length some crucial points—for example, speaking of things or people never seen—as if Skinner had ignored them, when any reader of *Verbal behavior* will come across detailed discussions of precisely these points? Should Chomsky be blamed for neglect; for indulging more or less consciously in the old strategy of building straw men in order to promote his own ideas; or even for some flaw with respect to intellectual honesty?

## SKINNER'S SILENCE

In fact, Skinner did not care to reply: this has sometimes been interpreted as admission of defeat,[5] and has probably contributed to the widespread habit among psychologists and psycholinguists of relying on Chomsky's text without going back to Skinner's book itself. After all, Chomsky had had the last word, and presumably this was the truth. Skinner's silence, however, did not mean acceptance of the linguist's arguments. On the contrary, it reflected his belief that Chomsky was not talking about the same thing, and in my view a feeling that his approach would eventually be adopted. Perhaps he felt intuitively that an open debate with Chomsky was pointless, with little chance of influencing him and eventually changing his mind.

Skinner rarely commented about his attitude, but on one occasion, he disclosed his motives in a humorous way. The passage is worth extensive quotation. Skinner was addressing an audience of poets and writers in New York City, in 1971:[6]

> Let me tell you about Chomsky. I published *Verbal behavior* in 1957. In 1958 I received a 55-page typewritten review by someone I had never heard of named Noam Chomsky. I read half a dozen pages, saw that it missed the point of my book, and went no further. In 1959, I received a reprint from the journal *Language*. It was the review I had already seen, now reduced to 32 pages in type, and again I put it aside. But then, of course, Chomsky's star began to rise. Generative grammar became the thing—and a very big thing it seemed to be. Linguists have always managed to make their discoveries earthshaking. In one decade everything seems to hinge on semantics, in another decade on the analysis of the phoneme. In the Sixties, it was grammar and syntax, and Chomsky's review began to be widely cited and reprinted, and became, in fact, much better known than my book.
>
> Eventually, the question was asked, why had I not answered Chomsky? My reasons, I am afraid, show a lack of character. In the first place, I should have had to read the review, and I found its tone distasteful. It was not really a review of my book but of what Chomsky took, erroneously, to be my position. I should also have had to bone up on generative grammar, which was not my field, [. . .]. A few years ago *Newsweek* magazine carried the disagreement further, going beyond linguistics and structuralism to the philosophy of the seventeenth century. I was said to be a modern disciple of John Locke, for whom the mind began as a clean slate or *tabula rasa* and who thought that knowledge was acquired only by experience, while Chomsky was said to represent Descartes, the rationalist, who was not sure he existed until he thought about it. *Newsweek* suggested that the battle was going my way, and the reaction by the generative grammarians was so violent that the magazine found it necessary to publish four pro-Chomsky letters. Each one repeated a common misunderstanding of my position. One implied that I was a stimulus-response psychologist (which I am not) and another that I think people are much like pigeons (which I do not). One had at least a touch of wit. Going back to our supposed seventeenth century progenitors, the writer advised *Newsweek* to "Locke up Skinner and give Chomsky Descartes blanche". But Chomsky cannot use a *carte blanche*, of course; it is too much as a *tabula rasa*.[7]

## FUNCTIONAL VERSUS FORMAL ANALYSIS OF
## VERBAL BEHAVIOUR

That Chomsky missed the point will be obvious to any reader, even of only the first chapter of *Verbal behavior*. It is an introductory chapter, significantly entitled "A functional analysis of verbal behavior". This title immediately follows the section title of the first part of the book, that is "A program". Skinner states clearly what he is dealing with: not language, as usually studied by linguists, but verbal behaviour, that is an individual's activity in speaking and/or listening. Having been persuaded of the heuristic validity of principles of behaviour discovered in animal research, and especially of the functional approach, aimed at describing the variables that contribute to the production of behaviour, Skinner attempts to apply them to verbal behaviour. He does not claim that he is proposing a theory, nor does he claim to draw empirical arguments from experimental evidence. As is unequivocally stated at the end of the chapter: "The present extension to verbal behavior is thus an exercise in interpretation rather than a quantitative extrapolation of rigorous experimental results".[8]

Chomsky was not ready to entertain such views, having already chosen the strictly formal approach to language, and he remained definitely (deliberately?) blind to the nature of Skinner's endeavour by objecting to any scientific study of verbal behaviour that would be based on animal experimentation, and framed in a deterministic concept of human conduct. He also strongly rejected, throughout his career, any theory of language use or of language acquisition that would resort to environmental variables, and defended instead an inneist conception, appealing to some internal Language Acquisition Device, an assumed cerebral structure or machinery innately prepared to acquire and use any natural language. He developed the curious idea that language can be compared, or better assimilated, to an anatomical organ, as the stomach or the liver, which needs no interaction with the environment to be formed during embryogenesis.[9]

Under Chomsky's dominant influence, for almost two decades, i.e. in the 1960s and 1970s, psycholinguistics has been the arena for debates about the formal *vs* functional issue, and about the radical inneism issue. We will not discuss the latter here, because we already know Skinner's general position with respect to the innate *vs* acquired issue. Although he undoubtedly emphasised environmental variables, he never denied the genetic equipment of animals or humans, and would have welcomed, for that matter, any evidence produced by modern psychogenetics. But he knew, as do all informed psychologists today, that the classical controversy between radical environmentalists and radical nativists had lost its meaning in the context of modern genetics. Chomsky appears to have obstinately ignored this.

The formal *vs* functional issue is a very complicated theme in linguistics and the psychology of language, and it is indeed difficult to treat it in a non-technical way without falling into oversimplifications; nor is it easy to capture the core of the problem without a little of the history of the sciences involved, namely the various fields of linguistics and some fields of psychology. Such an account would take us far beyond the scope of the present chapter. I shall limit myself to giving an intuitive view of the debate, but the reader, if uninformed, should keep in mind that things are far more complex; for instance, when I oppose linguistics and psychology as the typical fields of formal analysis and of functional analysis, respectively, this is somewhat oversimplified, as not all linguists limit themselves to formal accounts, and some psychologists have become quite formal!

Linguists, although they use native speakers' production as their raw material, are essentially interested in accounting for the properties of a given language, say English or Chinese, or of any natural language, which is the ambition of general linguistics. Particularly since the seminal proposals made by Saussure early in this century (Saussure, 1916), they have adopted what is called a *synchronic* approach, based on the assumption that natural languages function, at any moment in their history, as whole systems, whose parts are all interdependent, and must therefore be described and explained by reference to each other, rather than by reference to an earlier stage in their evolution, as assumed in the traditional approach of historical or diachronic linguistics. By collecting a fairly representative sample of verbal utterances, linguists aim to describe as adequately as possible the properties of the linguistic material, and, if they are working along the lines of general linguistics, at abstracting properties common to all languages. To that end, they usually engage in fairly formal accounts of grammars (viewed as sets of rules at work in the language system, not as normative prescriptions for good speaking). Various types of such accounts, at varying levels of generality, have been proposed throughout the history of linguistic science. They differ, among other things, in their degree of abstractness with reference to the sequences of whatever elements—sounds, words, phrases, etc—compose utterances: some do keep as close as possible to the surface structure; others, on the grounds that such a strategy does not allow many important difficulties to be resolved, appeal to inferred levels, or deep structures, after the concept popularised by Chomsky. Deep structures must be invoked, Chomsky argued, if one is to account for sentences having the same surface structure, with obviously different values, as in his famous examples "John is easy to please" *vs* "John is eager to please". Theories also differ in their emphasis on one or another aspect of the linguistic material: phonology has focused on basic sounds; Chomsky's generative grammar was syntax-centred; other theories give priority to semantics. All this is important, but it does not tell us the whole story about what happens when people speak, which in most cases means speak to each other. Language is normally implemented in speech, in *"parole"* as opposed to *"langue"*, as emphasised by Saussure, using a French word that could be appropriately rendered by "verbal behaviour".

The study of *"parole"* or verbal behaviour obviously requires a functional approach, that is to say an analysis of the variables that lead to the production or reception of a given utterance on a given occasion. Although things are far more subtle than that, it is easy to represent what a functional analysis is about by imagining under which circumstances the same simple sentence, for instance, "I would like a cup of tea", can be pronounced. In the most probable case, the speaker will be ordering in a coffee-shop, or answering his host's request. He might also suddenly interrupt his work, because he feels thirsty, and simply say that to himself, or to his colleagues, if any, while getting up from his chair and going to prepare some tea. But it could as well be pronounced as an exercise by the foreign student in an English class repeating after the teacher, or the reader of this page reading aloud, for her own solitary pleasure. The utterance, formally defined, has not changed; what has changed is the context and the function of what is said in that particular context. The context involves physical and social aspects, variables inside the subject (in the case of feeling thirsty) or outside (the presence and request of the host; the teacher's invitation to repeat; the written text). What makes the difference between the four cases are those events that take place before, during, and after the sentence is produced.

Conversely, the choice of a given occurrence by the speaker is not, as Chomsky claimed, a matter of caprice, besides the constraints imposed by linguistic rules; it is obviously determined, again, by factors linked with context, with the subject's and the audience's history, social status, previous or anticipated success in comparable situations, etc. A formal grammatical, linguistic account does not suffice to explain it. For example, a speaker saying "Her Excellency be blessed for having listened to my humble request" is evidently conforming to the rules of English, but the selection of the royal style third person is itself context dependent, an extralinguistic variable.

An essential difference between the formal and the functional approach is that in the first one, all possibilities can be considered, there is no limit to the number or complexity of utterances *theoretically* possible, except that they must be acceptable in the language being considered, whereas in the second, only what actually occurs has to be accounted for. The formal approach operates at the level of potentialities; the functional one at the level of realities. This basic distinction was completely ignored by Chomsky, when he argued that stimuli are unimportant in what a speaker decides to say. To quote an example that is now classic in the debate, it matters little to the psychologist that an infinity of verbal utterances (*clashes with the wallpaper, I thought you liked abstract work, never saw it before, tilted, hanging too low, beautiful, hideous*, or what not) are possible in the presence of a painting hung in a salon; what matters, and needs to be explained, is that the actual speaker has said "Dutch", reacting with his own history to a particular situation. That other utterances were *theoretically* possible does not modify the causes of the response that has *actually* been produced.

## SKINNER'S ESSAY IN INTERPRETATION

Verbal behaviour was what Skinner was interested in. He certainly did not deny that the work of linguists and grammarians was important (for obvious chronological reasons he did not mention Chomsky's work in his book), but pointed to the fact that they had little to say about what he thought was the domain of the psychologist. He was not satisfied either with previous attempts by his fellow psychologists and he tried his own way. He first emphasised the "global verbal episode", which typically looks for language as produced or received in context. He further attempted to build his own functional classification of verbal behaviours, using newly forged labels totally different from linguistic terms: *mand* to designate all verbal behaviour leading to a listener's actions in favour of the speaker (putting it more concisely, "reinforced by the listener"); *tact*, defined as verbal behaviour describing part of the subject's universe; *autoclitic*, referring partly to verbal units that occur because of intraverbal links (part of the autoclitic concept covers grammatical dependencies); and *echoïc* behaviour, which is simple reproduction of heard verbal behaviour. These categories are not without their own difficulties, but they were given, let us remember, as the result of an "essay in interpretation", not as a decisive invention. We shall see that they addressed a central question that has been dealt with by other investigators, including some linguists. At this stage, let us stress a crucial aspect of these categories, as opposed to formal ones: their structure is not strictly defined, neither in length nor pattern. A *mand* can be a short imperative verb form, giving an order, or it can be a lengthy political harangue, engaging the audience to a certain course of action.

Of course, as linguistic systems themselves were not invented for the sake of formal linguists, but rather emerged from some functional evolution in living organisms' behaviour, it is no surprise that they contain many elements (it can indeed be argued that they contain *only* elements) endowed with functional value, whatever the formal description given of them. Imperative verb forms, for instance, usually have the functional value of *mands* in Skinner's categories. But other verbal forms serve a similar function, and are more probable in some situations: a polite guest might declare "This Bordeaux is exceptional" thus drawing the host's attention to an empty glass, rather than order: "Would you fill my glass". Functional analysis cannot be mapped in any simple way onto formal analysis.

## THE COMPETENCE VERSUS PERFORMANCE ISSUE

It would seem, at first sight, to a straightforward observer, that the distinction between functional and formal analysis is fairly sound, and, once recognised, should not result in any conflictual tensions. However, a lot of confusion has arisen in contemporary linguistics and psycholinguistics, and more specifically in the debate around Chomsky and Skinner, because of Chomsky's opposed concepts of *competence* and *performance*. These are not strictly linguistic concepts, that could be taken, more or less, as synonymous to Saussure's notions of *langue* as opposed to *parole* (Saussure, 1916). They have much deeper psychological implications, or perhaps, pretensions. Speakers are said to possess an internalised replica of their language rules, defining their (linguistic) competence, which they will implement in actual speech productions, or performances. The latter are frequently poor testimony of the former, because the subject's competence is hampered by the limitations of the psychological functions involved in performance, such as memory, attention, vocal and articulatory motor skills, emotion, etc. A person's competence is supposed to provide a cognitive capacity that, in principle, enables linguistic material to be dealt with by applying rules, as linguists would do; this implies, among other things, the capacity to produce utterances of unlimited size, consisting of an infinity of embedded propositions. Grammar authorises sentences of the type "The cat that caught the mouse that ate the cheese that was left on the breakfast table in the kitchen died". They are rarely, if ever pronounced, not (or not only) because they are inelegant in style, but mainly because they put an excessive load on memory and decoding. This gap between the cognitive apparatus, endowed with competence, and actual behaviour, is really the crucial issue that divides the formal approach typical of Chomsky and the functional analysis proposed by Skinner.

Competence refers, as we have seen, to an internalised set of rules that the individual will apply more or less perfectly. For Skinner, the behaving subject does not apply rules, no more than cells do in their immunological reactions: what is done, or said, can be described by rules, in the sense that it can be accounted for in a lawful way—this is, indeed, all what science is about—but the subject is not drawing on some set of rules deposited in the mind in order to turn them, with more or less success, into behaviour. A language is certainly an organised system that can be described consistently, and that is what linguists do. In so far as the individual's verbal behaviour is controlled by the habits in strength in a verbal community, the rules define the linguistic contingencies, not an internalised machinery distinct from its behavioural byproducts.

The debate takes us back, of course, to the issue of mentalism. Skinner's objections to Chomsky's view were the same as those he had addressed before to all sorts of mentalistic theories: what is the status of the mental entity called "linguistic competence"? Of which stuff is it made, and where does it reside? More important, who is the subject who exploits it? From where does he operate? Does he escape scientific analysis? How can we account for him and for what he does without falling into the infinite regression of the homunculus?

Saussure had been wise enough to limit himself, as a linguist, to the study of language, of *"langue"*, although assuming that it is, in one way or another, deposited in the speaking subject's brain. He left open the study of *"parole"*, or verbal behaviour, admitting that a complete science of language—he called it *séméiologie*—encompassing both aspects, would be completed only after psychologists, or some other specialists, had carried out the study of verbal behaviour. He did not give any definite psychological or neurobiological status to the *"langue"*, nor did he claim that the linguist's contribution had any sort of priority in accounting for *"parole"*. Chomsky took a totally different stand: not only was linguistic formal analysis said to be a prerequisite for any psychological enquiry into verbal behaviour, but a concept, i.e. competence, typically derived from such analysis, was also given psychological, and even neurobiological status.

Enthusiastic investigators belonging to the first generation of psycholinguists of the post-Chomskyan era spent much of their time trying to demonstrate the psychological reality of deep structures, and of the grammatical transformations appealed to in generative grammar. Their attempts were generally unsuccessful. This did not disprove the validity of generative grammar(s)—an issue left to linguists themselves. It did however demonstrate that an apparently adequate formal account of the linguistic system, as such, need not be of help in describing the subject's functioning when speaking or listening. Although they maintained some distance from Chomsky, most psycholinguists remained within the cognitive movement, and did not really adopt the type of functional approach advocated by Skinner. Some of them, however, came across similar problems and eventually turned to a very similar approach, although they ignored the resulting kinship.

## THE CHILD ACQUIRING LANGUAGE: THE TOUCHSTONE

Skinner rejected the concept of linguistic competence because of its mentalistic status. The objection was logically in line with his most constant theoretical position. The inadequacy of the concept for psychological use was soon evidenced, moreover, in empirical context. Students of language acquisition, although they had been especially receptive to Chomsky's message, discovered that they could go nowhere, methodologically, with the distinction between competence and performance. Competence, as we have seen, is inferred from the assumption that the speaker of a given language has internalised the grammar of that language, which is only one among many actualisations of something more abstract, i.e. a general grammar common to all languages (which in turn is supposed to have its corresponding physical counterpart in the brain, making language literally comparable to a physical organ). The drift from the notion of grammar, as a linguistic description, to the notion of competence, with its psychological connotations, is probably due to the traditional methodology used by linguists in collecting relevant data. Generally, when working on well-known languages, linguists collect utterances from normal adult subjects, and when there is any hesitation, they forge a sentence that they propose to their subjects, asking them simply whether it would be acceptable or unacceptable in their language. When linguists work on their own language,[10] as Chomsky mainly did, for all practical purposes they can short-cut the process by using themselves as subjects, and simply refer to their own "linguistic intuition". Thus, they can tell what is potentially part of the language from what is not.

For obvious reasons, the method does not work with young children at the stage of language acquisition. They cannot answer the ritual question "Is that acceptable in your language?" Theirs is no stable language, but a language in the process of being acquired: its form will change from day to day. Children produce all sorts of utterances that would be rejected by adults, but which are, for the time being at least, part of their language. There are no criteria by which a choice could be made between those utterances presumably reflecting competence, which should be retained, and those pertaining to imperfect performance, which should be rejected. The only solution consists in retaining everything as a legitimate component of the child's language, and ignoring the distinction between competence and performance, because it lacks operational value.

The contribution of developmental psycholinguistics to the "global episode" approach to verbal behaviour has been even more important. Those who record and attempt to analyse babies' speech productions are confronted with the very difficult problem of decoding what they mean. They cannot ask young children, as they would normal adults, to paraphrase, give another version, or comment on what has been said. What children say is not enough to account for their productions, even in purely formal terms. One must listen and look at what is said to them, to whom they speak, on what occasion, in which particular physical and social situation, with what gestures or mimics, what emotional expression and motor action, and with what result. Taking such variables into account means of course turning to functional analysis, changing the emphasis from an abstract linguistic system to the behaving subject.

This was a major shift in developmental psycholinguistics in the 1970s, with almost all researchers unanimously sharing a view that had been defended a few years before by a handful of forerunners only. Investigators who adopted this new line, because it was inescapably imposed by the matter under study, often came from the most radical Chomskyan circles, and would not admit anything in common with behaviouristically oriented investigators. They had simply been confronted with reality, which changed them into behaviourists unaware of their behaviourist style, just as M Jourdain in Molière's comedy was unaware that he was speaking in prose.

This is not the place to go into details of developmental psycholinguistics.[11] We will pinpoint three topics, typical of the evolution described earlier, for their special relevance to basic issues in Skinner's functional analysis: the concept of the global (social) episode; the definition of functional categories of verbal behaviour; and the stimulus variable as a research strategy to appraise the child's linguistic system.

Under Chomsky's influence, the verbal environment of a child was referred to vaguely as the linguistic community, responsible for the fact that he or she would eventually speak English rather than Finnish or Dutch. Its characteristics were not further described, as it was assumed that it provided a general input that would trigger into activity that part of the child's mind and brain innately prepared to produce language. It was even suggested that the input was more often than not of poor quality—comparable in the proportion of ill-formed sentences to what can usually be observed in discussions among linguists!—but that nothing better was needed, given the relatively secondary importance of environmental factors in language acquisition. Not all psychologists were satisfied with that view, and looked at the linguistic environment in some detail. They identified each of the protagonists usually interacting with the child (mother, father, older children, etc.) and recorded their speech together with the child's productions. They discovered very interesting features for the psychology of learning. Adults, or older children, addressing babies use a specific way of talking, that has sometimes been called baby-talk. Contrary to an early popular intuition, this is by no means an imitation of the child's language by adults. It is a special sublanguage, universally used by adults in the situation of talking with babies. Motherese, as it has been called by Newport, exhibits peculiar formal properties: utterances are slower, with more frequent and longer pauses; they are pronounced at higher frequencies, with more emphasis on prosodic contours; syntax is better (that is with less disruptions, unfinished sentences, etc.) and simpler (with shorter sentences and fewer subordinates, simplification of the pronominal system, etc.); it is semantically highly redundant and contains a limited number of lexical items, the selection of which is obviously adjusted to the child's level; it makes extensive use of diminutive forms, marked with an affective value. Despite minor variations and despite occasional traits bound to each particular natural language, this sublanguage shows very constant properties throughout the world, in both sexes, in parents and non-parent adults, in adults and older children (as early as the fourth year of age) addressing younger children. These properties reflect implicit teaching procedures, which could be taken as illustrations of applying principles of the psychology of learning to real life. All the formal characters alluded to here (redundancy, simplified and clear syntax, limited vocabulary, and so on) can be analysed as such. Along the same lines, it is quite remarkable that this sublanguage is constantly adjusted to the child's progress, always being a little ahead, which is the very nature of any good educational procedure, as rightly noted by Vygotsky; and, in that sense, a much more adequate device than educational procedures in which children are offered model behaviour exactly in tune with their present level, or, at the other extreme, already at the final, desired level, but clearly too distant from the present stage.

As well as analysing the formal properties of adult talk to children, psychologists have also observed various aspects of the conversational interactions that take place between a child and an adult, only to discover other implicit teaching procedures. For example, approvals and disapprovals are frequent in adult speech to children. They obviously have a reinforcing function on the child's behaviour. They seem to be delivered more according to the semantic relevance of the child's utterances than according to grammatical correctness—an indication that the priority given to syntax by Chomsky is not justified, in this context at least. In most cases, however, the adult's answer to the child is not limited to yes or no, to right or wrong. The dialogue includes a number of utterances, on the part of the adult, that extend the immediately preceding child's utterance, rephrasing what the child has said while completing or correcting the syntax or morphology, or bringing in some new semantic component. To a large extent, the subtle reinforcing system involved in early verbal communication is based on affective reinforcers. Keeping the (meaningful) conversation going is also an essential point. Verbal behaviour acceptable in a given linguistic community would be shaped, not by explicitly approving or correcting each bit of grammatical production from the child, but by inducing a lot of talk, providing the child with a more and more efficient tool for enlarging communication with others. A refined analysis of the global verbal episode, to use Skinner's expression, has revealed basic aspects of language acquisition, and clearly shown that, whatever the nature of the human specific disposition to master natural languages and whatever its part in language acquisition, it does not follow that learning processes are not at work, in an important sense, in the development of the behaviour most typical of our species.

Students of child language have been confronted with the functional aspects of verbal communication, and have led to the identification of preverbal behaviours that prepare the use of language proper to deal with the social environment. Various attempts have been made to order these preverbal and verbal behaviours, by building functional classifications. Well-known contributions along these lines are those of Halliday, and of Bates.[12] None of them, any more than authors of other parallel endeavours, refers to Skinner, although they take inspiration from Austin, the famous philosopher of language, whose work on speech acts has undoubtedly been seminal, but possibly more limited in scope than Skinner's. For instance, Bates has applied Austin's classification to the evolution of imperative and declarative sentences, showing a developmental progression from perlocution to illocution and then to locution. Perlocutory and illocutory acts cover, in Austin's terminology, part of what Skinner put together under the label *mands*.[13] In his very detailed analysis of preverbal and early verbal behaviour, Halliday identifies what he calls instrumental, regulatory, and interactional functions, which have much in common, to say the least, with Skinner's category of mands, whereas so called personal and informative functions have something in common with Skinner's *tact*. The similarity between the first three functions and the mands becomes all the more striking in the course of development, where Halliday admits the difficulties in making clear-cut distinctions, and groups them under the general term *pragmatic function*.

Overlapping is, of course, no argument for claiming that these classifications are really helpful. They overlap, perhaps just because they are all too crude. Indeed, none of the available functional classifications of verbal behaviour appears totally satisfactory, and one might ask whether recent attempts really add anything important to more traditional categories, such as Jakobson's. The famous linguist used to oppose three primary (i.e. conative, referential, and expressive) and three secondary (i.e. poetic, phatic, and metalinguistic) functions, with the conative function covering much the same things as Skinner's mands or Halliday's pragmatic function.

If we want to set things in proper perspective, we must be aware of the persistent concern for functional aspects of language inside the field of linguistics long before structuralism, and later Chomsky, tended to reduce the study of language to its purely formal aspects. Many linguists before and after, even among those who contributed to formal analysis in one way or another, kept an interest in the other side, the functional side. Before Jakobson, Saussure himself was undoubtedly one of them, when he envisioned a more general science of *langue* and *parole*, as was the American linguist-anthropologist Sapir. The French linguist Benveniste elaborated the same theme in his theory of enunciation, and eventually modern pragmatics developed with an emphasis that language cannot be accounted for unless the practical context of its use is considered. Such evolution is linked, beyond doubt, with the intrinsic characters of the things studied, which sooner or later, in spite of opposite theoretical assumptions, impose a different, appropriate line of attack. It would not make sense to give Skinner exclusive credit for having foreseen this major turn; he deserves credit, however, for having located insufficiencies in the treatment of verbal behaviour in his time, especially on the part of psychologists, and for having stated, in his own terms (which admittedly, were not very widely received), his own proposals, converging on essential issues with other trends in the modern study of language.

It is worth pointing out here that linguistics and psycholinguistics are not the only fields in which that sort of evolution took place. At about the same time, logics experienced a parallel move. After having been neglected for a long time, rhetoric, as it was called by ancient Greeks, received renewed attention under the name of *theory of argumentation*, as developed, among others, by Perelman.[14] In an attempt to account for the properties of discourse that make it efficient, that is persuasive, rather than true or false, the theory of argumentation considers not only the discourse in itself, but also the interaction with the audience, coming close to a functional analysis and to a substantially psychological interpretation.

A last illustration drawn from developmental psycholinguistics will show, ironically, how cognitive research on the rules of child language resorts to precisely the sort of manipulation of the stimulus that Chomsky had declared irrelevant to the productions of the speaking subject. A child's language, at any level of its development, may be seen as a provisional, imperfect approximation to the final stage to be attained, represented by adult language—an ever-changing system itself when looked at carefully. This is typically the way child behaviour was viewed before specialists of development imposed an alternative approach, in which child behaviour is seen, at every stage of development, as exhibiting its own consistency, however transitional it may be in a changing organism.[15]

How can an investigator describe or infer the rules in strength at successive stages of a child's language? A simple example will tell us. The use of verb tenses and modes, in English, French, and most Indo-European languages, obeys a number of rules, among which temporal relations proper are generally given priority: the verbal form is first selected according to time—present, past, or future—of the action or state described. Other features are taken into account, but are felt to be secondary to time proper, such as duration, repetition (iteration), real or potential status of the action, etc. These are called *aspects* by grammarians, and they can be marked by grammatical modes, by specific tenses, or verbal forms (e.g. in English: *he walked down the street* vs *he was walking down the street*). The methods designed to find out what the rules in strength are in child language involve an analysis of non-linguistic accompaniments of the speech acts. The experimental procedure is based on a very simple principle: the child is shown a scene with objects and/or personages, and asked to describe it in words (production test), or is requested to act out with available objects and/or personages a scene closely corresponding to a sentence proposed by the experimenter (comprehension test). In exploring the value of verb forms, an experimenter can show the child actions performed by small dolls or animals, such as going home, jumping over fences, knocking down someone or something, etc. and invite the child to describe the scene, either immediately after, or after a delay (say of 2, 7, or 25 seconds). The actions shown may differ in duration, in their continuous *vs* repetitive character, their result, the space covered, or any other property hypothetically important in determining the verb form selected. The results of such an experiment on French-speaking children revealed that they use verbal forms mainly according to the *aspectual*, rather than to the *temporal* features.[16] Verb forms are selected as a function of the character of the action to be described—completed *vs* uncompleted, successful *vs* unsuccessful, punctual *vs* durative or repetitive, etc.

As can be seen, the inquiry bears on changes occurring in verbal utterances when specific aspects of the stimulus are modified. The experimenter obtains relevant material from which to infer the grammatical system typical of the child's developmental stage by inducing small changes in the stimulus; that is, by doing the sort of thing that Chomsky so assertively ridiculed in his criticisms of *Verbal behavior*, discarding the characteristics of the stimulus as irrelevant to the speaker's decision to produce a given utterance. Taking for granted that what a speaker would say in front of a painting would be determined exclusively by the speaker's own will, he ironically questioned Skinner's interpretation that subtle properties of the painting or of the whole situation might induce the verbal response "Dutch school". According to Chomsky, as already alluded to, the speaker might as well have said "hanging upside down", "horrible" or "doesn't match the wallpaper".

Unfortunately, no behaviouristically oriented psychologist undertook, at that time, an experiment where the situational factors would have been manipulated very finely, so that variables important in determining the selection of verbal responses could be identified. How obliquely should the frame of a painting be positioned to induce in an otherwise polite guest the response "askew" rather than "marvellous"? This is exactly what the experimenter did in the investigation summarised in the preceding paragraph, in a research tradition that has been, from its beginning, clearly seen as part of the cognitive approach.

## WHY IS *VERBAL BEHAVIOR* STILL IGNORED?

How is it that Skinner's anticipatory ideas have not been recognised, not even in retrospect, as a historical acknowledgement, when we know how convergent they were with major trends in the field of language studies? Reference to authorities of the past has become fashionable after Chomsky's appeal to the Grammar of Port-Royal—and, later, Fodor's use of Gall's phrenology. Skinner was still alive, not remote enough in history to serve as prestige reference. Worse, he had been eliminated from the scene of serious students of language. Few specialists were ready to take the risk among their peers of alluding to Skinner, and even less to suggest that he had foreseen some of the current developments in psycholinguistics. Exceptions could probably be counted with the fingers of one hand. One of them was the Austrian-born American psycholinguist Moerk, whose book *Pragmatic and semantic aspects of early language development*[17] is one of the most balanced and most complete accounts of developmental psycholinguists published in the last two decades. He dares to note that Skinner's conceptualisations have again been accepted in (then) recent work on language, "whereas Skinner's system and his terminology are still mostly refuted".

Chomsky's attack, however, is not the whole story. Other factors, concerning Skinner or his students, should, I think, be mentioned as having contributed to the quasi general neglect of the important content of *Verbal behavior*. In the first place, the book did not generate significant empirical research among followers of Skinner. Most of them were busy exploring schedules of reinforcement in animals, and were neither ready nor prepared to switch to verbal activities in humans. Those who did so, did it in a rather naïve and simplistic way, limiting themselves to experiments in which elements of verbal behaviour were reinforced by a "Hmm!" type approval on the part of the experimenter. Skinner did not himself engage in empirical work, and his students were almost totally absent from the rapid growth of the field, marked by a sudden blossoming of imaginative experimental procedures.

A second factor has been the neglect, by Skinner and by his followers, of the developmental dimension, as discussed in Chapter 7. As we have seen, Chomsky's theses, although enthusiastically received by developmental psycholinguists, were soon revealed as especially inadequate in their field, where investigation methods as well as theoretical issues soon converged with what Skinner had suggested earlier. Again, the neglect of development appears in this context as the major flaw in Skinner's thinking, given the themes he was interested in, and the type of original contribution he had to offer.

In the third place, Skinner (and his followers) have been ignored by most psycholinguists because they did not pay much attention to the cross-fertilisation between psychology and linguistics that occurred in the 1950s and 1960s, which undoubtedly received a decisive impetus from Chomsky, whatever the intrinsic value of his theory. From what he knew of linguistics (but it is difficult to appraise with some precision how much this may have been),[18] Skinner was not satisfied with their way of solving the type of problems he addressed as a psychologist. He did not question the importance nor the legitimacy of their work (no more than he did of neurophysiologists' work). He explicitly noted, when discussing *autoclitics*, that these (or at least the category he labelled *relational autoclitics*) were the traditional subject matter of grammar and syntax. But what he was interested in was different, and, from what he knew, of little relevance to them. Perhaps a closer look at their work would have revealed to Skinner some of their concern for the issues he himself considered as crucial. This would have been the case with "classical" linguists, and still more so with some of those whose work eventually led to modern pragmatics at the time he wrote *Verbal behavior* or in the years after.

To summarise, I would contend that Skinner's contribution to the study of language has been a major one, in the sense that it opened new avenues for approaching previously unexplored and little understood aspects of the psychology of language, and that it deserves rehabilitation. He was right when he stated that Chomsky's critical review "missed the point". But he missed the chance to influence contemporary psycholinguistics by keeping himself away from the interdisciplinary dialogue that was established between linguists and psychologists, who eventually came close to his own views by following different paths. This, of course, is what really counts in the progress of knowledge.

## NOTES

1. Chomsky and Miller, 1963; Miller and Chomsky, 1963.
2. Sinclair-De Zwart, 1967.
3. Mehler, 1969.
4. It is worth noting, with respect to the fluctuations of judgements in the scientific community, that Mehler, although not converted to behaviourism, has recognised, 20 years later, Skinner's contribution in a different context,

namely selectionism, by putting it on equal level together with Piaget and Changeux. See Chapters 6 and 8, and Mehler and Dupoux, 1990.

5. Proctor and Weeks (1990) argue that Skinner's ignorance of his opponents reflected his intellectual poverty as well as the blindness of a sect leader to any contradiction. I have discussed this interpretation in Richelle (1991).

6. *Verbal behavior* is often mentioned in Skinner's memoires, especially in *A matter of consequences* (1983); Chomsky's review is discussed in the latter book, pp.153–154.

7. Quoted from "A lecture on 'having' a poem", as reprinted in *Cumulative record*, pp.345–347.

8. *Verbal behavior*, p.11.

9. The case has been made in an especially non-metaphorical manner, in the debate with Piaget (Piatelli-Palmarini, 1980).

10. Whether to describe its particular grammar, or to build a general grammar, as Chomsky did. The legitimacy of using only one language to capture so-called universals of language and formulate a general grammar has been questioned, of course, by linguists with a comparative inclination, who believe, with sound arguments, that a general grammar can only be derived from careful comparative studies. We can note that a similar issue has existed for many years in psychology, with respect to the possibility of drawing general laws from the study of one single species, or, consequently, of defining the psychology specific to one species, say humans, without previous comparative inquiry. Cognitive psychology, possibly after Chomsky's questionable model, has, more often than not, neglected the comparative dimension.

11. For a more technical account see Richelle (1971; 1976b) and Moreau and Richelle (1981).

12. Halliday (1973; 1975); Bates (1976).

13. We leave out here the important and difficult problem of intentionality, the solution of which is very different in Skinner and in Austin.

14. See, among other sources Perelman & Olbrechts-Tyteca 1958, *Traité de l'argumentation*, Paris, Presses Universitaires de France (2 vol.).

15. The crucial difficulty raised by the developmental approach has always been, of course, in reconciling the notion of structural consistency at any stage of development and the fact that development is, by definition, an uninterrupted flow. One solution, exemplified by Piaget among many others, has been to characterise a limited number of consistent stages ("*stades*") separated by transition periods lacking structural consistency; on the other hand, viewing development as a continuously (although not necessarily evenly) changing process makes it extremely difficult to account for structural consistency at any moment. Developmental psychology is still in search of its own infinitesimal calculus technique.

16. Bronckart, 1976.

17. Moerk, 1977.
18. Very few linguists are quoted in *Verbal behavior*, and when they are the citations are generally anecdotal rather than focusing on substantial points of their theory. We occasionally meet Jespersen or Sapir, never Saussure, Bloomfield, or Jakobson.

# 11 Thought Processes and Creativity

## A BEHAVIOURAL APPROACH TO COGNITION

Skinner is not usually viewed as an expert on problem-solving and other higher order cognitive processes. His contribution to psychology is felt to end at the point where intelligence begins. If his work on elementary learning in animals is recognised, he is not generally credited with any significant advance in the field of human thought. This judgement is often expressed, of course, by cognitivists who discard his non-mentalistic approach as irrelevant to the understanding of intellectual activities, today more fashionably labelled *cognition*. But it is more widely shared by many psychologists who simply note that Skinner does not offer much empirical work in that particular area. It is true that Skinner did not engage in experimental research on problem-solving and similar issues. His contribution has been, in the same vein as for verbal behaviour, at the level of interpretation. It went equally unrecognised, although it was not as strongly attacked as *Verbal behavior* was by Chomsky; it was simply left aside by specialists in the field, presumably because they already had an impressive bunch of experimental data to deal with and to incorporate in theoretical constructs, and also—as quite correctly noted by Hunt[1] commenting in 1984 on a paper delivered in 1965—because Skinner did not use the right metaphor for thought. He extrapolated from animal studies, which implicitly meant using the animal organism as a model, at a time when the computer metaphor was already the unanimously adopted reference.

As for language, the concern with thought processes was not new in Skinner; it was not simply a response to the increasing interest in problem-solving in psychology. The last chapter of *Verbal behavior* was devoted to Thinking, as was one chapter, in 1953, of *Science and human behavior*. These were certainly products of a reflection initiated in the concluding chapter of *The behavior of organisms* (1938). In these very illuminating pages—illuminating as to Skinner's intellectual project—he refers to "cognition" (yes, the word is there already, under Skinner's pen) as one of those concepts that need to be approached with the type of analysis he has used in his book in accounting for some aspects of the rat's behaviour—that is to say one of those concepts that must be dealt with in a non-mentalistic manner if we want to provide a scientific description and a scientific explanation of the reality to which they refer.

> The traditional description and organization of behavior represented by the concepts of "will", "cognition", "intellect" and so on, cannot be accepted so long as it pretends to be dealing with a mental world, but the behavior to which these terms apply is naturally part of the subject matter of a science of behavior. What is wanted in such a science is an alternative set of terms derived from an analysis of behavior and capable of doing the same work. No attempt has been made here to translate mentalistic or philosophical concepts into the terms of the present system. The only value of the translation would be pedagogical.[2]

Most of his later writings on the subject were indeed attempts at such translation, and no doubt they were done with pedagogical intention. They should not be evaluated with reference to the explosion of empirical and theoretical studies in the field of problem-solving from the late 1950s until now, but as answers to the challenge of extending the radical (as opposed to methodological) behaviourist approach to the most complex levels of human activities. Whether the challenge has been met is a matter of debate; as we shall see in a moment, here as in the field of language, looking from a distance in a dispassionate way can reveal unsuspected foreshadowings of, and convergences with, current work, carried out within the cognitivist framework.

## THE STATUS OF THOUGHT

Let us first characterise the main features of Skinner's "translation". In discussing convergencies with Piaget, in a preceding chapter, we have already pointed to Skinner's underlying general epistemology, anchored in action, rather than derived from sensations, as would be expected from an empiricist—which he was not, at least in the classical sense. This is the core of his analysis of thought. It is, however, fundamentally distinct from the concept of thought as proposed in other behaviourstic accounts, especially in Watson's. The founder of behaviourism, embarrassed with the mental appearance of thinking, solved the difficulty by assimilating thought to subvocal speech. Speech can be treated as behaviour, if clearly of a particular kind; and if it is assumed that thinking can be equated with speaking, we can go one step further and treat all covert thought—and thought is more often than not covert—as subvocal, covert speech, and therefore as behaviour.

Skinner unequivocally rejects that view. In a sound analysis of verbal behaviour addressed to oneself, the speaker and the listener being inside the same skin, he discusses the status of inaudible (to others) *vs* audible speech, pointing to the labour-saving value of subvocal speech, but also to its function in avoiding punishment. These, and other variables, account for the distinction between the two levels, overt and covert, but, as he concludes:

> they do not greatly affect other properties (of speech). They do not suggest that there is any important distinction between the two levels or forms. Nothing is gained, therefore, by identifying thinking with subaudible talking. This was done in certain early behaviouristic analysis, apparently in an effort to find replacements for the so-called mental processes.[3]

Thinking is no more the precursor of behaviour than covert speech is the precursor of overt speech:

> There is no point at which it is profitable to draw a line distinguishing thinking from acting on this continuum [ranging from overt behaviour, verbal or non-verbal, to covert, possibly unconscious behavior, again verbal or non-verbal].[4]

The following quotation encapsulates the substance of Skinner's views on thinking, while it clearly shows his awareness of the different levels to be distinguished when dealing with human higher processes. The final sentences illustrate once more the convergence with Piaget:

> The simplest and most satisfactory view is that thought is simply *behavior*—verbal or non-verbal, covert or overt. It is not some mysterious process responsible for behavior itself in all the complexity of its controlling relations, with respect to both man the behaver and the environment in which he lives. The concepts and methods which have emerged from the analysis of behavior, verbal or otherwise, are most appropriate to the study of what has traditionally been called the human mind. Tradition and expedience seem to agree in confining the analysis of human thought to operant behavior [as opposed to reflexes, conditioned or otherwise]. So conceived, thought is not a mystical cause or precursor of action, or an inaccessible ritual, but action itself, subject to analysis with the concepts and techniques of the natural sciences, and ultimately to be accounted for in terms of controlling variables.[5]

And this truly "systemic" statement:

> We can disregard the troublesome dissection of human thought into the familiar pattern of (1) a *man* possessing (2) *knowledge* of (3) a *world*. Men are part of the

world, and they interact with other parts of it, including other men. As their behavior changes, they may interact more effectively, gaining control and power. Their "knowledge" is their behavior with respect to themselves and the rest of the world and can be studied as such.[6]

# THE OPERANT AS PROBLEM-SOLVING

In a sense, any operant, in the process of emerging, can be seen as a simple case of problem-solving; an organism is confronted with a situation arranged in such a way that a given behaviour will produce food, which is what the subject is looking for at the moment. What it can do is modify the situation or modify its own way of behaving in the situation, in other words its interaction with the environment. Eventually, it will emit the adequate bit of behaviour that will be reinforced. If the response has not been shaped, i.e taught, it may have been produced "by chance", one of the behavioural variations exhibited by the subject happily hitting the goal, i.e. solving the problem. Once emitted, the response will eventually be produced again in a similar situation, and become a quickly available, automatic solution to the same problem.

This is not all that is usually under consideration when psychologists study problem-solving in humans. Hitting the solution by chance can be seen as a good outcome of random trials—the fact that the subject tries, rather than stays inactive, is already an important part of most operant adaptive behaviour, and an essential one when no other procedures are available—but humans have developed many more sophisticated and efficient ways of solving problems. Skinner has emphasised two of these ways, which could be called strategies, were the word free of mentalistic connotation. One is the building of discriminative stimuli that modify the situation or the type of interaction the subject has with it; the second is the appeal to verbal descriptions and instructions that Skinner has called rules. Rules are often involved in the construction of discriminative stimuli, so that disentangling both types of strategies is not always easy, but we will keep them separate for the sake of clarity.

In solving a problem, a subject will usually organise, rather than leave to randomness, the exploratory activities that will make the discovery of the solution more probable. Suppose subjects have to solve a mechanical problem, repair an engine, for example, or assemble pieces into a device. Manipulating the material at random gives little chance of finding the solution. Subjects will observe the material systematically, maybe by checking those parts already looked at carefully; they will sort items and mark them while trying to fit them to the device; they will operate successive manipulations, of which they will keep traces, and so on. Throughout individual history, more or less generalisable "precurrent behaviours" develop, that can be successfully applied to a wide range of problems. For instance, looking at things in a fresh way—in Piaget's language, performing a decentration—usually helps towards a solution; breaking down the problem into simpler components sometimes proves effective, and so on. Language will generally be involved in the process: describing what is observed, what has already been done, what could be done, are ways of changing, in reality or in thought, aspects of the situation, until eventually the solution will emerge. All this amounts to describing the contingencies, and describing one's own behaviour in relation to them. Such description can be used to control further one's own behaviour, thus taking the function of *rules*.

Rules, in Skinner's terminology, are verbal statements (which includes any of the specialised languages of science, as elaborated in logics or mathematics) that describe aspects of the world or of the relation of the subject to the world, and that can be used efficiently in acting. They play a major role in human adaptation. Many of them are part of the cultural context, others are constructed by the individual in coping with the environment. Teaching is to a large extent a transmission of rules for dealing with various kinds of domains.

## RULE-GOVERNED BEHAVIOUR

The difference between behaviour resulting from direct exposure to physical and social conditions and behaviour resulting from following rules is most important. Skinner has drawn a very basic distinction between what he termed contingency-shaped behaviour and rule-governed behaviour. The first refers to the process at work in animals, and also in humans when behaviour is acquired and maintained by direct interaction with the world. We all have acquired various motor skills in that way, such as climbing stairs or riding a bicycle. But this most natural process has its limits when it comes to adapting to more sophisticated man-made situations, such as driving a car or piloting an aircraft, or to mastering high-risk situations. Such adaptations are possible only by resorting to verbal instructions usually provided by persons with expertise. They are typical of rule-governed behaviour.

The advantages of rules so conceived are numerous, and easy to identify. As we have just seen in the examples given, they allow for the safe acquisition of skills that would expose the learner to high, possibly fatal risk if in direct contact with the contingencies. They are economical, in the sense that they spare the individual the energy- or time-consuming efforts of going alone through the stages that others have already mastered: they shortcut an important part of individual learning. They are obviously the basis of the cumulative character of human culture: none of us is able to reconstruct single handed the whole of mathematics or cabinetmaking; we can, however, take over from the current state of the art a synthesis of the past in a finite set of rules. Advantages remain when rules are constructed by the subject in the course of coping with a given situation or solving a problem. They are, of course, the key to hypothetical anticipation of action, that makes it possible to foresee outcomes of various strategies, until one is eventually selected as the most appropriate solution. They make it possible to put present behaviour under the control of remote consequences. A typical example in daily life is subscribing to insurance policies, to protect oneself against risks to which most subscribers are unlikely to be exposed during their lifetime. These policies follow rules stated by insurance companies, who base their estimations on statistical inferences concerning rare events, which an individual usually does not experience directly often enough to get under the control of concrete consequences. This is one case where humans are able to adopt a behaviour controlled by very low-probability events. Ecological risks present the same properties, and safety will be reached only when modern societies genuinely make decisions based on estimations of consequences remote in the future, and therefore ineffective in controlling behaviour directly.

The concept of rule-governed behaviour is related to a major classical problem in psychology, the problem of articulating verbal and non-verbal behaviour. In so far as verbal behaviour is assigned a higher status in the hierarchy of behaviours, the problem is generally stated in terms of control of motor action by language, or to use Luria's phrase, of regulation of motor behaviour by language. In the framework of contemporary cognitive psychology, it is a case of top-down causation. The importance given to it by Skinner reflects his deep interest in one of the most distinctive features of human psychology, and would suffice to discard the idea that he took the rat as a model of human beings.

Rules offer an alternative to contingencies, but the behaviour emerging from the control by rules is not identical to the behaviour shaped by the contingencies. The latter keeps its genuine properties, which Skinner has characterised by drawing a parallel between the opposition of contingency-shaped *vs* rule-governed behaviour on one hand, and other classical dichotomies, on the other hand. Rule-governed behaviour is more on the side of the intellect as opposed to emotion, of logical argument as opposed to intuition, of deliberation as opposed to impulse, of knowledge as opposed to know-how, of word as opposed to deed, of reason as opposed to faith, of truth as opposed to belief, of rationality as opposed to passion, of consciousness as opposed to unconsciousness, of culture as opposed to nature. Each of these contrasts captures some aspects of the difference that remains even when the behaviour derived from the two types of control is at first sight identical. Their origin and history are different, and therefore they have functionally different status. The contrast becomes striking in cases where rules can fairly easily be stated, but do not succeed in controlling behaviour. Skinner quotes Pascal's famous example:

> The greatest philosopher in the world, standing on a plank broader than needed to support him but over a precipice, will be controlled by his imagination even though his reason convinces him that he is safe. [Skinner comments:] It is not his imagination but earlier contingencies which evoke the behavior of being afraid (and some of these contingencies may be phylogenic).[7]

We have all experienced similar situations, even though of a less dramatic nature. The description of a dance step, or of a sporting performance, is not necessarily all that is needed to reproduce them correctly. Stating the rules for solving a mathematical problem does not always suffice to have the student solve it. The relation of rules to action is a complex one, and to talk about rule-governed behaviour implies that the subject *behaves*. Action is still an essential part of the process.

## CURRENT TRENDS IN PROBLEM-SOLVING

Are these formulations of thought and problem-solving relevant to the current trends in the field? In so far as the field is now part of cognitive psychology, and in so far as cognitivism has to some important extent defined its own identity by contrast with behaviourism, one cannot expect that students of problem-solving, or, more generally speaking, of intelligence today would give Skinner credit for having developed seminal ideas. More often than not, they simply ignore his contribution—as they ignore many other, non-behaviourist contributions of the past that would appear surprisingly modern in many respects—or, when they allude to it, they discard it as irrelevant, for not giving due place to mental states or processes, such as thought, intention, will, and the like. Thus, they show that the traditional debate has not come to an end, and they also reveal that they have not read Skinner carefully, if they have read him at all. Had they done so, they would have discovered that Skinner did not deny the reality behind terms such as thought, intention, or will, but that he objected to taking them as self-explanatory entities and as explaining the behaviour they are supposed to cause. Their position often pertains to what I have called in a previous chapter epistemological cognitivism.

In that context, it is interesting to pinpoint the opinion of some commentators on Skinner's ideas on that particular issue. I shall refer to two of them, reputed authorities in the field of intelligence. To Robert J. Sternberg, Skinner's account of problem-solving appeared, when he first read it as an undergraduate, as:

> an analysis to be refuted, at that time, by what I believed to be the white knight of information-processing psychology. On rereading the piece, my reaction was quite different. I think Skinner has provided an ingenuous analysis of problem solving that just happens to address relatively few of the issues that I and many others view as our primary concern today. This is not to say that our concerns are right and Skinner's wrong—simply that they are addressed to different aspects of the phenomena of problem solving.[8]

The questions that Sternberg is interested in are not, in fact, questions dismissed by Skinner, but redefined by him, "in a way", Sternberg adds "that begs the questions that I hope to see answered. Thus, for example, he states that 'to speak of the purpose of an act is simply to refer to its characteristic consequences,' . . . I do not believe that goals can be subsumed by characteristic consequences . . ."

Sternberg's objections bear on the status of mental events, on the legitimacy of having one category for thought or goal seeking as mental entities or processes, as distinct from behaviour. He comes back, as do most cognitivists, to a loose mentalistic use of the terms that Skinner thought it necessary to clarify by proposing a functional analysis of the realities referred to. Sternberg shares the widespread belief, again scientifically dignified in cognitivism, that these realities are of a different nature from behaviour, but the belief is not critically supported against Skinner's reasons for not sharing it. Many biologists and philosophers did not believe that life could eventually have emerged from physicochemical processes; or they did not believe that species might have evolved through a process of natural selection rather than having been created by the will of God. Science has shaken many of our beliefs, and those related with our self-image are more tenacious than others. No wonder that they recur on any possible occasion before leaving the stage for ever.

In spite of these basic divergences—which he calls "this sense of irrelevance"—Sternberg admits that Skinner had emphasised aspects of problem-solving regrettably overlooked by information-processing psychology. The following paragraph of his comment is worth quoting in full:

> . . . I did find Skinner dealing with questions that I think were often too quickly shoved aside in the first flush of enthusiasm with information-processing research. For example, Skinner shows quintessential sensitivity to the effects of the situation upon behavior; information-processing psychologists have often treated tasks as though they occur in isolation, without reference to a variety of situational constraints. Moreover, Skinner shows a concern with issues of learning that have often been ignored or explained away by information-processing psychologists, most recently, by claims that experts differ from novices in, it seems, little else but the knowledge they bring to bear on the problems they solve. Certainly it was their superior learning strategies that helped them acquire their enormous knowledge; I suspect Skinner would have more to say about how this learning took place than would those who start their analysis only after the learning has taken place.

Sternberg undoubtedly reflects a swing of the pendulum towards a more balanced position on problem-solving.

Hunt, already quoted earlier, goes one step further, by tracing parallels between Skinner's treatment of problem-solving, and the formulations adopted by some of the influential leaders in the field of cognitive psychology. He does not hesitate to use the expression "internal representation" as an equivalent to "discriminative stimulus", especially to designate the labelling of the goal to be attained when a subject engages in solving a problem, and is able to describe the change in the situation that the solution should bring. The importance of that step is clearly exemplified in problem-solving simulations, in which students of cognition resort to the concepts of pattern-action rule: a "pattern" P, in this context, is a symbolic statement of the goal state, the presence of which in the internal representation of the problem produces action A. Hunt notes:

> Production systems can appear to be teleologically driven toward a goal. In fact, they are evoked by our statement of the problem and its goal. The learning theorists of the 1940s and 1950s (and Skinner) had the impoverished notion that problem solving could be stated in terms of an S→R notation. Modern cognitive psychologists find that P→A is more appropriate. Skinner could justly claim that his paper had the essentials of the modern idea![9]

Another analogy is between precurrent behaviours, building new discriminative stimuli, and the manipulation of a physical symbol system by the modern problem-solver. Hunt also points to the close resemblance between Skinner's emphasis on labelling responses and aspects of the situation, and the role of labelling in the expert's way of solving a problem, as contrasted with the novice's. He suggests that "there is no reason why Chi, Larkin and their colleagues could not have used Skinner's language instead of terms borrowed from computer science!"[9] Finally, Hunt underlines the similarities between the contingency-shaped *vs* rule-governed behaviour distinction and Schneider and Shiffrin's distinction between automatic and controlled processing.

These remarks are all the more significant because their author is working within the cognitivist paradigm, and has nothing to gain from venturing into a rehabilitation of Skinner. They simply stem from a lucid and honest reading of Skinner's work, and from Hunt's awareness that deep continuities link even successive and apparently opposite trends in psychological science—an awareness that a large part of the conflicts within contemporary psychology are but debates on metaphors.

## CREATIVE BEHAVIOUR

Although problem-solving, in the classical sense, by definition always involves some novelty, it is widely admitted that it can be submitted to scientific analysis, and it could even be conceded that it can be profitably analysed in behavioural terms, as proposed by Skinner. One area of human higher activity, however, will certainly escape for ever any attempt at causal explanation; that is the domain of creativity. Would it not appear especially paradoxical to suggest that pieces of art, literature or music could be accounted for within a deterministic psychological theory mainly concerned with conditioning?

Since the 1950s there has been a widespread interest in creativity, in educational, industrial, and even political circles. This was not exactly a sudden concern of an opulent society for drawing the best from otherwise satisfied humans by promoting artistic and intellectual creation. It was to a large extent a response of American society to the disturbing discovery that a rival power, the Soviet Union, had preceded them into space. Education and industry were blamed for neglecting creativity, which became a favoured theme in conversations, as did oil some 20 years later; nobody speaks of it until there is a shortage.

In spite of this impetus, psychological research on creativity hardly took us beyond traditional ideas defining creativity as a sort of faculty of the mind, eventually measurable with appropriate tests, or as the happy result of mental aptitudes combined with favourable circumstances. Others preferred to look at it as an innate characteristic equally shared by all humans, that would flourish better when left untouched by educational control. In the 1960s the myth of creativity was linked with the anti-school movement in education, and with the non-directivist approaches in psychology. In that perspective, you don't educate creativity, you have only to free it from any control.

Needless to say, such views, essentially mentalistic as they are, were alien to Skinner. This does not mean that he was not concerned with the problem of creativity. But, as may be expected, he took a completely different approach, which will be easily understood because the bearing of the evolutionary analogy has been thoroughly elucidated earlier. Rather than trying to capture some mysterious mental faculty that would be the source of so-called creative productions, Skinner preferred to talk of creative behaviour, to identify the properties of the behaviour we agree to qualify that way, and to look for the variables that allow its emergence in some individuals or groups, at some times in history, in some cultures, etc. He saw no reason why such behaviours should be dealt with in any basically different way from other types of behaviour.

An obvious common characteristic of all creative behaviours is that they imply some novelty, a concept that needs to be defined, of course, with reference to some previously defined set: a behaviour observed in a child may be new compared to previous behaviour—this is developmental novelty, but not creative behaviour in the usual sense—and artistic creation usually implies novelty with reference with previous productions in a given culture (pieces of art inspired from other cultures may look creative only to members of the borrowing culture, not to members of the culture from which they were borrowed). Some human cultures have developed in which creative productions, under conditions of acceptance, are highly praised by the community. This might induce individuals to produce objects, texts, or music marked by novelty, for which they will be rewarded, not necessarily financially, but socially; not necessarily immediately, but in a remote, sometimes posthumous future; not necessarily from outside, but from the intrinsic satisfaction of making a new piece of work. Cultural selection works in this case to encourage diversity.

This appears to be simply a special case of the general process underlying operant behaviour. The parallel with biological evolution applies in a peculiarly striking manner to creative behaviour, which results in productions almost as diverse and fascinating as living species. Far from raising a difficulty for a theory of behaviour, creativity, quite to the contrary, provides an exceptionally clear illustration of what it is all about. The following quotation from Skinner summarises the point:

> Novelty and originality can occur in a wholly deterministic system. A convenient archetypal pattern is the theory of evolution. The living forms on the earth show a variety far beyond that of works of art. The diversity was once attributed to the whims and vagaries of a creative Mind, but Darwin proposed an alternative explanation. The word "origin" in *The origin of species* is important, for the book is essentially a study of originality. The multiplicity of living forms is accounted for in terms of mutation and selection, without appealing to any prior design. There are comparable elements in the behavior of the artist who produces original works.[10]

We are far from the image of Skinner as a defender of conformism. He was, on the contrary, quite aware that the selection of a piece of art, literature, or science does not necessarily come from the majority, nor from contemporaries: cultural mechanisms have evolved that seem also to operate the selection through the judgements of very few individuals, whose opinion is nevertheless decisive, or with a delay that can extend beyond one generation. He was himself exposed to so many and so violent attacks from his peers, or from the laypeople, that he would have withdrawn from the scene were it not for the conviction that he was right, and that it would eventually be recognised. He pertained to that category of people who, even in the scientific domain where rigour is usually praised at the expense of fantasy, take as fair evidence of their own value the fact that others treat them as fools. An anecdotal paper is worth quoting in this context. It was published in 1960 under the title "Pigeons in a Pelican". It tells the story of the Pigeon project, an applied research programme aimed at exploring the technical possibility of detecting or later guiding missiles using living organisms (pigeons). Skinner, then at the University of Minnesota (in the early 1940s), tested the pigeon's capacity to respond in such a way as to keep a missile (the candidate was called Pelican) moving towards a target. Experimental work took place, of course, in a simulator. Incidentally, this piece of research was often mentioned later as evidence of Skinner's involvement in military affairs, an allegedly logical consequence of his theoretical stand. The accusation appears rather ridiculous when one thinks of the time when the project was carried out, of the much more far-reaching involvement of most American scientists in defence research-projects, and of the outcomes. Although the results were rather encouraging they never quite reached practical applications in warfare, because of the electronic solutions worked out concurrently by engineers.

The concluding paragraph of the paper is revealing of Skinner's character as a scientist, and of his conception of creative research. It reads as follows:

If I were to conclude that crackpot ideas are to be encouraged, I should probably be told that psychology has already had more than its share of them. If it has, they have been entertained by the wrong people. Reacting against the excesses of psychological quackery, psychologists have developed an enormous concern for scientific respectability. They constantly warn their students against questionable facts and unsupported theories. As a result the usual Ph.D. thesis is a model of compulsive cautiousness, advancing only the most timid conclusions thoroughly hedged about with qualifications. But it is just the man capable of displaying such admirable caution who needs a touch of uncontrolled speculation. Possibly a generous exposure to psychological science fiction would help. Project Pigeon might be said to support this view. Except with respect to its avowed goal, it was, as I see it, very productive; and this was in large measure because my colleagues and I knew that, in the eyes of the world, we were crazy.[11]

I pointed out in the introduction to this book, that in my long experience as a student, Skinner was the least authoritarian teacher I ever met. He was also the most adventurous creative researcher, and occasionally the more inclined to uncontrolled speculation. This is probably why we owe him so many well established data, well argued theoretical proposals, and stimulating sources of speculation.

## NOTES

1. Earl Hunt, "A case study of how a paper containing good ideas, presented by a distinguished scientist, to an appropriate audience, had almost no influence at all", *Behavioral and Brain Sciences*, 1984, 7, 597–598. Hunt's paper is an invited peer commentary to "An operant analysis of problem-solving", reprinted in *Behavioral and Brain Sciences* (and before that in *Contingencies of reinforcement*, 1969).
2. *The behavior of organisms*, p.441.
3. *Verbal behavior*, p.437.
4. *Verbal behavior*, p.438; parentheses are mine, and summarise the content of the preceding paragraph.
5. *Verbal behavior*, p.449, parentheses are mine.
6. *Verbal behavior*, p.451.
7. *Contingencies of reinforcement*, p.171. This, as the summary of contrasted couples that precedes it, is drawn from extended notes to the paper "An operant analysis of problem-solving" reprinted in the volume given. Part of the material of these notes has been included in a more concise form in the article as reprinted in *Behavioral and Brain Sciences*, 1984.
8. Sternberg, 1984, p.605.
9. Hunt, 1984, p.597.
10. From "Creating the creative artist", reprinted in *Cumulative record* (1972a), p.339.
11. From "Pigeon in a Pelican", reprinted in *Cumulative record*, (1972d), p.590.

# IV THE CONCERN FOR REAL LIFE: A VENTURE INTO UTOPIA

# 12 Mental Health

## SCIENTIFIC PSYCHOLOGY IN CLINICAL CONTEXT

Psychology is probably best known to the layperson through its applications to the treatment of psychological disorders. This is the professional field of clinical psychologists and psychotherapists (two categories that tend to merge in the same persons). The field is often confused in the public's mind with psychoanalysis and Freud's tradition, but throughout the century, many other practices have developed, some of them derived from Freudian sources, others of a rather different nature. They show a wide range of variations, with respect to the procedures used, the types of patients or clients addressed, the underlying philosophy, and the reference made (or not made) to scientific criteria in defining the rationale for the therapeutic strategy and in evaluating the outcome of treatment. Behaviour therapy is one of the main varieties, with a number of subvarieties, including so-called behavioural-cognitive or cognitive-behavioural therapies, at first sight a somewhat unexpected hybridisation.

Behaviour therapy was born before Skinner's contribution: its origins can be traced back to Pavlov and to Watson.[1] But Skinner's influence was a decisive one, in the 1950s, in the rapid extension of what has been viewed as an alternative to psychodynamics and psychoanalysis. His major writings on the subject are, once again, parts of *Science and human behavior*, and half a dozen papers published in the same decade. His contribution was twofold: on the one hand, he criticised some aspects of Freud's theory; on the other, he promoted the experimental analysis of behaviour as a possible tool for understanding and for modifying abnormal behaviour.

We have seen in Chapter 5 the place given to Freud in Skinner's writing, both to credit the founder of psychoanalysis for his search for determinants of human behaviour, and to blame him for his mentalistic theory. By appealing to the psychic apparatus, Freud has reified as mental entities what should, in Skinner's view, have been more fruitfully analysed in functional terms. It had

> a damaging effect upon his study of behavior as a dependent variable. Inevitably, it stole the show. Little attention was left to behavior per se. Behavior was relegated to the position of a mere mode of expression of the activities of the mental apparatus or the symptoms of an underlying disturbance.[2]

Skinner argues, as have other critics of Freud, that by resorting to internal psychic structures rather than keeping close to the sequence of events that eventually produced neurotic behaviour, one runs the risk that part of the relation between actual behaviour and its antecedents in the individual's history will be lost, and consequently that therapeutic attempts will become more difficult. Although psychological disturbances are viewed as originating in the details of an individual's early interaction with the surrounding social world, they are soon, in the theory, attributed to constructs such as complexes, defence mechanisms, or conflicts between components of the personality, the Id, Ego and Superego.

It is important to underline that Skinner never expressed any objection to Freud's idea that current troubles derive from early events, even if behaviour therapy has often been accused of a-historicity, in the sense that it has sometimes overlooked the fact that psychological dysfunctioning frequently has its roots in the (remote) part of a person's life. This was never Skinner's position, and in any case it is completely alien to a psychology of learning, which is by definition concerned with how an organism is changed through time.[3] However, there is no reason to look for the causes of psychological disturbances exclusively in the early stages of life. There are many psychological problems linked essentially with current or recent causes in the individual's life, and many of those problems originating in a remote past would remain minor, and possibly go undetected, were it not for present conditions that contribute to amplifying and exacerbating them. One consequence of the psychodynamic approach had been that the treatment was aimed at changing the patient's psychic functioning; the question was not asked whether removing some of the current conditions would not make for faster and more effective improvement. It was assumed that if, at the beginning, the world around might have been responsible for the patient's problem, by the time of the treatment the patient could but adjust to the world as it is.

By proposing to apply to psychologically ill people the same kind of functional behavioural analysis that he had applied successfully to normal organisms, Skinner was suggesting that their condition could be better understood, and that they could eventually be helped more efficiently than before. One must remember that by the time Skinner entered the field of psychological disease and treatment, clinical psychology was dominated by the psychoanalytic tradition, which exhibited unusually rich theoretical elaborations but very limited therapeutic indications and successes, compared with the number and variety of cases demanding help. On the other hand, psychiatry was only beginning to benefit from the recent discovery of the first psychotropic drugs.

Although his theoretical attacks against Freud were clear enough, Skinner was quite cautious in venturing into the territory of psychiatrists and clinical psychologists. In introducing one of his papers, he honestly emphasised his lack of credentials, if evaluated in terms of clinical experience. He had no new classification of mental diseases to offer, and he would not question the importance of the search for biological correlates or causes of psychological dysfunction. But he contributed to a shaking of some of the comfortable beliefs in psychiatry and psychopathology, by pointing to the possible importance of environmental factors that should be carefully explored before assigning a patient to a nosological category with a given degree of severity, and more or less pessimistic prospects of improvement.

## A PRAGMATIC APPROACH TO SYMPTOMS

Admittedly, Skinner's approach might look theoretically poor, compared with speculations on the origins and structures of mental disease in various orientations of psychiatry and psychopathology. It was an essentially pragmatic approach, mainly to the problem of treatment, with little direct impact on the issues of nosological classification or of etiology. The basic hypothesis has been a very simple one, even a simplistic one, as viewed by practitioners of some schools of thought: knowing as little as we do about the true nature and causes of so-called mental disorders, we should not focus too much on defining the various pathological conditions, but concentrate instead on modifying those behaviours that lead to the labelling of an individual as a psychiatric or psychological case. If those behaviours can be changed favourably, why bother about classification or theory? Why insist that the disorder is still around, as if it were distinct from the disordered behaviours, which are taken as mere symptoms of an underlying disturbance?

In applying functional analysis to abnormal behaviour, putting nosological classification in parentheses, Skinner eventually suggests that, in some cases, it can be accounted for by simple mechanisms at work in the control of behaviour in general, but pushed to some extreme point, or involved in unusual contingencies. For instance, emotional by-products of aversive contingencies, possibly adaptive if they do not pass a certain level, can generate really abnormal conditions when aversive control is excessive. Fear is a normal healthy reaction, that helps keep us away from dangerous situations, but it becomes abnormal when stimuli are so threatening, or when other factors increase their threatening power to such point as to generate phobia. Many "abnormal" behaviours can be explained by "normal" behavioural mechanisms, if we refrain from cataloguing them pathologically instead of analysing carefully the conditions that account for their origin and their maintenance. For example, drug addiction may appear as an escape or avoidance from otherwise intolerable social or affective conditions; some depressive states can be understood as a drastic reduction of behaviour in situations where subjects have lost the chance to be positively reinforced for whatever they do, where they stop coping with the world around because success never follows; aggressive behaviour towards others or oneself sometimes has no other function but to draw social attention not otherwise obtained. This type of analysis displaces the emphasis from the disease category to the context in which the individual has lived and is currently living. It moves the responsibility from the subject's personality or psychological structure to the environment, usually the social environment. If the importance of such environmental factors is confirmed, it radically modifies the whole conception of the psychological disorder being considered. It will eventually be concluded that it is a by-product of society rather than an internal disturbance, and efforts will naturally be made to identify and change the social factors, rather than to multiply individual psychological treatment. Prevention will quite naturally also take priority over remediation. If it is too late to change the abnormal behaviour generated by exposure to earlier abnormal contingencies or impossible to modify it by changing the present situation, all that is left is to prevent similar psychological damage for people in the future. In spite of the prolific development of treatment procedures in the behaviour therapy movement in the 1950s and 1960s, Skinner did not engage himself in much practical contribution to remediation techniques as such. He was much more attracted by the long term effects on mental health of revised cultural design.

Starting with an apparently modest contribution to the difficult field of psychiatry and psychopathology, Skinner advocated positions quite similar, although for quite different reasons, to those defended at about the same time by antipsychiatrists. Antipsychiatrists contend that psychiatry is, to a large extent, a social instrument for putting aside those individuals with supposedly deviant behaviours, who would disturb social order, or for avoiding the responsibility for changing social conditions that generate psychological disorders by putting a medical label on those individuals who are victims of them. This is an extreme view, which gives an exclusive causal role to social factors in mental diseases. Skinner did not go that far, and he never denied the possible importance of biological, including genetic factors, in psychopathological disorders. But he certainly contributed to pointing out the hopelessness of increasing medical and psychological care for increasing numbers of patients if we know, from a behavioural analysis, that the source of their disorder is mainly in their social environment. All efforts should be put into changing that rather than into training an increasing number of therapists.

## BEHAVIOURAL TREATMENT IN BIOLOGICALLY DETERMINED DISORDERS

Even in cases in which genetic or other biological factors are likely or certain to be the cause of the psychological disorder, the behavioural approach to treatment remains important, as long as an effective biological treatment has not been discovered, and even after such treatment is available. Genetic engineering was still in its infancy when Skinner first dealt with these problems, and in spite of the astonishing progress made since that time, it still does not have the solution to most genetically determined mental diseases. Drug treatment has similarly progressed since the early 1950s, but is rarely by itself a satisfactory solution if other procedures, psychological in nature, are not combined with it. And it is well known that, sometimes, drug treatment can contribute to masking the real problem by giving a more radical medical and biological status to what is essentially a socio-cultural problem. Prescribing pills can be easier, and less costly, than changing housing or working conditions, and it has the advantage of leaving the disorder inside the patient.

Contrary to widespread belief, a behavioural (or for that matter any psychological) approach is not mutually exclusive to a biological, including genetic, approach to mental disease. If an individual's psychological state is abnormal, or their potentialities limited because of genetic factors the effects of which cannot be reversed (a miracle perhaps not out of reach in the future, but not currently realised), we have no other way to help than by putting to work all possible behavioural strategies. This principle is easy to understand in the case of mental deficiency. Mental retardation can be traced, in a limited proportion of cases, to identified genetic factors, and in a larger proportion, with various degrees of certainty, to biological factors linked with various organic diseases, growth conditions, nutrition, etc. The only way to compensate, unfortunately not perfectly, for these determinants consists in applying behavioural procedures more intensively and more deliberately than is usually done with normal subjects—who will eventually adjust to their environment with even a minimum of external (educational) intervention.

## OPERANT TECHNIQUES IN THERAPY

If behavioural treatments already existed before Skinner, he gave them a new impetus, not only by entering the theoretical debate, but by enriching them with operant techniques. A pioneering work by Fuller, in 1949, had shown the effectiveness of operant principles in a case of severe retardation. Skinner himself supervised studies carried out by Lindsley on chronic psychotic patients, demonstrating that they were sensitive to positive reinforcement. Soon after, an operant approach was applied by Ayllon and Azrin on a psychiatric ward, under the label of "behavioral engineering".[4] After a detailed analysis of the behaviours displayed by a group of chronic patients, and a study of possible positive reinforcers, the investigators organised a "token economy". Applying principles from the laboratory, they reinforced—by tokens, exchangeable for attractive items or for opportunities to engage in some much appreciated activity—desirable behaviours that were presumably good for the patients, for other inmates and for the personnel in charge of them. The general organisation of daily life improved, patients' dependence on the nursing staff decreased, and constructive and autonomous activities increased accordingly. No aversive contingencies were used, no constraints were imposed. Adequate behaviours were shaped, such as attending meals according to a regular schedule, or feeding oneself rather than depending on a nurse; undesirable behaviours were eliminated by extinction procedures, by the shaping of competing behaviours, or by satiation, as in the case of a patient who collected all the magazines he could in the ward and stored them under his mattress: a huge number of magazines were made available, which he collected until his room was full of them, and he eventually gave up his mania. While the project was carried out in a group, operant principles were applied to individual patients: behaviours were first analysed, then modified on the basis of individual observation and management of individual contingencies.

From then on, behaviour therapists elaborated more and more sophisticated procedures, applied to individuals or groups, sometimes aimed at altering a target behaviour, for example self-mutilation or aggressive activities, sometimes at building up a lacking repertoire, the presence of which would eliminate or offer an alternative to the abnormal condition. Verbal procedures, using instructions or self-instructions, were developed. The field of application, initially limited to the classical range of mental disorders, was extended to include many health problems in otherwise normal people, such as obesity, smoking, addiction, and family or couple difficulties.

The first practical attempts raised objections and criticisms that are still heard today, in spite of the accumulated empirical evidence and of the repeated elucidating arguments. Most of these objections and criticisms had already been addressed to Skinner's proposals.

## OBJECTIONS

A first objection, mainly from those who follow the psychodynamic tradition, is that, if superficial improvements in behaviour can indeed be observed, the disorder itself is not really cured. The objection is based on the theory that overt behaviours are but symptoms of a deeper internal conditions, which has to be removed first if the symptoms are to disappear. If they disappear first, because of direct action on them, one must suppose that they are only masked, and that the underlying disorder is still present, ready to manifest itself again, for instance in displacement—some other symptomatic expression taking the place of the suppressed symptom. The debate on this issue usually turns to a dialogue of the deaf, unless the objector can demonstrate the existence of the inferred internal condition after the symptoms have been removed.

The objection, however, can be answered in a more pragmatic style. Psychological disorders are usually not an all-or-none matter. They cannot be compared with infectious diseases that can be totally eliminated by antibiotics, or well-located tumours that can be completely removed surgically. They can be alleviated to various degrees, some behaviours can be changed, others not, and there is often a high risk of relapse. Then, to the question: "Have you really cured the patient?" the behaviour therapist (as any honest therapist) will reply: "I am not sure, but what I do know is that he has improved". This statement is not based on one's own intuitive judgement as a therapist, but on empirical evidence that the goal of the treatment, or of one part of the treatment, explicitly defined before the treatment was started, has actually been reached. This is a major difference between behaviour therapy and other types of psychotherapies: goals can be less ambitious, less global, but they are clearly stated, so that it can easily be checked whether the treatment was a success or a failure.

A second objection has to do with the notion of control. The word is a familiar one in Skinner's prose, and it is frequently used in behaviour therapists' vocabulary. The objection does not come so much from psychoanalysts as from therapists of the Rogerian non-directive tradition. Although it is admitted that only positive rewards are used (some critics obstinately refuse to admit this, persisting in comparing Skinner and the behaviour therapists working along his lines to dangerous punishers, resorting to such unethical stimulation as electric shocks!), the whole approach is rejected as typically based on deliberate control by the therapist of the patient's behaviour. At first the objection sounds a strong one, because it appeals to our sense of respect for the patient's freedom. It appears all the more strong when it is also claimed that alternative types of treatment are available. Can we advocate coercive procedures when we can reach the same end with permissive ones? The fact that control is based on positive reinforcement is usually viewed as even more suspicious: freedom is all the more threatened when the control of it is made pleasant. Framed in the general ethical issues of the medical and the psychological professions, the debate is a difficult and a complex one. Some patients are simply unable to express their own desires concerning the treatment they like: severe retardates, some psychotics, or deteriorated elderly people cannot be left without care because they cannot negotiate their treatment. With these as well as other cases, behaviour therapists do not pay less attention to ethical problems than with others; on the contrary, it could be argued that they apply more rigorous standards, by specifying their goals more explicitly and by evaluating their therapeutic successes according to experimental criteria. But we will credit therapists of all persuasions with equal ethical concern. Skinner's reply to that objection was on different grounds: those who oppose controlling techniques to non-directive approaches are simply cheating, because there is no type of psychological intervention that can claim not to exert an influence on the patient's behaviour. Apparently non-directive techniques in fact resort to mechanisms for controlling others' behaviour, which can be detected and described as can those overtly put to work in behavioural analysis and derived therapies. The psychoanalytic couch, where the patient is invited to say whatever comes to mind, is typically a situation from which all stimuli associated with repression are tentatively removed, with the consequence that the patient will eventually be free from disturbing inhibitions. The face-to-face dialogue of Rogerian therapy, with the therapist intervening very little, and exclusively by mild approval and encouraging signs, also creates favourable conditions for alleviating inhibitions, increasing verbal productions, and through mild social reinforcement reinstating a sense of self-esteem, usually linked among other things with the opportunity to be listened to. There is of course nothing wrong with this type of control, but it would be fair to state clearly what is going on, rather than flatter the patient with the illusion of freedom. After all, the patient or the client has the right to know about the processes involved in the treatment. They can choose a given procedure, as they would decide on a surgical operation, because it is most probably effective, of a reasonable timespan, and not exceedingly expensive, as compared with other therapies of which the objectives are not defined in advance, the duration is not limited, and the cost hence uncertain. Current ethical practices in behaviour therapy generally include a clear and fair contract with the patients: they are informed of where they should go with the therapist, what will be the mechanisms involved, and what is their own part in the therapeutic process. This could explain the success of behaviour therapies all over the world: clients have used their freedom to choose what they have considered the most promising treatment.

It should be made clear at this point that the merits of other treatments are by no means denied. Opinions differ as to the real nature of psychological disorders, and as to the best methods to reduce them. No theory or practice proposed up to now can claim universal validity. It must be remembered that, as has often been the case in the history of medicine for organic diseases, a treatment can be effective for other reasons that those believed by their users; some theories can prove to be wrong, and the treatment derived from them efficient, and conversely some theories can be correct but the derived treatment without any effect. Today clinicians tend to adopt an eclectic approach, recognising that some cases benefit best from one type of treatment, others from another type. This is not inconsistency; on the contrary, it is both the most ethical and most pragmatic position, given the limitations of our present understanding. It is not alien to Skinner's own open-minded position, as expressed in the following sentences, pointing to some basic commonalities between behavioural and psychodynamic approaches:

Causal factors important in understanding mental disease are, however, to be found among the independent variables to which the psychologist characteristically turns. An excessive emotional condition, a dangerous mode of escape from anxiety, a troublesome preoccupation with sex, or an excessive enthusiasm for gambling may be nothing more than extreme cases of the effects of environmental conditions. These aspects of the personal history and the current environment of the individual are commonly taken to be in the realm of psychology and within reach of the psychologists' techniques. Modes of behavior characteristic of mental disease may be simply the result of a history of reinforcement, an unusual condition of deprivation or satiation, or an emotionally exciting circumstance. Except for the fact that they are troublesome or dangerous, they may not be distinguishable from the rest of the behavior of the individual. Insofar as this is the case, the etiology of mental disease and the possibility of analysis and therapy lie within the field of psychology proper. (At this point an overlap with psychodynamics is obvious. The distinction between the psychological and psychodynamic view is not basically a distinction in subject matter or in the range of factors studied. The distinction is primarily one of method, and it is possible that these two fields will eventually fuse or at least become very closely associated).[5]

## PSYCHOTHERAPY AND SOCIAL CONTROLS

In his analysis of the psychotherapeutic process, Skinner insists on its role in correcting in the individual the damaging consequences of various cultural controls; political, economic, religious, and most frequently punitive in nature. Psychotherapies are compensating for negative controls exerted by other agencies. In some sense, they imply almost necessarily a questioning of those controls. They are, in some way, inevitably subversive. They may, however, fulfil that function in different ways. The same society, that is the same set of controlling agencies, generates the psychotherapists and the patients, and there is a risk that the first will feel their role as one of adapting the second to social norms. The subversive side inherent in all psychotherapeutic projects gives then way to conformisation. The history of the main methods of psychological intervention show that they have bred two diverging tendencies, one favouring the adjustment or reinsertion of the individual, the other promoting their liberation.

What is paradoxical is that those schools of psychotherapy that rely on the subject's internal resources and do not make controls explicit, are especially exposed to being supported by the controlling agencies, the excesses of which have made them necessary. By emphasising the individual's autonomy, they are in fact supporting the very controls they should, instead, expose, as they are committed to correcting their effects. The main task of psychotherapy, as the main task of medicine, in the long term, ideally consists in rendering itself useless by provoking the changes necessary to avoid the problems it tries to remedy. It is in the nature of mentalistic psychotherapies that they maintain what they should tend to eliminate, with the beneficial consequence that, in doing so, they perpetuate themselves. Excesses of various powers in society are a source of psychological problems, and indirectly of psychotherapeutic practices that attempt to solve them in individuals, and themselves become a power among others.

## EXPERIMENTAL APPROACH TO THERAPIES

Skinner's contribution to psychotherapy has certainly been instrumental in introducing an experimental orientation in a field that had been left, traditionally, to the intuition and empathy of the clinicians. This has been the common emphasis in all trends of behaviour therapies, but the impetus given by Skinner has been, in this respect, decisive. First, it has extended the range of relevant concepts and procedures transferred from the laboratory to clinical situations. This is not unique to Skinner's influence, but he has made important additions to the contributions made by others, from Pavlov to Liddell, Harlow, Miller, or Seligman. Second, it has given its credentials to the experimental approach to individual behaviour, and Skinner has largely contributed to establishing single case studies as part of recognised experimental designs, applicable in behavioural treatment. This point might appear as secondary to the central issues of psychological treatments, but it has been of major importance. Experimental psychology has been dominated by the methodological obsession of drawing general laws from group studies, developing to that end sophisticated experimental designs and appropriate statistical procedures. The fact that behaviour takes place in individual organisms, and that its controlling variables should be looked for there has been widely overlooked by orthodox research and teaching. Experimenters have conceded to practitioners the exclusivity of individuals, admittedly unamenable to rigorous analysis. This opposition has not favoured the mutual interaction between the laboratory and the clinic. As we have seen before, Skinner took a completely different stand, by carrying out in his laboratory experimental work on individual organisms, an academic risk at a time when all respected psychologists working in animal laboratories were studying groups of subjects. His experimental procedures were strong enough to show that behaviour can be modified by a given variable, then reinstated in its initial state by removing the variable, modified once more, and so on. This simple but very convincing A–B–A design is based on the alternation of a baseline state A and a modified state B, followed by a return to A. It has been applied extensively to the experimental study of the effects of drugs on behaviour, and it is easy to see how it can be usefully applied to treatment, including psychological treatment (with the important obvious condition that the effects of the variable under study are reversible). Other designs applicable to single subjects—which is the rule in clinical work—are available, but need not be detailed here. The important point is that the behavioural treatment itself is approached as an experiment, in which the therapists have to demonstrate that they are really doing what they claim to be doing.

Third, along the same lines, the clear definition of the partial or final objectives of the treatment is also one major aspect of the experimental approach to psychotherapy. Defining the objectives makes it possible to evaluate the outcomes. This has been a crucial concern in the behaviour therapy movement. The validation of therapeutic action can be made only if the goals have been clearly stated in advance. This implies more than mere sympathy for the patient's suffering: it is nothing less than a statement about the desired changes. Great progress has been made in psychological treatment since validation studies have been systematically carried out. Evaluation of outcomes has not, however, become a routine control in most psychotherapeutic practices, a neglect that would be declared unethical in medicine. It is, however, inherent to the methods of behaviour therapy, at least as Skinner thought of them.

## NOTES

1. For a historical survey of behaviour therapy, see Kazdin (1978), and Schorr (1984).
2. *Cumulative record*, p.243. Reprinted from *Scientific Monthly* (1954).
3. Early attempts in behaviour therapy already recognised the historical determinants of abnormal behaviour, for instance by developing procedures to extinguish long-established undesirable behaviour such as is observed in phobias. Desensitisation remains one of the most widely used and efficient procedures of behavioural treatments applied to a type of disorder that has proved especially resistant to the psychoanalytic approach.
4. Ayllon and Azrin, 1968.
5. From "Psychology in the understanding of mental disease" in *Cumulative record*, p.252. Reprinted from Kruse (1957).

# 13 Education

## A FORERUNNER

Education is another field in which Skinner's contribution has perhaps occurred ahead of his time. He was best known in the 1960s, and since then has been widely and strongly attacked, for his proposal to use teaching machines. He worked out the idea of building inexpensive electromechanical devices, which were rejected because they were said to dehumanise schools. A few years later, the cheap personal computer was popularised, and computer companies invested time and effort in all sorts of computer assisted learning or teaching, which received wide and uncritical acceptance, with very few ethical objections. The pioneering work of Skinner is rarely acknowledged in that context. The principles applied are those he had painfully attempted to implement in home-made gadgets, and tested on his own students.

Teaching-machines, however, were but one part of a much wider and persistent concern for educational problems. In the last book of collected papers he published in his lifetime,[1] he opened a chapter entitled "The School of the Future" by claiming the right to repeat himself with a quotation from Borges: "What can I do at 71, but plagiarize myself?" and referring to his writings on education in the last 30 years. His chronology was at fault, with an underestimation of about 10 years, since he first expressed his views on education in important sections of his novel *Walden Two* (1948),[2] and he discussed the issue further in *Science and human behavior* (1953). Several papers published or read as lectures from 1954 were included, together with new material, in the book *The technology of teaching* (1968), and he continued to engage in educational debates until the end of his career.

165

Two levels must be distinguished in characterising Skinner's views with respect to education. Many of his reflections are part of his wider views on society and culture, and as such they are related to the function of social agencies, the type of control at work in fulfilling their goals, successes and failures as measured with reference to their overt goals, or with reference to higher order consequences, including survival of the culture or of the species; the issue of countercontrol. All this is at a general, and indeed quite ambitious level. Teaching machines are at a different, more technical level, closely related to the psychology of learning proper. The question Skinner is addressing is: given the choice of educational goals, especially in the school system, are we applying what we know about the learning processes in such a way as to maximise the results? We shall first deal with this more technical aspect.

## TEACHING MACHINES

Skinner once observed an arithmetic class in the school attended by one of his daughters, and was shocked by the fact that almost all the laws of learning derived from the experimental laboratory were constantly being violated. He did not blame the teacher; she was actually among the best trained and most devoted. She simply did her job in a context which she had no power to change, applying methods that were believed adequate, but were obviously inefficient. So the potentialities of 20 valuable young organisms were lost. Skinner thought about the problem, and the result was his designing of teaching machines and programmed instruction.

The search for concrete, practical solutions is worth emphasising. Skinner diverted much of his time from his laboratory work and from his theoretical reflections to engage in tedious efforts to build efficient, although crude, mechanical teaching devices. Most famous psychologists have been, at some time in their career, involved in educational problems; they have written and talked about the improvements to be expected in education from taking psychological knowledge into account, especially as available from their own contributions; they have often been called as experts, on the ground that they know better about the child, about learning processes, about cognitive mechanisms, about the growth of mind, and so on, than ordinary school teachers traditionally doing their best by applying rules of thumb. However, it has rarely been the case that they have really engaged in practical work.

What was wrong with the classroom situation, as appraised from the point of view of a learning psychologist? (There are, clearly enough, other points of view that can also help identify defects and suggest solutions, for example the points of view of developmentalists, of social psychologists, of specialists in problem-solving; but, given that schools are supposed to be places where pupils or students learn, all these different points of view are relevant only in so far as they bring their contribution to better learning.) Defects identified by Skinner must be understood, of course, in the framework of his concept of the learning process, as it has been characterised in the preceding chapters. If we recall the importance of an organism being active in order to learn anything, a major defect of the traditional class is that pupils have very few occasions to actively and overtly produce responses that can be followed by clear evaluation. This is simply a consequence of the ratio between teacher and pupils, and of the place given to monologue teaching (the *ex-cathedra* style in universities). Not only is the overall number of opportunities for a whole class exceedingly small, but it is proportionately still smaller, and close to zero, for some pupils in the class—for those who, for various reasons, escape questions from the teacher.

Not being active in responding gives little chance to be rewarded, or reinforced. Reinforcement in the school context may mean receiving social approval on the part of the teacher, or recognition from peers, getting good marks, reaching final success, having access to the next step in training towards a profession, etc. Rewards remote in time can be mediated by more immediate signs, as in secondary reinforcers used in the laboratory. In intellectual activities, knowledge of results, sometimes called feedback, is in itself a reinforcer, and success itself seems to function as an intrinsic reinforcer, as already shown in monkeys who work on manipulation problems with no other reward than access to the next problem.[3] Unfortunately, reinforcers in school are scarce, and they are delivered in an inconsistent manner. This is a second important defect.

A third defect is the levelling of individual differences. A teacher confronted with two dozen pupils cannot adjust the teaching methods to the particular level of each of them. The teacher can take a medium stand, adapted to the average, the best pupils getting bored and the bad ones getting lost; or adjust to the best or to the poorest, causing more boredom for opposite reasons. Skinner, who had objected to group experiments and studied learning in individuals, where it actually takes place, could not be satisfied with the waste inherent in non-individualised teaching.

Finally, Skinner had the feeling that the school-system does not take advantage of technological advances that could be put to work to alleviate the task of teachers and free them for more attractive aspects of the job. A large part of the teacher's time in school is spent transmitting basic information that could be imparted as efficiently, or even more efficiently, by using other techniques. Schools fail to develop rich interchanges between teachers and students of the kind that can only take place between people, because too much time is wasted in teaching multiplication tables in arithmetic, or the name and place of bones in anatomy. This is important information, but it could be transmitted without mobilising the teacher for hours and hours. The result is that teachers and students are easily frustrated, having few occasions to discuss problems encountered in the various fields taught.[4]

Part of the solution was teaching machines. The idea had already been worked out in the 1920s by Pressey, an American educationist. It did not possess, however, all the features Skinner thought important to put in his own project. Several experimental versions were designed, one of which was used to teach undergraduates at Harvard part of Skinner's own course.

The subject matter was divided into a large number of small items or frames (an early use of a word that would later become part of the cognitivist lexicon), organised in a progressive way—according to the hypothesised logic of the learner rather than to the logic of the material. Each step consisted of one or several propositions, and a question that the student had to answer by writing in the accessible space of a paper strip. Items were disposed radially on a disk and presented one at a time through a window. Students could not move to the next frame unless they had answered the one presented. They could compare their answers to the correct one, grading themselves, the grades being automatically recorded. The machine would keep track of any failed frames, which would be presented again in new learning of the same material until complete mastery was achieved.

The machine remedied several of the defects observed in the classroom. Students worked at their own pace, and were free to repeat—and indeed encouraged to repeat—sections of the material they had not mastered. They were active throughout, their own answers being the condition to move to the next step. They received immediate reinforcement by being given the chance to check their answers. Moreover, they could work on the machine at the most convenient time for them, and as long or as little as they liked. The teacher, liberated from the task of teaching that particular material, was freed for more stimulating types of interchanges.

Skinner had his own conception of what a good programme should be. For example, he insisted on building the required behaviour with as few errors as possible, the ideal being errorless learning. This was subject to debate among the first generation of specialists, some of them arguing, on the contrary, that errors have some virtues and that in any case they can never be completely eliminated in practice. One must admit that a natural life environment does not provide many occasions for errorless learning, and that education should prepare for real life, which implies some tolerance of failure and frustration. It might be advisable to maintain a certain degree of tension in activities like problem-solving, lest the individual turns away because of boredom when things are just too easy and not enough of a challenge. In practical terms, designing errorless programmes for all possible individual students is not feasible; a better strategy consists in having an average–high level programme, with remedial loops at various points for those who get into difficulties. This important issue is one that, in principle, can be decided empirically.

Skinner also emphasised the importance of a very gradual progression in the programme, the student being taken step by step from one difficulty to the next. As a general rule, this is sound pedagogy that very few people would object to. When it comes to practical cases, however, it is not always easy to define how small or how large a step should be. Excessive fragmentation could be as counterproductive as exceedingly long frames. Some have objected to teaching machines because they leave little place for a synthetic view of the material to be assimilated. Skinner would have agreed that the size of steps could vary depending on the goal to be reached, and that, again, solutions should be found through experimental inquiry.

Teaching machines did not have any magic in Skinner's mind. He talked about *technology* of teaching not so much becaue machines were involved, but because he viewed that contribution to education as applied science, to be compared with the field of engineering in its relation to basic physics or chemistry. He saw the machine as a simple exploitation of modern technical progress, parallel to the changes following Gutenberg's invention of movable printing type. He eventually developed, as many others did after him, machineless versions of programmed instruction, in the form of programmed texts. His own course, implemented on his teaching machines, was later published in that form.[5] But when machines are available at reasonable cost, they provide possibilities in programming the material and in self-evaluation that make them highly preferable to books.

## OBJECTIONS AND OBSTACLES

Teaching machines and programmed instruction had their enthusiastic supporters. A number of research projects were carried out and various types of devices were proposed in the years following Skinner's initial publications. The development of computers, that would eventually lead to the present age of inexpensive personal computers for all, soon made early technical endeavours obsolete. But there was an intermediate period in which the new computer technology was too heavy and too expensive to meet the demands of educational applications. The few attempts to commercialise non-computer versions were failures, probably because of the excessive investments required for uncertain returns. And returns were uncertain because the education establishment as a whole was not receptive to the new proposition.

The threat to the teacher's position was of course one main objection. Machines performing humans' jobs are readily accepted when they are seen as alleviating the burden of unpleasant work, and insofar as they do not result in the suppression of jobs. The latter risk is usually the source of corporatist reactions, which, in the case of teaching machines, were not expressed as such, but disguised under more noble arguments, such as repelling the danger of dehumanised education.

Another major objection was that learning at school was more than accumulating step by step overt performance levels related to specific subjects. There is an old persisting belief in educational circles that teaching means developing or building mental faculties of some general nature that will later be put to work in life or professional activities. The cognitive approach, giving a new look to mental constructs, has taken over that traditional conception of school education concerned with training the mind, inculcating judgement, providing the student with mathematical or literary competence, developing creativity, etc. All these goals are distinct from objectively defined performance; they look more ambitious and dignified, but they are essentially more vague. In spite of the insistence from a number of educationists on objectively defined goals of teaching, so that it can be clearly decided whether they have been reached or not, the school system keeps functioning with the assumption that intellectual education is guaranteed when general mental capacities have supposedly been developed in the students.

The school system is paradoxical in the sense that it is, in some respects, exceedingly inert and unreceptive to novelty and reforms, and yet sometimes quite ready to adopt the most unfounded practices that suddenly become fashionable. Infatuation for new methods or ideas is generally the result of economic or political influence, rather than the consequence of objective research. Teaching machines were not popular, not only because of the objections already alluded to, but because their success would have required extensive research and an experimental approach that neither the school system nor the economic agencies were willing to adopt at that time. Programming material to be learned is not simply dividing and organising it in a way that seems appropriate to the programmer; it means adjusting it to the student and to individual learning processes and pace. This can only be done by testing the programme on the students, and by correcting it as needed. This is not an easy task, nor can it be carried out rapidly, and has been an obstacle to the extensive use of early teaching machines. One can imagine the work and time needed to change a dozen items in the radial presentation of the Holland-Skinner machine.

## COMPUTERS: "IDEAL TEACHING MACHINES"

These technical problems have since been solved by the computer, the "ideal teaching machine" as Skinner himself called it in 1989. It has invaded modern life, and school is no exception. However, the attention to psychological aspects of their use in teaching does not always match their technical potential. Skinner rightly noted, in the same recent paper, that:

> . . . [the computer] still tends to be used as a substitute for a lecturer and to teach as teachers of large classes do. It can bring 'real life' into the classroom, at least in schematic form. That is one way it is used in industry. Employees cannot be taught to act appropriately during a meltdown in a nuclear power plant by creating real meltdowns, but meltdowns can be simulated on computers. Computers can teach best, however, by leading the students through carefully prepared instructional programs. They cam prime and prompt behavior and reinforce it immediately. In addition, computers can move the student on to the next appropriate step. Those are the essentials of good teaching. They are what a tutor with one or two students could do and what teachers with large classes simply cannot do.[6]

Skinner points to the difference between the effective use of computer-assisted training in industry and its often inefficient use in schools. The contrast is evident, and is due to the difference in consequences of good and bad management between the two environments. Economic factors lead industry to expect returns from investments in training, and therefore serious preliminary research as well as continuous validation tests are willingly carried out. Agencies responsible for school teaching do not traditionally devote much effort or money to method validation studies, although they often pay lip service to objective evaluation of teaching practices.

Most schools now have computers. Not all teachers know what to do with them, besides helping their maths colleagues. As potential teaching tools, they are obviously underemployed. Especially in low grades, they still are largely used with ordinary textbook type material, not real teaching programmes. The financial cost of the equipment has been accepted (computer companies had more influence on education policy makers than did Skinner!), but the psychological and didactic research needed to justify the investment has been overlooked. Looking back, at the end of his life, at what happened to his seminal idea of delegating part of teaching to machines, Skinner could only deplore that it had not yet been generalised, while the available machine, the computer, offers unforeseen possibilities.

The last sentence of the quoted passage reflects, once more, Skinner's concern with the individual: teaching machines, contrary to one of the strongest early objections, are not a way to level down education; they are a way to adjust teaching to the individual, who will benefit from the best possible education; an ambition perfectly compatible with the ideal of leaving no-one out of the school system. The respect of individual differences, besides being met by teaching machines, is part of Skinner's general philosophy of education. We shall now turn to some major tenets of the latter.

## THE SCHOOL SYSTEM QUESTIONED

Skinner was very critical of the school system in Western society. As a scientist, he could not accept that certain defects would be perpetuated, when we know how to remedy them by applying scientific knowledge. As a learning psychologist, he could not understand why even basic principles of learning are neglected, when principles of elementary hygiene are applied routinely in medical care. As a pragmatically oriented mind, he could not be content with the general inefficiency of the system as evidenced by the rate of failures, and by the overall low level of scientific or other skills in the population after complete school education. As an opponent of aversive controls and punishment, he was shocked by the extent to which schools still resort to punitive controls. As a thinker concerned with the future of the world, he was anxious at the levelling down of individual differences and the resulting loss of original talents and potentialities. As an individualist, he was unhappy with the constraints of the educational establishment, which leave little room for personal achievement.

The criticisms Skinner addressed to the school system had some common points with those expressed by other thinkers at about the same time. Some of them concluded that, if schools are not good, one should get rid of them.[7] Their position was based in the belief that a human being, if left unrestrained, would naturally develop toward self-realisation, showing curiosity for knowledge, love for beauty, and altruism. If school not only failed to impart these traits, but impeded their normal growth, we should dispense with it. The anti-school movement, as illustrated by Illich, went as far as proclaiming the dictatorial nature of the school system, viewed as one form of oppression. The underlying philosophy gives credit to humans for what they are and can become. Skinner was very critical of the movement for a school-free society, especially when it was supported from inside schools by some teachers in the late 1960s and early 1970s: "The free school is no school at all. Its philosophy signalizes the abdication of the teacher".[8]

Skinner, confident as he was in the action of the environment, and disbelieving the autonomous sources of self-fulfilment, took a diametrically opposite stand: a human culture, being characterised by the transmission of acquired behaviours, includes, by definition, educational agencies of one sort or another; it does not make sense to deny it, but at some point it is useful to evaluate how these agencies really fulfil the promises they claim. Schools, or instruction agencies, are not to be suppressed; they must be changed, according to better defined goals and by resorting to methods better fitted to reach them.

This does not mean bringing in more authoritarian procedures. On the contrary, punitive devices, physical or moral, should in fact be eliminated. Skinner always objected to punitive control, and advocated the exclusive use of positive incentives. He argued that punishments may reduce or abolish undesirable behaviour while they are in strength, only to have it reappear when they are discontinued. Furthermore, education is not concerned essentially with suppressing existing behaviour, but with shaping and building new behaviours: to that end, positive reinforcements are far more powerful, and they do not, as punishments do, generate emotional responses that usually are inimical to rich and refined acquisitions in whatever field of knowledge or skills. School and learning should be made attractive.

Given what we know of Skinner's psychological theory, we can expect that he could not conceive of good learning at school unless the student is active. This was one of the characteristics of teaching machines, but the concept should pervade all aspects of education.

It is true that before and besides Skinner, many educationists have defended the idea that schools should be both attractive and active. In many cases, however, they have emphasised somewhat superficial aspects in attempting to implement these characteristics. Pleasant buildings (although plausibly one important factor, readily accepted and taken into account for bank buildings or shops, but not given such importance where school buildings are concerned) can attract students to school, as exciting group activities can keep children quite active throughout school days. Skinner does not object, but he insists that these should not be taken as sufficient signs of success. One must make sure that one has not displaced attractiveness onto irrelevant, purely contextual aspects, and neglected the primary goal of schools—that is to endow the pupils with specific knowledge and know-how, that can be put to work in real life. The main difference, if any, between Skinner and most advocates of active schools is that he maintained the emphasis on an unequivocal definition of objectives, and the search for efficient techniques to reach them. He had no objection to the idea that the maths class would be a funny social happening, provided that students eventually solve mathematical problems adequately. This is not necessarily achieved because the class has been a memorable party. Skinner has always been aware of the danger of mistaking accessory, though positive, aspects of school life for real fulfilment of objectives.

That is why, for Skinner, one essential ingredient of successful teaching is leading students to find their own pleasure and satisfaction in learning activity proper. Progressing in knowledge acquisition should soon become an *intrinsic reinforcement*, as he called it. This can be done only through mastery of what is learned, through successful problem-solving, which in turn implies progressive and carefully paced instruction.

Skinner has often been blamed for his supposed intention to get rid of the teacher, but he made it clear on many occasions that this was by no means part of his approach. On the contrary, he was especially lucid in diagnosing teachers' problems in modern schools. They are expected to produce perfect results, both in terms of number and quality, but they are not given the minimal conditions to meet that ambition. They are underpaid, they have a socially undervalued job, and even supposing these factors are not important to them, they do not have the technical conditions for success: they face too many students in a class, they do not receive adequate resources to ensure good teaching, they receive little support to try new methods, and still more discouraging, they are not told exactly what type of result will be called a good one. Paying teachers much higher salaries, or appointing many more of them, is no solution: Skinner, quite realistically, was aware that the educational budget of modern nations cannot expand indefinitely. If there is any chance for teachers to receive better salaries, it is by demonstrating better productivity: like it or not, education has its economic aspects that cannot be avoided or ignored. In the meantime, we must do better with approximately the same resources, essentially by using them differently.

To have students learn more within the same total time spent in school, Skinner obstinately emphasised simple rules, contrasting these with the sophisticated proposals from cognitive psychology, which can be reduced to rather trivial statements. In a paper entitled "The shame of American education", first published in 1984, he strongly criticised the emptiness of cognitivist educational advice, and then formulated once more his own simple principles, captured in the following four points:

1. *Be clear about what is to be taught.*[9] This is emphasising once more a pedagogy based on the definition of objectives, a trend that had been developed by several prominent educationists in the 1960s, but eventually gave way to a revival of loosely defined goals, along the lines of the mentalistic tradition.

2. *Teach first things first . . .* This sounds quite trivial, but some approaches to teaching, especially sciences and mathematics, have been tempted, as Skinner comments, to moving quickly to what is considered as the most general, achieved state of the field. A case in point is the "new math": new math was not introduced after empirical demonstration that children learned mathematics better that way, but because of arguments from some mathematicians that having learned the most general aspects of mathematics, pupils would have no problem in entering any specialised branch. This had, however, never been established. What is at stake here, and it is admittedly a very difficult issue, is how to decide which are those "first things" to be taught first. Again, the logic of the subject matter, as conceived by an expert in the field, can be completely alien to the logic of the learning individual.

3. *Program the subject matter.* This has been covered in detail earlier, in relation with teaching machines.

4. *Stop making all students advance at essentially the same rate.*

The latter point brings us back to the respect of individual differences. It deserves the final comments of this chapter.

## INTER-INDIVIDUAL DIFFERENCES, DIVERSITY AND CREATIVE ACTIVITIES

Because of the erroneous connotations of the word conditioning, and because of the persistent misrepresentations of Skinner's thought; because of the confusion between the term teaching machines and mechanistic educational principles, it is usually not accepted that Skinner was a defender of the individual. So he was, however, and with conviction, as testified abundantly in his writings over many years. His respect for individual differences had various facets. Focus on the individual had been one of his most distinctive attitudes in the laboratory, separating him from the tradition of American experimental psychology of his time, which endured after him in most investigations within the cognitive psychology school, carried out as a rule on group of subjects rather than on individuals. Many students who are subjected to the same "phalanx" system throughout their school years experience the negative feelings of not being permitted the self-achievement that their talents would allow, or of being left behind because they cannot keep up with the "average" student. As already said, negative control has been rejected from Skinner's ethics, on the basis of scientific arguments. Individual happiness converges here with the future of the species: education, as concerned with the future of society, should aim at preserving diversity, which is recognised as an essential factor in survival, in a Darwinian sense.

The importance Skinner gave to individual differences is well exemplified in the detailed discussions in *Technology of teaching* quoted earlier, and, among many others, in the following passage:

> Failure to provide for differences among students is perhaps the greatest single source of inefficiency in education. In spite of heroic experiments in multi-track systems and ungraded schools, it is still standard practice for large groups of students to move forward at the same speed, cover much the same material, and reach the same standard for promotion from one grade to the next. The speed is appropriate to the average or mediocre student. Those who could move faster lose interest and waste time: those who should move more slowly fall behind and lose interest for a different reason. . . . The unhappy consequences of this phalanx system have been aggravated by the use of mass media. Television reaches large numbers of students, but the apparent gain is more than offset by the fact that they must all move at the same speed. It is not only differences among students which is at issue. One student must move at the same rate in several fields, although he may be able to move rapidly in one but should move slowly in another. Little or no room is left for idiosyncratic talents or interests, in spite of the fact that many distinguished men have shown an insularity not far from that of the *idiot savant*.
>
> Problems of this sort are no doubt prodigious, but they may nevertheless be soluble . . .
>
> By supplementing defective environmental histories and by making sure that instructional contingencies are complete and effective, a technology of teaching will solve many of the problems raised by differences among students. It will not, however, reduce all students to one pattern. On the contrary, it will discover and emphasize genuine genetic difference. If it is based on a wise policy, it will also design environmental contingencies in such a way as to generate the most promising diversity.[10]

The theme of diversity in education, in its relation with the dynamics of a culture, is extensively elaborated in other places of the same book:

> a policy designed to maximize the strength of a culture must encourage novelty and diversity. It is true that many cultures, like many species, have survived without appreciable changes for long periods of time, but both cultures and species increase their strength with respect to a far wider range of contingencies when subject to variation and selection. . . . those who encourage the student to inquire, to discover for himself, and in other ways to be original are enlarging the supply of mutations which contribute to the evolution of a culture. Although some mutations are useless or even harmful, diversity is essential. The same principle applies to educational policy. A wide range of goals, derived from a wide range of conditions which determine what it is to be taught, is a particularly likely source of diversity among students.

Diversity is not, however, a strong point in current policy. Regimentation appears to be a more likely consequence of the curricula, syllabuses, requirements, and standards imposed upon educational systems by governments, parents, employers, and other supporting agencies. We do not worry about regimentation, as we have noted, so long as we know that such specifications will not be met, but ineffective teaching is only a temporary solution. So are other equally unplanned sources of diversity. Different schools teach different things in different ways, teachers are different, and students have different genetic and environmental histories. The resulting diversity no doubt has survival value, but in the long run, an effective diversity must be planned. There is no virtue in accident as such, nor can we trust it. The advantages of a planned diversity have been abundantly demonstrated in science. Men first learned about the world through accidental contacts under accidental conditions and, hence, only within the range of accident. Scientific methods are largely concerned with increasing the diversity of the conditions under which things are known.[11]

Encouraging diversity is the key to educating students to be creative. By definition, we cannot teach creative behaviour itself, because we do not know it before we see it occurring and until we see its product. The solution is not to detect supposedly "creative personalities", using tests of creativity; there is little evidence that creativity is a characteristic of individuals that can be validly inferred from the responses to such instruments. If there are any individual talents that prepare for creativity in arts, literature or science, the more people are taught to perform these activities, the more chance there is that those talents will emerge. Skinner cites Diderot, one of his favourite authors:

Other things being equal, a culture will be more likely to uncover an original artist if it induces many people to paint pictures, or to turn up a great composer if it induces many people to compose. Great chess players tend to come from cultures which encourage chess playing as great mathematicians come from those which encourage mathematics. The contingencies of positive and negative reinforcement which encourage activity in a given field no doubt yield much mediocre behavior, but mediocrity, as Diderot, said, is valuable just because it gives genius a chance to discover itself.[12]

In contrast with the pedagogy of creativity that prevailed in the 1960s and 70s, according to which creativity is not something that can be taught but that can only be liberated,[13] Skinner emphasised the necessity of technical mastery in a given field before creative behaviour can emerge. He objected to a naïve belief that free play with paints, with clay or other material, with notes, etc. would eventually allow great painters, sculptors or musicians to emerge. He saw artistic and musical creation as much like the transmission of craftsmanship, a domain in which laws of learning have for centuries been very skilfully and efficiently applied by intuition. He stated his view once more in one of his latest writings on education:

The origin of millions of species was to be found not in an act of creation, but in the selection of otherwise unrelated variations. Truly creative individuals, if any exist at all, behave in ways that are selected by reinforcement, but variations must occur to be selected. Some variations may be accidental, but students can learn to increase the number and, in that sense, to be more creative. Like all the creative people of the past, however, they must first be taught something to be creative *with*.[14]

This is far from the concept of the robot-like student that Skinner was supposed to have promoted.

## NOTES

1. *Recent issues in the analysis of behavior*, 1989.
2. See Chapter 14, this volume, and especially pp. 187–189.
3. This is only one classical example, from Harlow (1959), of maintaining activity by giving the organism the chance to continue it, or to be stimulated, or to explore.
4. Some teachers, following philosophies of education that give little weight to the transmission of basic skills, have chosen to concentrate on those more motivating aspects of their task, such as discussions with the students, leaving to chance the acquisition of basic skills.
5. Holland and Skinner, 1961
6. *Recent issues*, p.94.
7. This was the radical position defended by Ivan Illich (1970) (*Deschooling society*, New York: Harper & Row)
8. Quoted from a paper entitled "The free and happy student" (1973, reprinted 1978), which contains an ironical discussion of the drop-out ideology.
9. Statements in italics in points 1 to 4 are reproduced from Skinner (1987b), pp.122–124.
10. *The technology of teaching*, pp.242–243
11. Ibidem, pp.235–236.
12. Ibidem, pp.182–183; the reference to Diderot is from *Le Neveu de Rameau*.
13. This idea has been implicitly the basis of a number of practices in art and musical education as well as being explicitly proposed by most famous specialists of education; a case in point is the French influential educational thinker Bertrand Schwartz (1973).
14. In "Programmed instructions revisited", reprinted in *Recent issues*, pp.97–103. For other developments on Skinner's view on education, and more specifically on the issue of diversity, see Richelle, 1979, 1986b.

# 14 Society and Utopia

## A VENTURE IN SOCIAL PHILOSOPHY

We shall turn now to what has been called Skinner's *ideology*. It is, with some justification, the aspect of Skinner's work in which the layreader is most interested, but the essence of Skinner's ideology can be difficult to grasp, let alone appraise or criticise, without a clear prior knowledge of the methodological and theoretical concepts from which it is derived, or is claimed to be derived. For this reason I have devoted much of previous chapters to discussion of consciousness, verbal behaviour, creativity, education, psychotherapy, etc—this, I hope, will be sufficient to discard the classical argument against Skinner's social philosophy, i.e. that man is neither a rat nor a pigeon. However, a number of questions remain to be asked concerning the sociopolitical writings of Skinner.

Do they derive from scientific data and concepts as logically as their author claims they do? Are they not, on the contrary, vague and hazardous extrapolations, or, less conspicuously, a product of the infiltration of an ideology with no relation whatsoever to scientific evidence? Has science been appealed to as a mask for ideology?

At another, somewhat less fundamental level, one might ask: is Skinner not simply ignoring a number of essential dimensions of social reality, so that any attempt to change society according to his views would prove to be completely futile and doomed to failure? This is another way to ask whether the passage from an experimental analysis of human behaviour to political action is possible at all.

If we want to answer these questions, we must first have a close look at those texts that reflect Skinner's views on these matters. Whichever answers we shall choose to give thereafter, we shall have to admit that a scientist's "ideological writings" deserve attention. When a man of science expresses in that way his concerns for the world around him, one should not remain indifferent. Scientists are frequently blamed for isolating themselves in an ivory tower; when one of them makes the effort to go out, it might be worth paying attention. In 1930, Freud wrote a small book entitled *Civilization and its discontents*. Undoubtedly, Freud had the conviction that his ideas, as expressed in that book, were closely related to his clinical experience and to his psychoanalytical theory. Whether this conviction was founded or not, whether the relation was as obvious to his readers as it was to him, might not be crucial questions, compared with the message of the book itself. It deserves careful reading and reflection. The same holds for Skinner's *Beyond freedom and dignity* (1971a): even if the arguments and the proposals exposed in the book have little basis in scientific analysis, there they are, and they are challenging enough not to leave anyone indifferent.

They have obviously shaken a number of important personalities, as shown by the selected quotations reproduced at the beginning of Chapter 1, to which many others could have been added. The reactions were usually strongly negative. They were indiscriminate condemnation, inviting future readers to join in the same vigorous judgement, and thereby protect themselves from being infected by so dangerous a plague. Critics and commentators concurred in dissuading people from reading *Beyond freedom and dignity*, as Chomsky had succeeded in doing earlier with *Verbal behavior*. More than that, suspicion was eventually transferred onto the use of operant methods in strictly fundamental laboratory research. For example, a reviewer in the reputable monthly magazine *Le Monde de l'Education* published in Paris devoted a long and essentially laudatory paper to a study on cognitive development in which issues raised by Piaget's theory were approached using methods derived from operant laboratory procedures. At the end of her review, she felt it necessary to insist: "Any psychologist or educationist interested in cognitive development should read this study . . ., *even if, for ethical and political reasons, he cannot dispense with a certain suspicion towards Skinnerian principles*".[1] She undoubtedly had in mind those principles on which the social views of Skinner are based, not the principles underlying the scientific experimental procedures applied by the authors—which could hardly provoke any suspicion of an ethical or political nature. Let us now see what these disturbing principles are.

Two major works, as already mentioned, are available to help us forge our judgement. The first, *Beyond freedom and dignity*, is an essay. It was published in 1971, translated shortly thereafter into a number of languages and widely publicised. It is a critical discussion of a number of notions that play a central role in our social system. Skinner develops a view of human beings, and of causal agents determining human conduct, that shakes many accepted principles founding modern society. He also denounces some illusions on which social and political life is currently based. No programme is offered for practical action: the book is by no means a political platform. It is neither a revolutionist manifesto nor a reformist proclamation. The well-disposed reader who is not familiar with Skinner's work is likely to ask the question: "What can we do with that in the real world? What sort of society would Skinner actually build if he were given the chance to shape mankind as he shaped rats and pigeons in the laboratory?" Belittlers claim they have the response, and it is a frightening one: Skinner's world would resemble a vast concentration camp or some as yet unforeseen form of totalitarianism. To so horrible a prospect, they oppose the (to them) undeniable happiness of our society, or, as an alternative, their own Utopian dream, which they usually do not care to qualify in practical terms. Thus, Chomsky envisions that:

> In a decent society, socially necessary and unpleasant work would be divided on some egalitarian basis, and beyond that people would have, as an inalienable right, the widest possible opportunity to do work that interests them. They might be 'reinforced' by self-respect, if they do their work to the best of their ability, or if their work benefits those to whom they are related by bonds of friendship and sympathy and solidarity. Such notions are commonly an object of ridicule—as it was common, in an earlier period, to scoff at the absurd idea that a peasant has the same inalienable rights as a nobleman. There always have been, and no doubt always will be people who cannot conceive of the possibility that things could be different from what they are.[2]

But Skinner also, long before Chomsky, had formulated his dream. And he went as far as to show us how that dream could be put to work, not by writing a political programme, but by composing a utopian novel. The genre is admittedly less practical, although it could be of more significance.

## WALDEN TWO

The title of this utopian novel refers to the name of a pond—Walden—near Concord, Massachusetts, where the nineteenth century American writer Henry David Thoreau retired for one year to experience solitary life, as something between Robinson Crusoe and a modern ecologist. Without elaborating on the literary affiliation between Thoreau and Skinner, it is worth noting that Thoreau is also the author of a short piece of prose entitled "On civil disobedience", in which he argues against the right of the state to raise excessive taxes (needless to say, what was excessive to him would appear quite tolerable to us).

*Walden Two* was written almost a quarter of a century before *Beyond freedom and dignity*. When it was first published in 1948, it encountered mild success. It took some years until it became a bestseller, but it has since sold more than one million copies in English and has been translated into several languages. French, the mother-tongue of the present author, is unfortunately not among them; for some reasons, publishers were reluctant, the officially advanced argument being that it is not a literary masterpiece. This is hardly a serious reason, as literary excellence is certainly not the criterion for deciding which books should be translated, but I am ready to admit that *Walden Two* is not the best of Skinner's work with regard to style. I would without hesitation give preference to some chapters of his strictly scientific writings. But this is not the point. What is of interest here is Skinner's utopian design of the ideal society; the sort of society he would have proposed, or imposed, if he had been endowed with full authority. Would it have been closer to the concentration camp, or to the decent society called for by Chomsky?

The plot that provides the background for describing the social rules at Walden Two does not have much importance and need only be sketched here: it simply sets the stage for a "guided tour". The visitors: two young men, with their girl friends; Burris, a psychology professor who has left his academic duties to accompany them; and a colleague of Burris' called Castle, an historian and a sceptic. The guide: Frazier, founder of the community. The site: a big village, called Walden Two, where 2000 people of all ages live together according to principles developed by Frazier. The time: the visit takes place at the end of the Second World War. The two young men have just been discharged from the army; they are freshly back from Europe in an American society with the strong hope of those who have been fighting—that they will find in peace the justification for the heavy wartime sacrifices. Shortly after their return, faith in the future has given place to bitter disappointment: post-war American society is a mess. This is the state of affairs that induces them to get in touch again with their former teacher, Burris, and to ask his help in locating Frazier's community. Theirs is, of course, Skinner's discontent: he was already, at that time, dissatisfied with the illusions of freedom and of social justice that were offered to the American people as the fruits of victory. If Skinner in 1945 wrote a utopia rather than a programme for political action, it was because, in his view, classical approaches in politics doom to failure any attempt really to change things in a positive sense:

> You can't make progress toward the Good Life by political action! Not under any current form of government! . . . What you need is a sort of Nonpolitical Action Committee: keep out of politics and away from government except for practical and temporary purposes. It's not the place for men of good will and vision.
>
> As we use the term these days, government means power—mainly the power to compel obedience. The techniques of government are what you would expect—they use force or the threat of force. But that's incompatible with permanent happiness—we know enough about human nature to be sure of that. You can't force a man to be happy.
> [This was Frazier speaking.]
> But there have certainly been many happy men under governments of one sort or another. [This is Burris' objection.]
> Not *because* of government—in *spite* of it. Some philosophies of life have made

men happy, yes, because they have set forth principles which I want to be taken seriously as principles of government. But these philosophies have come from rebels. Governments which use force are based upon bad principles of human engineering. Nor are they able to improve upon these principles, or discover their inadequacies, because they aren't able to accumulate any body of knowledge approaching a science. All that can ever be done by way of "improvement" is to wrest power from one group and transfer it to another. It's never possible to plan or carry out experiments to investigate the better use of power or how to dispense with it altogether. That would be fatal. Governments must always be right—they can't experiment because they can't admit doubt or question.[3]

This has a flavour of anarchy, does it not?—as Castle himself observed after this conversation had been going on for some time.

But let us leave ideology for a while, and follow our visitors in their promenade through Walden Two.

## WORK: 24 HOURS A WEEK AND A FLEXIBLE SCHEDULE

Walden Two is an agricultural community. It lives in a half-closed economy. It has to find among its own members the working force to carry out the variety of tasks that have to be done in any social group. All members of the community who are physically able are required to work a few hours a day for the community. Three or four hours will eventually do, as will become clear. They receive in exchange all the goods and benefits provided by the social organisation in which they live: housing, food, clothing, education, medical care, free access to all sorts of creative leisure activities; in short, they enjoy a style of life that compares with the usual standard of American citizens, though quite different in many respects and far more rewarding. How can this be, when the amount of time allocated to "work" in the usual sense of the word is reduced by some forty percent?

In fact, these four daily hours per capita turn out to be much more productive at the scale of the whole population than the eight hours or so required in our society. First, as is well known, productivity is highest early in the working day; tasks are performed all the more quickly when there is no obligation to keep on working beyond a certain limit in time for the sake of conforming to some prescribed schedule. Secondly people who work for themselves rather than for somebody else or for a company work better and faster. This is what happens at Walden Two: private property has no place in the community, and there is no place either for exploitation of others' work. Third, if each individual works on average four hours a day, the total amount of time allocated to work in the whole population well exceeds half of the total time devoted to work in an equivalent population working eight hours a day in our society. The reason for this is simple enough: everyone works at Walden Two. There is no privileged class; there is no early retirement; there are no alcoholics, no delinquents, very few ill people;

last but not least, there are no unemployed, who are the by-products of defective planning. "No one is paid to sit idle for the sake of maintaining labor standards. Our children work at an early age—moderately, but happily." *(Walden Two* p.60.)

Another gain in working time is obtained by rationalising tasks, by resorting to appropriate skills and competences, and by permanently improving everyone's capacities and know-how. Walden Two also dispenses with a number of jobs, which simply do not find any place because there is no need for them: there are no banks, no advertising companies, no insurance companies—insurance is not needed because the community protects its members against all serious risks, such as illness, infirmity, old age, and so on. It also dispenses with the excess of facilities of all sorts, restaurants, shops, bars, theatres, transportation, currently found in modern cities.

Finally—and this is not the least source of pride at Walden Two—women have a completely different condition as compared with society at large (remember, we are in the mid 1940s). Traditional domestic work has been drastically changed, rationalised and automatised, so that more than half of the women's time is free for other, more rewarding activities. This is only one aspect of a woman's life at Walden Two. We shall come to other aspects later.

Walden Two is characterised by moderate working obligations and by an enviable standard of living. For these two characteristics to fit together, a third one is needed, namely drastic elimination of wastage. Awareness of and fighting against, the wasteful habits of our consumer society—which have since become the tenets of ecological movements—were central to Skinner's message as early as 1945. Walden Two residents:

> . . . practice the Thoreauvian principle of avoiding unnecessary possessions. Thoreau pointed out that the average Concord laborer worked ten or fifteen years of his life just to have a roof over his head. We could say ten weeks and be on the safe side. [Their] food is plentiful and healthful, but not expensive. There's little or no spoilage or waste in distribution or storage, and none due to miscalculated needs. The same is true of other staples. [They] don't feel the pressure of promotional devices which stimulate unnecessary consumption.[4]

Good radio programmes are picked up and broadcast free of charge for all members, though after having been cleared of ads!

The reduction of working time is not the only innovation in Walden Two labour organisation. In addition to that qualitative difference, work is also qualitatively lighter, because of two other characteristics: each member is offered a wide variety of tasks and an ingenious form of flexible schedule is practised.

Members are not scheduled to work a definite number of hours, but to accomplish a definite number of credits. Each task that has to be performed is given a certain credit value, which is a function among other things of how attractive it is and consequently how frequently it is chosen. A task that is usually considered unpleasant, such as cleaning the floor or dishwashing, has higher credit value than a pleasant and therefore much sought-after task, such as seeing to the upkeep of the flower gardens. Those who want to fulfil their obligations quickly and enjoy more leisure time can choose to work no more than a couple of hours at a task with high credit value. This value is, of course, not fixed once and forever, but is adjusted according to the choices made on an offer/demand basis. Tasks are, with few exceptions, offered to all and are interchangeable, which does not mean that people will not spontaneously develop expertise in a field of their choice and tend to perform tasks appropriate to their competence.

Whenever it is feasible, work can be done at any time throughout the day. The concept "From 9 a.m. to 5 p.m." is unknown at Walden Two. This provides another way to avoid monotony. Everyone is free to combine to their taste the most flexible schedules. Work, as well as meals and leisure activities, takes place all through the day. Disrupting the schedules in that way has two important consequences. Common facilities are fully exploited: there is no need to build very large dining halls, or a great number of bathrooms or tennis courts, so that all users can be accommodated simultaneously at peak hours. Small dining rooms, a limited number of bathrooms, tennis courts, etc. will do. This in turn has another advantage: contrary to what occurs when collective restaurants are expected to serve 2,000 meals between 12 and 2, or when cinemas are open only from 7 to 11 p.m., people do not gather in crowds at Walden Two. Crowds are costly, they are occasionally dangerous, and, more important, they are not favourable to the most valuable forms of social relations (Skinner was, let us recall, an individualist).

There is still another rule in the organisation of work that is worth noting. Each member must accomplish part of their credits in the form of physical work, whatever their own inclinations and specialised competence. This rule guarantees a balance, both at the individual level and at the level of the community, between the two aspects of productivity. It also avoids the risk of having a caste of "brain workers" deciding how to organise the jobs of "handworkers" without being familiar with these jobs from inside.

All these regulations result in reducing, alleviating and simplifying the labour required for the community to survive; they are not, of course, intended to suppress work. The general philosophy underlying the system is clearly summarised in the following declaration by Frazier:

There's nothing wrong with hard work and we aren't concerned to avoid it. We simply avoid uncreative and uninteresting work. If we could satisfy our needs without working that way at all, we'd do so, but it's never been possible except through some form of slavery, and I don't see how it can be done if we're all to work and share alike. What we ask is that a man's work shall not tax his strength or threaten his happiness. Our energies can then be turned toward art, science, play, the exercise of skills, the satisfaction of curiosities, the conquest of nature, the conquest of man—the conquest of man himself, but never of other men. We have created leisure without slavery . . .[5]

Can we be closer to the decent society called for by Chomsky? It will become even more convincing if we take a look at the ways people spent their leisure time at Walden Two.

## ART AND SCIENCE AT WALDEN TWO

Walden Two provides its members with the best facilities for practising and enjoying the arts. Buildings are embellished with paintings and drawings of local artists, which compare favourably with works exhibited in reputed art galleries. Records and instruments are available for amateur musicians and from string quartets to symphony orchestra or choirs, there is a variety of musical ensembles of high quality. Such a proliferation of creative activities is the byproduct of conditions favourable to their emergence: extended leisure time, emulation without rivalry, availability of technical facilities, and above all a social context in which artists and performing musicians meet their public. These conditions are in fact far more effective than occasional honours or awards offered to a few creative individuals in our competitive society.

> Prizes only scratch the surface. You can't encourage art with money alone. What you need is a culture. You need a real opportunity for young artists. The career must be economically sound and socially acceptable, and prizes won't do that. And you need appreciation—there must be audiences, not to pay the bills, but to enjoy. All in all, we really know a lot about what is needed. We must get to the artist before he has proved his worth. A great productive culture must stimulate large numbers of the young and untried. Philanthropy can't do that. It may produce a few great works of art, but it's only a start.[6]

Besides arts and music, and, of course, sports and games, members of Walden Two are offered another form of leisure activity: scientific research. If various kinds of technological research—essentially research applied to improving agricultural practices, education, health, industrial transformation of some raw materials—are listed among necessary activities, and as such are credit-earning jobs, basic research is considered a leisure time activity. This is by no means a way to neglect it. As with the arts, optimal conditions prevail: people have plenty of time, and their minds are remarkably free; as a result, scientific creativity is much higher than in most places where basic research is organised on a professional basis. One might wonder whether institutions really do exist in our society, where pure research is carried out without scientists having to pay for their right to search freely by also accepting utilitarian tasks. By the time *Walden Two* was written, that sort of question might have seemed overcritical towards the organisation of science in the United States. It was a premonition of the trend that since then has invaded policies of science in all contemporary Western countries.

There is at first sight something suprising in the fact that individual creativity is encouraged, not by mere exhortation but by arranging a highly favourable environment, in a community designed by a behaviourist on the basis of the laws of conditioning. If the usual connotations of that word are correct, one would have expected instead a collection of identical beings all behaving in exactly the same fully predictable manner, whose life would unroll according to a strictly preprogrammed course, as pictured in some futuristic fiction. But on the contrary, the emphasis is on diversity, tolerance to idiosyncrasies, receptivity to change. We must not forget that Walden Two is not the implementation of some theory of government imposed on more or less benevolent subjects, but an experiment in cultural design in which the individual's satisfaction is the foundation of social equilibrium, and where diversity is viewed as the best guarantee of vitality.

This unexpected diversity strikes the visitor to Walden Two in the clothing women wear. Rather than conforming to the fashion of seasons, which changes four times a year but makes the women all alike, women dress in the way that they feel fits them best. There is no compulsion perpetually to modify one's clothes just for the sake of being in fashion. The financial advantage is, needless to say, important. But more important, this does not prevent women from taking care of their charm and of their beauty: as they do not feel constrained to adopt a fashion that more often than not does not suit them, they avoid the ridicule that is frequently the result of following fashion at all costs; they can put the emphasis on the most personal features of their personality. Thus, the small community of Walden Two offers the most pleasant spectacle of a cosmopolitan society, in which variety in clothing is both tolerated and admired:

> Here we are not so much at the mercy of commercial designers, and many of our women manage to appear quite beautiful simply because they are not required to dress within strict limits . . . Going out of style isn't a natural process, but a manipulated change which destroys the beauty of last year's dress in order to make it worthless. We opposed this by broadening our tastes. But the required change has not yet taken place in you. In a day or so you will know what I mean. Little touches which now seem out of style and which, in spite of what you say, must mar your appreciation, will then appear natural and pleasing. You will discover that a line or feature is never in itself dated, just as you eventually come to regard the dress of another country as beautiful, even though you first judge it comical or ugly.[7]

## EDUCATION VERSUS SELECTION

Children at Walden Two exhibit happiness, activity, and curiosity. There is no need to impose on them the content of a school curriculum. It suffices to teach them techniques for learning and thinking, and besides that to provide them with opportunities for learning and with occasional counselling, as they might request. Fewer teachers are needed, but education is better.

There is no definite curriculum, with pre-established steps; there are no age classes, no compartmentalised types of school. Every child has the possibility to develop at its own pace, to cultivate its aptitudes and its interests. It will find in the community the help it needs. Education is part of the life of everyone. Members of Walden Two never stop learning, as they never refuse to teach their fellows. Here is lifelong, permanent education, long before it became the popular idea—practice is still another story—it is today.

A large part of what a child or an adolescent eventually learns is acquired through real life activities. Workshops, laboratories, study rooms, libraries with reading halls, rather than classrooms, are provided. The doors and windows of these buildings are wide open, so that children come and go freely, without tension, in a self-disciplined style. They live in groups, each of them being stimulated by older children. They take care of their own quarters. This autonomy is introduced progressively: after the complete dependency of the nursery, educational control is faded away gradually up to the age of 13 or so, when the adolescent is practically integrated in adult life, with adult responsibilities.

Punishment is banished from education and character training. A child never experiences unpleasant situations or adversity as a result of the deliberate intervention of a teacher or of some other adult authority. As adversity is a fact of life anyway, children must be prepared for it, but by resorting to methods that progressively enable them to cope with it.

> In most cultures the child meets up with annoyances and reverses of uncontrolled magnitude . . . We all know what happens. A few hardy children emerge, particularly those who have got their unhappiness in doses that could be swallowed. They become brave men. Others become sadists or masochists of varying degrees of pathology. Not having conquered a painful environment, they become preoccupied with pain and make a devious art of it. Others submit—and hope to inherit the earth. Traditional practices are admittedly better than nothing . . . Spartan or Puritan—no one can question the occasional happy result. But the whole system rests upon the wasteful principle of selection. The English public school of the nineteenth century produced brave men—by setting up almost insurmountable barriers and making the most of the few who came over. But selection isn't education. Its crops of brave men will always be small, and the waste enormous. Like all primitive principles, selection serves in place of education only through a profligate use of material. Multiply extravagantly and select with rigor . . . In Walden Two we have a different objective. We make every man a brave man. They all come over the barriers. Some require more preparation than others, but they all come over. The traditional use of adversity is to select the strong. We control adversity to build strength.[8]

Cooperation is preferred to competition, and this choice is crucial in educational methods.

We carefully avoid any joy in a personal triumph which means the personal failure of somebody else. We take no pleasure in the sophistical, the disputative, the dialectical. We don't use the motive of domination, because we are always thinking of the whole group. Triumph over nature and over oneself, yes. But over others never.[9]

We are opposed to personal competition. We don't encourage competitive games, for example, with the exception of tennis or chess, where the exercise of skill is as important as the outcome of the game: and we never have tournaments, even so. We never mark any member for special approbation. There must be some other source of satisfaction in one's work or play, or we regard an achievement as quite trivial. A triumph over another is never a laudable act.[10]

The educational system at Walden Two is, of course, designed to meet Skinner's discontent with the school system in operation in his country. Being a professor, and part of that system himself, he questions with unusual clear-sightedness the usefulness of exams and marks, the efficiency of learning by exposure to lecturing teachers, the rationale of a universal curriculm imposed on all children, equally constrained to study matters or to read books in which they have no interest. In the narrative, Burris does not reflect on all those problems spontaneously: in fact, he replies to questions posed by a group of girls, well prepared by their Walden Two education to ask relevant and somewhat embarrassing questions.

In fact, the educational practices to which Skinner objects and which he remedies in the imaginary society of his Utopia have been repeatedly denounced since then in other contexts, including the 1968 student movement and a number of reforms (and counter reforms) in most Western countries. As we have seen in Chapter 13, Skinner later elaborated his critical views on school education and developed his alternative approach in terms of the technology of teaching.

## WOMEN'S LIBERATION

The community organisation drastically changes the role of the family. Here again, Skinner is guided by his perceptiveness of a social evolution that is taking place under his eyes:

The significant history of our time is the story of the growing weakness of the family. The decline of the home as a medium for perpetuating a culture, the struggle for equality for women including their right to select professions other than housewife or nursemaid, the extraordinary consequence of birth control and the practical separation of sex and parenthood, the social recognition of divorce, the critical issue of blood relationship or race—all these are parts of the same field. And you can hardly call it quiescent.[11]

This aspect of social organisation is undoubtedly one of the most difficult and delicate. And here, even more than in any other domain, Walden Two is a field of experiments, always open to improvement and change. It does not offer any definitive and rigidly fixed solution. The traditional importance of the family as an economic, socioaffective and educational unit is fully recognised; but it is also recognised that the family is no longer capable of fulfilling these functions. Something must be done at the level of the community.

Marriage is maintained, and is no less permanent than it is elsewhere (remember that divorce was becoming more frequent and more accepted in American society right after the Second World War). In fact, marital bonds are more resistant in the particular conditions of life of Walden Two. One interesting detail is the right of all members, married or not married, to live in a room "of their own". There is of course no obligation, and some couples do prefer to live under the same roof, but generally married individuals continue to live more or less permanently in their room.

> Many of our visitors suppose that a community means a sacrifice of privacy. On the contrary, we've carefully provided for much more personal privacy than is likely to be found in the world at large. You may be alone here whenever you wish. A man's room is his castle. And a woman's too.[12]

This echoes Virginia Woolf's preoccupation, symbolically encapsulated in the title of her feminist essay *A room of one's own* (1929). The right to individual residence, perhaps paradoxically, contributes to lasting fidelity and affection. It does not eliminate possible attraction towards other sexual partners, with resulting problems for the abandoned partner. However, other aspects of daily life help to solve these problems and reduce their undesirable consequences. Friendly and affectionate relationships between people of the opposite sex are widely encouraged, and no one expects that they would, as a rule, lead to sexual intimacy. (Again, remember we are in 1945!). Of course, they sometimes do, but in that case, the abandoned partner is at no risk of suddenly finding him or herself completely isolated and lost in the world. He or she has normally established many highly satisfying affective ties with members of the community, which help compensate for the loss of the loved one. Moreover, he or she is protected from any form of gossiping: gossiping on private affairs is totally unknown at Walden Two (a typically utopian proposition!).

On the other hand, education in the realm of affectivity has been aimed at reducing feelings of jealousy, of irreparable failure, of loss of self-esteem. Attenuating some forms of emotional reactions has advantages beyond the domain of love. It contributes to minimising inter-individual tensions as well as internal conflicts. Like most modern psychologists, Skinner recognises the stimulating value of a certain, optimal level of arousal in positive emotions like joy or love; but he also emphasises insistently the generally negative consequences of anger, hate, pain, and fear. Such emotions undoubtedly had a function in the remote evolution of human beings, or of their biological ancestors, but they are no longer useful in modern life. How can such emotions and related feelings be reduced? Exhorting people not to indulge in them will not do, and punishing them will not be very effective either. Conditions must be arranged in which they are not likely to occur. For example, for every crucial choice of life, such as choice of a profession or of a love partner, each individual should be offered a wide array of attractive possibilities:

> The fact is, it's very unlikely that anyone at Walden Two will set his heart on a course of action so firmly that he'll be unhappy if it isn't open to him. That's as true of the choice of a girl as of a profession. Personal jealousy is almost unknown among us, and for a simple reason: we provide a broad experience and many attractive alternatives. The tender sentiment of the 'one and only' has less to do with constancy of heart than with singleness of opportunity.[13]

> "It doesn't imply that we get everything we want. Of course we don't. But jealousy wouldn't help. In a competitive world there's some point to it. It energizes one to attack a frustrating condition. The impulse and the added energy are an advantage. Indeed, in a competitive world emotions work all too well. Look at the singular lack of success of the complacent man. He enjoys a more serene life, but it's less likely to be a fruitful one. The world isn't ready for simple pacifism or Christian humility, to cite two cases in point. Before you can safely train out the destructive and wasteful emotions, you must make sure they're no longer needed." "How do you make sure that jealousy isn't needed in Walden Two?" I said. "In Walden Two problems can't be solved by attacking others," said Frazier with marked finality.[14]

Let us come back to the family. Marriage in Walden Two usually takes place much earlier than in our society, but it must be remembered that education brings adolescents to adulthood also much earlier. Planners of Walden Two are not too concerned with the possible consequences of early marriage on population growth (in days when contraception was not as simple nor as widespread as it is today).

> It's no solution of the Malthusian problem to lower the birth rate of those who understand it. On the contrary, we need to expand the culture which recognizes the need for birth control. If you argue that we should set an example, you must prove to me that we shall not all be extinguished before the example is followed. No, our genetic program is a vital one. We don't worry about our birth rate, or its consequences.[15]

The Walden Two community structure certainly weakens parents-children relationships. But this is by no means an undesirable by-product: family relations are traditionally too confined and too restrictive to guarantee adequate education to all children. The family home, with parents exhausted by their job and more often than not completely unprepared for their educational responsibilities, is no ideal place in which to educate children. Affective ties, when they are too close and too complex, are frequently a source of conflicts, and eventually of persistent problems. In spite of these difficulties, the exclusivity of the family cell is a cause of frustration for those who are deprived of it: children without parents and adults without children. At Walden Two, the sort of affective ties that are typical of the relations between parents and children extend to the whole group, and are typical of the relations between adults and children. Being an orphan or the child of divorced parents is no longer a trauma. Similarly, sterility is no longer a malediction: it does not prevent relations with children, just as varied and rewarding as natural parents would enjoy. In this context, deliberate sterility, on a strictly voluntary basis, on the part of individuals presenting identified genetic risks, does not appear as dramatic renunciation. Blood ties are given less emphasis, in favour of affective ties of a more psycho-cultural nature. Biological filiation might eventually be ignored.

What about the danger that looser relations between parents and children have adverse effects on personality development, on identification processes, on feelings of security, on all those aspects of psychological well-being usually thought to derive from the quality of parental care? Frazier rightly observes:

> We know very little about what happens in identification. No one has ever made a careful scientific analysis. The evidence isn't truly experimental. We have seen the process at work only in our standard family structure. The Freudian pattern may be due to the peculiarities of that structure or even the eccentricities of the members of the family. All we really know is that children tend to imitate adults in gestures and mannerisms, and in personal attitudes and relations. They do that here, too, but since the family structure is changed, the effect is very different.
>
> Our children are cared for by many different people. It isn't institutional care, but genuine affection. Our members aren't overworked, and they haven't been forced into a job for which they have no talent or inclination. What the child imitates is a sort of essential happy adult.[16]

The reader familiar with psychology will have noticed the emphasis on the distinction between "institutional care", that is the sort of care an infant or a child would be likely to receive in the best possible nursery, children's hospital, etc., and "genuine affection". With a few exceptions, specialists in child care, and developmental psychologists, were not really aware of that distinction until the famous Bowlby report on maternal care and mental health was published in 1951. *Walden Two* was written, remember, in 1945. And the author had no academic expertise in child care and development, being known as a "rat psychologist".

Skinner also anticipated further evolution of educational practices in American society with regard to the role of male adults. At Walden Two, adults specifically in charge of young children belong to both sexes, and the balance between them has been carefully observed in the nursery as well as in school. In that way, problems resulting from the asymmetrical relationship to the mother are eliminated.

To children born and raised in the Walden Two community, the feelings of insecurity are unknown, which are so common among children raised by "an overworked or emotional mother, or living with quarrelsome parents, or sent to school unprepared for needed adjustments, or left to get along with children from different cultural levels" (p.145).

Substituting the community for the family has drastically changed the conditions of women's lives. Or, more precisely, the concern with the status of women in society has guided the founder of Walden Two in shaping a new style of marital and parental relationship. This concern was Fred Skinner's concern, and it might have been his major motivation to write *Walden Two*. In fact, it is listed first among the "personal dissatisfactions" that led him to turn to such an unusual literary genre. These are his own words in a preface to a new printing of Walden Two published in 1976:

> I had seen my wife and her friends struggling to save themselves from domesticity, wincing as they printed 'housewife' in those blanks asking for occupation.[17]

Without indulging in psychological interpretations which have no place in the present volume, I feel it important to mention a detail, showing how persistent that concern has been for Skinner. The 1976 Preface has been reprinted, in turn, in a collection of papers published in 1978 under the title *Reflections on behaviorism and society*; the book is dedicated to his wife, Eve, in a short dedication, half in French, "To Eve, *renée"—"renée*", an adjective and a forename meaning "reborn". The importance of the theme of the status of women in *Walden Two*, a few years before Kate Millet and the Women's Liberation movement, has generally been overlooked, and it makes the quotation of a few paragraphs of Frazier's words appropriate:

> The world has made some progress in the emancipation of women, but equality is still a long way off. There are few cultures today in which the rights of women are respected at all. America is one of perhaps three or four nations in which some progress has been made. Yet very few American women have the economic independence and cultural freedom of American men. What does the ordinary middle-class marriage amount to? Well, it's agreed that the husband will provide shelter, clothing, food, and perhaps some amusement, while the wife will work as a cook and cleaning woman and bear and raise children. The man is reasonably free to select or change his work; the woman has no choice, except between accepting and neglecting her lot. She has a legal claim for support, he has a claim for a certain type of labor.
>
> To make matters worse, we educate our women as if they were equal, and promise them equality. Is it any wonder they are soon disillusioned? The current remedy is to revive the slogans and sentiments which have made the system work

in the past. The good wife is told to consider it an honor and a privilege to work in the kitchen, to make the beds every day, to watch the children. She is made to believe that she is *necessary*, that she has the care of her husband's happiness and health and also her children's. That's the stock treatment of the neurotic housewife: reconcile her to her lot! But the intelligent woman sees through it at once, no matter how hard she wants to believe. She knows very well that someone else could make the beds and get the meals and wash the clothes, and her family wouldn't know the difference. The role of mother she wants to play herself, but that has no more connection with her daily work than the role of father with his work in the office or factory or field.

Here, there's no reason to feel that anyone is necessary to anyone else. Each of us is necessary in the same amount, which is very little. The community would go on just as smoothly tomorrow if any one of us died tonight. We cannot, therefore, get much satisfaction out of feeling important. But there are compensating satisfactions. Each of us is necessary as a person to the extent that he is loved as a person. No woman gets much satisfaction out of feeling that she will be missed as one misses a departed cook or scrub woman. In a world of complete economic equality, you get and keep the affections you deserve. You can't buy love with gifts or favors, you can't hold love by raising an inadequate child, and you can't be secure in love by serving as a good scrub woman or a good provider.[18]

The difficulties encountered in transforming in depth the status of women have not been overlooked by the founder of the community:

Those who stand to gain most are always the hardest to convince. That's true of the exploited worker, too—and for the same reason. They both have been kept in their places, not by external force, but much more subtly by a system of beliefs implanted within their skins.[19]

Incidentally, the reader will have noted the behaviourist's reference to internalisation . . .

## IS DEMOCRACY DEMOCRACY?

These are only a few aspects of life at Walden Two, in that small fraction of mankind that has successfully eluded the malediction of work and used time thus spared for creative activities. I have not reviewed all the details of the guided tour, during which, incidentally, we never encounter any drunkard, any delinquent, any depressive person. We are shown no jail, no psychiatric hospital, not because organised guided tours would be strictly confined to places of interest officially defined as such for visitors, but simply because there are none. Where does that ideal harmony come from? Who governs, and how?

Contrary to most other social dreams, Skinner's Utopia does not rely on some innate virtues of human nature, heretofore left unused or repressed. Skinner does not believe in such virtues, any more than in ineradicable vices. Virtues, such as happiness, emerge from the conditions in which people live. These favourable conditions cannot be defined beforehand and once and for all in the absolute formula of an ideology. They have to be sought after empirically, and permanently readjusted. Walden Two is not governed on the basis of political doctrine, but of experimental attitude. That is why, as a community organisation, it never stops changing and being changed, as its members never stop changing their behavioural habits.

Whatever problem arises is solved tentatively, and the solution given is always open to correction, according to the observed results. If it proves to be inappropriate—that is to say, if people concerned are not satisfied with it—another solution will be looked for and tried out. As in the laboratory, the subjects are always right: if they do not behave as expected, or as wished, they are not to be blamed; administrators—or experimenters—are responsible for their bad predictions.

The search for optimal conditions favourable to the equilibrium of the whole community through satisfaction of each of its members is in the hands of a team of planners and managers. Their special charge is imposed on them by their competence only. They are not exposed to the usual temptation of politicians obsessed by the next elections: their office is strictly limited in time, to a maximum of 10 years. In any case, what sort of privileges could they think of keeping? Money is not in use at Walden Two; individual properties do not exist; pieces of art are available for everyone's enjoyment; every member has plenty of free time for leisure; and individuals in charge of managing responsibilities are not given any special attention or honour. And if there is any real satisfaction in dominating one's fellowmen, there is not much place for it, because force and coercion are excluded from the principles on which Walden Two is administered.

Managers, whose personal qualities and virtues have been shaped by education and are maintained by current circumstances, have not been chosen by popular vote. Walden Two is not a democratic regime, in the sense in which modern states, and especially the United States, are called democratic. Frazier (or Skinner) denounces vigorously the democratic illusion, the "pious fraud", the "travesty", in which voting has become a "device for blaming conditions on the people"; in which the only guarantee is that "the majority will not be despotically ruled"; in which "the majority solves the problem to their satisfaction, and the minority can be damned"; in which people are not invited to vote "for a given state of affairs, but for a man who claims to be able to achieve that state" (pp.265, 266, 268). Certainly, if democratic countries would appear as real democratic regimes, where representatives were actually elected for their competence and were actually under the control of the voters, we might be close to the ideal society. But most modern states offer only the caricature of that ideal:

> The government of Walden Two has the virtues of democracy, but none of the defects. It's much closer to the theory or intent of democracy than the actual

practice in America today. The will of the people is carefully ascertained. We have no election campaigns to falsify issues or obscure them with emotional appeals, but a careful study of the satisfaction of the membership is made. Every member has a direct channel through which he may protest to the Managers or even the Planners. And these protests are taken as seriously as the pilot of an airplane takes a sputtering engine. We don't need laws and a police force to compel to pay attention to a defective engine. Nor do we need laws to compel our Dairy Manager to pay attention to an epidemic among his cows. Similarly, our Behavioral and Cultural Managers need not be compelled to consider grievances. A grievance is a wheel to be oiled, or a broken pipe line to be repaired.[20]

Democracy, as we have come to live it in the Western world, has demonstrated its advantages over political systems based on force and exploitation. But it has had its time, at least in the form it has taken, and we must be aware of its present limitations, and be ready to move beyond it, if we do want to face problems that even coercion might not be able to solve. What is wrong with current democracy is that it is based on an erroneous conception of human nature:

A *laissez-faire* philosophy which trusts to the inherent goodness and wisdom of the common man is incompatible with the observed fact that men are made good or bad and wise or foolish by the environment in which they grow.[21]

The question inevitably arises, and indeed it does in the conversation between the founder of the community and his visitors: is that not Fascism? If we adopt the semantic looseness so common today in political discourse, and use the word uncritically to name any kind of social organisation that diverges from Western pseudo-democracy or from pseudo-egalitarian systems of Marxist obedience that have been collapsing recently, as "a convenient way to dispose of any attempt to improve upon a *laissez-faire* democracy", then, perhaps, Walden Two should be labelled "fascist". If, however, we feel it more appropriate to confine the term to designating totalitarian regimes, usually based on individual or oligarchic power, resorting to force and exploitation by one group on others as main principles of government, then it cannot seriously be applied to a small community where a handful of men and women have the charge, for a limited period, and with no personal benefits whatsoever, of administering public life to the satisfaction of all by resorting exclusively to the use of positive consequences. When a stage is reached where democratic regimes are no longer able to solve effectively the problems on which the survival of society depends, the best strategy for totalitarianism is to maintain the illusion of democracy.

Some will insist that it is fascism, in spite of the fact that there are no despots, that there is no exploitation, that all members are equal and receive their share of the common wealth, that the rights of the individual are respected, that people are happy; fascism because all these features of the social organisation are but the consequence of deliberate arrangement, rather than the product of free choice.

Freedom: here is the magical word, the major objection. Is the concept clear enough to decline to enter Walden Two? To what extent are the social systems we are cherishing really based on freedom? And what exactly do we mean by *freedom*? One need not read heavy philosophy treatises to understand that the word does not cover a single, consistent concept. One need only listen to candidates' declarations on the day before a presidential election.

Skinner has not elaborated an analysis of freedom in *Walden Two*. He would devote to it, a quarter of a century later, his essay *Beyond freedom and dignity*. We shall turn to this book in the next chapter to penetrate further his view on that central problem. He has, however, already shaped the premises in Frazier's words. As soon as one agrees to look at human conduct in a scientific manner, one expects it to obey laws. Then, the question is: what laws rule those behaviours, those situations, those feelings and ideas to which, with various meanings according to time and place, the term *freedom* is applied?

# NOTES

1. Paper signed by Evelyne Laurent (1976) on C. Botson and M. Deliège's (1975) book. Italics mine. For an example of the approach and material presented in this book published in French only, see Richelle (1977a).
2. Chomsky, 1972.
3. *Walden Two*, pp.193–194. Parentheses mine.
4. Ibidem, p.64. Parentheses mine.
5. Ibidem, p.76.
6. Ibidem, p.89.
7. Ibidem, pp.33–34.
8. Ibidem, pp.113–114.
9. Ibidem, p.112.
10. Ibidem, p.169.
11. Ibidem, p.138.
12. Ibidem, p.139.
13. Ibidem, p.54.
14. Ibidem, pp.102–103.
15. Ibidem, pp.136–137.
16. Ibidem, pp.144–145.
17. Quoted from the text as reprinted in *Reflections on behaviorism and society*, 1978, p.56.
18. *Walden Two*, pp.146–147.
19. Ibidem, p.148.
20. Ibidem, p.269.
21. Ibidem, p.273.

# 15 Freedom, at last . . .

## PSYCHOLOGY: THE AMBIVALENT SCIENCE

Skinner was 75 years old when he published an essay that made his name widely known among lay readers. The title was provocative, and might itself have stimulated negative reactions to the book: *Beyond freedom and dignity* sounded like a denial of two basic values of our society. Freedom is a magical term, with a flavour of absoluteness; we like to think that nothing can be, that no one can go, *beyond* freedom.

*Beyond* was not, originally, in the title. While he was preparing the book, Skinner referred to it simply as *Freedom and dignity*. He mentions it frequently, under that title, in his notebook between 1965 and 1970. The change came about, as is often the case, after a discussion with the publisher. Skinner suggested, as a more appropriate title, what eventually appeared on the bookcover. As he says in his autobiography, he was:

> aware that [he] was borrowing from Nietzsche's *Beyond good and evil* and Freud's *Beyond the pleasure principle*. It seemed right, Gottlieb [the publisher's man] liked it, and we let it stand. It was probably responsible for much of the controversy about the book and quite possibly for its success. It was, however, misleading. As a scientist I did not think of people as free initiating agents to be credited with their achievements, But I was proposing changes in social practices which should make them *feel* freer than ever before and *accomplish* more.[1]

From a scientific point of view, concerned with the search of determinants of what occurs in nature, the concept of freedom has always been a puzzle. Many scientists in fields of natural sciences such as physics or chemistry have left the issue to philosophers or theologians, admitting that they do not possess, from the information in their own domain, the knowledge needed to decide; they do not discard the idea that humans are made of a different stuff and escape the constraints of natural laws. Many others, while not entering the technical aspects of the debate, would make the assumption that humans, being part of Nature, obey natural laws. The problem becomes crucial, of course, in the science of psychology, because a field can hardly be a science at all if its subject matter is not studied with the hypothesis that it can be described and explained in a lawful manner. Therefore, it would seem that anyone who defines himself as a scientific psychologist should belong to the second category of scientists—those who assume that human actions can be causally accounted for. In fact, many psychologists are closer to the first category, and while they use apparently scientific discourse, they paradoxically maintain the belief that human actions proceed from the autonomous decisions of the self, the internal agent, or some irreducible core of the subject, not amenable to scientific explanation. The debate has been vivid throughout the history of psychology, but it is perhaps more vivid now than ever before. In fact, it has reappeared, overtly or covertly, in most philosophical discussions about artificial *vs* natural intelligence.

Skinner, of course, is unequivocally among those for whom a psychological science cannot assign itself any goal other than the search for causal relations in behaviour (or, for that matter, in cognition). To quote him again: "As a scientist I did not think of people as free initiating agents". Approaching psychology as a science implies a deterministic stand, whatever changes the notion of determinism has undergone in the past hundred years.

Such a position in Skinner should not bother us more than in any other scientific psychologist. If it does, it is because he has explicitly pushed it to its most extreme logical consequences, something very few others have done. It is not unusual for psychologists to apply their scientific credo inside their laboratory, when studying well defined and limited problems, but to overlook the full implications of their choice at the level of a general theory of human conduct; if asked, they would probably not commit themselves to betting on the scientific assumption, and would instead be ready to concede the credit to alternatives, such as philosophically oriented views proposed under the headings of phenomenology or humanistic psychology. As Konrad Lorenz put it:

> Probably the reason why people are so afraid of causal considerations is that they are terrified lest insight into the causes of earthly phenomena could expose man's free will as an illusion. (Lorenz, 1966, p.199).

## A PROTEAN CONCEPT

The word freedom is used today, and has been used in the recent past with many different and equally ill-defined meanings. It is part of political slogans on the most diverse and opposite sides. It is used as a commercial argument in advertising all kinds of products, be it cars, clothes, or cigarettes, with various, but equally attractive connotations. Under the name of freedom, nations and groups have fought to emancipate themselves or to prevent others from becoming emancipated. The same word applies to matters of individual privacy, of human rights, of market economy, of possibilities of choice in buying goods, taking a spouse, selecting a dwelling, using one's money, engaging in risky sports, driving at high speed on highways, etc. It is obvious that it does not refer to any unifying property common to such disparate contexts and situations. Confronted with such a state of affairs, a linguist would legitimately engage in a semantic inquiry, in order to characterise all these various uses of a single word, to trace the origin of each particular use in the past history of our languages and of our culture. A psychologist is equally entitled to lead a similar investigation, and to attempt the natural and cultural history of freedom. This is exactly what Skinner has undertaken, with the consequence that he came to denounce many of the myths attached to the concept of freedom both in our self-image and in our social and political systems. *Beyond freedom and dignity* is not a destruction, nor a denial, of some important things to which these words refer; it is an essay aimed at analysing lucidly what freedom is about, at identifying some of the contradictions in our passion for freedom, at warning mankind from the possibly self-destructive consequences of our uncritical veneration for freedom, and at helping humans to *feel* freer, while being aware of the importance of perpetuating such feeling to future generations.

## FREEDOM TO WIN . . . OR LOSE

This is, in short, the message of *Beyond freedom and dignity*. We shall deal with it in some depth in a moment, but before extracting the substance of that controversial book, a much simpler text on freedom is worth mentioning, because it captures, in an ironical style and in the form of a parable, part of the analysis found in *Beyond freedom and dignity*. The two-page paper was published in the *New York Times* in 1977 under the title "Freedom, at last, from the burden of taxation".[2]

It is about something familiar to many people living in Europe as much as, if not even more than, in America, i.e. lotteries. Lotteries run by the state, as is well known, are another way to raise money from the citizens, which they seem to accept more readily than taxation. Skinner argues ironically that resorting to lotteries could very well be developed to a point that would permit us to get rid of taxation, and that lotteries could be used extensively by agencies, such as the Pentagon, which need a lot of money but dislike being controlled too closely as to what it is used for. Pointing to the fact that people are not born gamblers but become gamblers if exposed to appropriate contingencies, he suggests we should train them from early in life to participate "voluntarily" in financing the state and all possible money-eating agencies. This is an extreme case of an illusion of freedom in individuals in fact strongly induced to bring "freely"—at least as far as their subjective feelings go—more money than through the (aversive) obligation to pay taxes. To an observer, the conditions responsible for gambling behaviour are clear enough, and paradoxically the behaviour is maintained in spite of the fact that, on the whole, losses by far exceed returns. This points to the strength of intermittent reinforcement, stretched *ad infinitum* in humans thanks to their ability mentally to anticipate possible rewards that will actually never come. Gambling can develop into something close to addiction, another case that illustrates the ambiguity of the relations between the concepts of causation, positive or negative reinforcement, control, and freedom.

One major difference, of course, between lotteries and taxation is that buying tickets is felt to be spontaneous action initiated by the individual's decision, whereas the taxation of income is imposed from outside and has to be fulfilled, like it or not. Organisers of popular lotteries and games of chance have correctly estimated how important it is for people to feel that they control their own actions. The success of numerical lotteries or bingo is probably due to the fact that, by writing down the numbers of their choice, gamblers feel they are controlling chance more surely than by buying a ticket bearing a preprinted number. Similarly, we feel free when we go shopping and buy all sorts of luxury goods, although it is well known, and perhaps *we* know, that our consumer behaviour is partly determined by advertising campaigns. The same is true when we elect political leaders: whatever the factors, to some extent well identified, controlling our decision from outside, the simple fact that we write down our choice and put it in the ballot box subjectively suffices to preserve the assumption of freedom.

## THE FREEDOM ISSUE AND THE FUTURE OF THE WORLD

To Skinner, what is at stake in a critical analysis of the concept of freedom is not just an old philosophical problem still debated among modern psychologists. It is nothing less than the future of the world. The book *Beyond freedom and dignity* does not start with an academic presentation of the various views about the concepts mentioned in the title. It opens with an evocation of the "terrific problems" mankind is confronted with, i.e. population explosion, nuclear holocaust, world famine, pollution of the environment, exhaustion of resources. Humans do not really seem ready to cope with them in any consistent and efficient manner. Yet, they do have the technological tools that would allow the solution of at least part of them. Demographic growth can be slowed down by birth control, famine can be alleviated by better distribution of available food and crops can be improved by adequate agricultural policy, environmental pollution can be reduced by turning to alternative solutions in industry, transportation, and energy production. Efforts are made in the right direction, but they appear hopelessly out of proportion with the ever extending problems they attempt to counteract. Such incapacity, Skinner argues, is not due to a lack of technical possibilities; it is due to our unwillingness to put ourselves in the right perspectives. We persist in perceiving ourselves as privileged creatures endowed with unlimited power over the world around us, and drawing our rules for action from our minds, by processes of free decision making. Although it is clear that all the dramatic problems we are facing today cannot be solved unless humans do drastically change their behaviours, we keep appealing to good will and to changes of mentality, as if these are the prerequisites for the solutions to be reached. We are blind to the fact that such an appeal to "change of mind" has been the traditional strategy, but that it has widely failed. And it has failed because behaviours are not the by-products of human will or mind: they are the results of humans' interaction with their environment. Awareness of that basic interdependency is the prior condition to solving contemporary problems, before it is too late. As long as humans will not accept that they are not perfectly autonomous beings, acting from sovereign internal initiative, they will be exposed to making their own world increasingly dangerous to themselves while believing that they are still controlling it to their advantage.

Skinner himself has pointed out that his view of human beings inflicts another wound to self-esteem, after those inflicted by Copernicus, Darwin, and Freud. It had not been easy to accept that the Earth was not the centre of the Universe, or that mankind was not born straight from the hands of God, but had evolved after a long process, with simple living forms eventually modifying into more complex ones, and none of them being entitled to eternity. At least Copernicus and Darwin had not shaken our pride in being truly rational beings, until Freud showed us that what we do, feel, and even think, is due to the turmoil of obscure emotional forces rather than governed by the conscious exercise of reason. Yet, autonomy, in a sense, was preserved: all that came from within, from the very depth of our being, all the more our "self" as it came untamed by rationality. Skinner gives the next blow: reason or passion, we are the behaving result of the interactions between our physical organism, as given at birth, and the physical and social environment in which our individual history has been taking place. By no means do our behaviours emerge from some mysterious and all-powerful individual freedom.

Such a reversal is not easy to admit, especially as freedom has become a magic concept. It has been used in recent human history to eliminate obvious constraints, but it might reveal, by its fetishist persistence, the real obstacle to freeing ourselves from the dangers that threaten modern society, and possibly the human species itself. It is worth making an attempt at describing, after Skinner, what sorts of "behaviour-situation" are referred to by the concept of freedom.

## THE STRUGGLE FOR FREEDOM: A NATURAL
## AND CULTURAL HISTORY

At a very simple level, animals obviously act to escape some situations, which are presumably aversive to them. For example, they withdraw from pain stimuli. Thus they "free" themselves from pain; and similarly from unusual physical constraints, which make them vulnerable to danger. They also act to avoid situations that are expected to be painful. If, for some reason, adaptive so-called escape or avoidance responses are prevented, one can say that the animal has limited freedom. But we should better phrase this the other way around, and say that the concept of freedom has its biological roots in the very primitive (in the sense of basic) behaviour of escaping or avoiding.

The human species has had its share of aversive situations, and a large part of its cultural development has been a progressive escape from them. Most ancient human technologies were designed to fight predators, protect from bad weather, be it cold or extreme heat, or to cure disease and so on.

The cultural environment in its turn has implied, presumably very early, a number of aversive controls of a social, rather than physical nature. Historians and prehistorians can sometimes trace their origin with some plausibility. In most political structures, some groups or individuals suffer aversive controls from others: one caste or class exploits another as a workforce, under the threat of whip, deprivation of food or salary, or of exclusion from happiness after death. Political power enforces the law by applying fines, putting into jail, suppressing rights and privileges. No wonder that these aversive controls, arising from cultural origins, lead to escape and avoidance responses similar to those provoked by physical aversive stimulation. Movements for freedom that have emerged in many places throughout history are in essence escape behaviours. They are just much more complex than animal responses, involving as they do intricate social structures and symbolic representations. They have eventually found formulations in philosophies of freedom or philosophies of liberation, as those elaborated in the eighteenth century and thereafter in Western societies. These philosophies, however, did not limit their concept of freedom to the elimination of aversive controls. They made a case for the individual's right to enjoy freedom. Going one step further, they defined freedom not simply as a right, which implies that it can be referred to real situations—freedom to vote, freedom to express one's opinion publicly, freedom to practice a religion, etc—but as a sort of inherent individual characteristic, that could fully blossom only by the suppression of all controls.

Such exalting of an abstract and almost metaphysical concept of freedom, although it made some positive contributions to freeing people from various constraints, had two peculiar consequences. On the one hand, in some social systems or social ideologies, it has contributed to the statement of the unlimited rights of the individual as a fundamental principle, which inevitably generates, sooner or later, new constraints for others: this is the case in the unlimited individual right to financial profit in completely free market economies (in which laws and regulations then tend not to define and ensure positive rights, but to limit them in such a way as to minimise the perverse effects of individual freedom). On the other hand, it has moved from the perfectly sound idea that one should get rid of aversive controls, to the debatable idea that any control should be banned, or in other words that all types of control are by definition aversive: they are happy whose actions and thoughts proceed freely from themselves, owing nothing to anything or anyone.

Now if we admit, on the basis of a scientific analysis, that such autonomy is illusory, that human action cannot be conceived of independently from its origins and its consequences in a complex social and physical environment, to suggest that any control should be discarded as alien to freedom is to deny those factors actually controlling individuals when they are supposed to have been freed from all controls. The claim of freedom, then, means nothing but leaving the stage to less visible controls, among which aversive controls are likely to sweep in again, surreptitiously. Paradoxically, freedom eventually generates enslavement. Mechanisms used in inciting us to consume in our society are a typical example. Addiction, whatever its object, drug, work, money, etc. refers to exactly that sort of process.

## MERIT AND DIGNITY

Let us turn to dignity. Autonomous human beings are endowed with another property: they are credited for their own actions and thoughts. They are attributed the merit if they are good, and responsibility if they are bad. The more mysterious the deeds, and the more difficult to understand, the more they will earn merit.

By analysing causes, however, we inevitably displace merit and responsibility. This is conspicuous in the evolution of criminal law. As our knowledge of the factors contributing to generate offences has developed, the notion of limited or attenuated responsibility has emerged, and some criminals have been recognised as not responsible. The individual's responsibility has been displaced either by biological factors, such as heredity or pathological conditions, or to social causes, be it the immediate social environment in which the individual has grown up, or society as a whole, that has allowed a particular social context to develop. As soon as we look for causes, and identify some of them, we can no longer hold the individual fully and exclusively responsible for their actions, the origin of which are obviously to be found elsewhere. Hence the idea that repression does not bring any real solution to criminality, and is at best a legitimate means of self-protection for society. In the long run, the only real solution is prevention: it consists in arranging society in some other way, in order to avoid crime-generating factors.

While the search of causal factors has become more or less accepted when dealing with deviant behaviours, so that those who so act are seen as victims rather than culprits, we dislike taking the same stand when positive behaviours are at stake. We like to retain total merit for them. We prefer to attribute to a good worker a sense of professional duty, zeal, and the will to perform the tasks well, rather than account for excellent performance by the amount of the salary, the status it provides, or even by the type of satisfaction derived from making a product of quality. We prefer to say of an honest person that their good actions arise from virtue rather than tracing them to the educational history that has built the person, or identifying the types of reinforcers that keep them behaving well. Autonomous people resist all attempts at analysing causes of their behaviour, so that they can preserve their merits, in the same way as they resist all efforts to demystify freedom, lest they lose such a valuable quality.

In his criticism of freedom and dignity, Skinner uses arguments parallel to his criticism of mentalism in scientific psychology. In this respect, the views expressed in *Beyond freedom and dignity* appear as a version applied to daily life, a political and social version of one of the core tenets of his behaviourism. Just as mentalism is the main obstacle to the progress of scientific analysis, so does it bar the way to any efficient solution to problems that mankind has to face today. Both aspects are, for Skinner, tightly linked together.

## FREEDOM AGAINST ITSELF

Why is it that the idea of autonomous human beings, and the notions of freedom and dignity that found them, are so difficult to eradicate? Perhaps the reason is, as many philosophies and ideologies assert, that it really defines the greatness of human beings, against reductionist scientific approaches. This argument, to Skinner, is but a disguise for the truth. The very reason for its persistence is that it is a useful fiction for those in power. It is an instrument all the more subtle because it entertains the illusion of escaping from power.

Throughout human history, as already pointed out, openly aversive controls have been amply resorted to: physical punishments and torture have sanctioned in turn the subject who did not prove as productive as expected, the culprit refusing to confess to the crime, the believer going astray from orthodoxy to heresy, the conquered people refusing to submit. The effects have usually been rapid and conspicuous, but they did not change in depth the individuals' behaviour in the desired direction. The heretic brought back to pure dogma by force will never be the most reliable of faithful believers, nor will the slave working under the whip be a collaborator to be trusted. Moreover, punishments are too visible, and they produce reactions aimed at escaping or avoiding them. They contain, so to speak, the seeds of their own eradication. Their results, imposed from outside by force, are alien to the subject, who is not responsible for them, and does not claim any credit for them. To the contrary, the subject feels justified in revolting.

A much better solution consists in making control less conspicuous, less decipherable, and less obviously external to the subject. If, taking advantage of the possibilities offered by symbolic activities, punishing mechanisms are transferred *inside* the subject, the goal will be reached: the control will not be less efficient, but it will be attributed to the autonomous person, who will keep full credit or responsibility for it. Correctly internalised, the threat of eternal hell is no less efficient than torture inflicted by the inquisitor, and the Superego advantageously replaces the physical punishment imparted by the parents. Advantageously, at least, from the point of view of the authority that has been transferred to within the subject. Those who really hold the power draw a twofold benefit from that change: charges and risks are alleviated (tyrants risk overthrow if their subjects rise up against them, but not if they are fighting with their own conscience); and secondly those in power maintain the belief in their own freedom and responsibility in their subjects (if they emerge victorious from their inner struggle they will credit their own will; if they come out defeated they will blame their own weakness). It can be seen here how the autonomous person, in fact, contributes to maintaining non-conspicuous forms of aversive controls. Freud had told us how to identify the origin and the mechanisms of the internalisation of punitive controls, but, it seems, neither his own lessons, nor the various socio-political interpretations that have been made since by his disciples, have succeeded in dethroning the autonomous person. Should that be taken as evidence that we cannot do without such a being?

Those in power take advantage of the idea of the autonomous person in still another way: they use it towards their own exoneration.

> The controller can escape responsibility if he can maintain the position that the individual himself is in control. The teacher who gives the student credit for learning can also blame him for not learning. The parent who gives his child credit for his achievements can also blame him for his mistakes. Neither the teacher nor the parent can be held responsible.[3]

The same is true of governments. If they discard the autonomous person, they have to endorse full responsibility in the case of failure of their policy. Skinner reminds us, in this context, of the evolution of Soviet Union, as analysed by Bauer:

> Immediately after the revolution the government could argue that if many Russians were uneducated, unproductive, badly behaved, and unhappy, it was because their environment had made them so. The new government would change the environment, making use of Pavlov's work on conditioned reflexes, and all would be well. But by the early thirties the government had had its chance, and many Russians were still not conspicuously better informed, more productive, better behaved, or happier. The official line was then changed, and Pavlov went out of favor. A strongly purposive psychology was substituted: it was up to the Russian citizen to get an education, work productively, behave well, and be happy. The Russian educator was to make sure that he would accept this responsibility, but not by conditioning him. The successes of the Second World War restored

confidence in the earlier principle, however; the government had been successful after all. It might not yet be completely effective, but it was moving in the right direction. Pavlov came back into favor.[4]

Perhaps one could apply the same kind of analysis to the current revival of mentalism in cognitive psychology, drawing a parallel with the incapacity of governments really to solve pending problems, and with their increasing tendency to hide their control under a claimed delegation of power to the citizens in democratic structures. It is clear that our societies are not exempt from those forms of exoneration. The latter have a place all the more important as they benefit from most official doctrines of freedom and of political responsibility. If the oil crisis was not solved by a general reduction of energy consumption, governments could always blame their citizens for their lack of civic responsibility, their inclination to waste, their lack of foresight. And if the citizens accused their government of carelessness, the latter could still reply that they gained office by the citizens' vote, so that, whatever way you like to put it, citizens can blame only themselves. The autonomous person appears as the indispensable alibi of the irresponsibility of power.

By exacerbating people's belief in their autonomy, one does, in fact, consolidate their enslavement. In this respect, the non-directivist doctrines popularised by various psychological and sociological schools might owe their success to the fact that, in spite of all appearances, they have served the powers in place extremely well.

> Permissiveness is not, however, a policy; it is the abandonment of policy, and its apparent advantages are illusory. To refuse to control is to leave control not to the person himself, but to other parts of the social and non-social environments.[5]

## MENTALISM AS A TOOL OF POWER

Those who govern by relying on autonomous people need not be concerned with changing the conditions in which people live. What counts is changing minds, as pointed out by a famous text stating that wars originate in people's minds[6]— as do all other nuisances about which they might like to complain. Paradoxically, attempts to change minds seem legitimate, whereas attempts to change people's actions and feelings by modifying their environment appear as a violation of their freedom:

> It is a surprising fact that those who object most violently to the manipulation of behavior nevertheless make the most vigorous efforts to manipulate minds. Evidently freedom and dignity are threatened only when behavior is changed by physically changing the environment. There appears no threat when the states of mind said to be responsible for behavior are changed, presumably because

autonomous man possesses miraculous powers which enable him to yield or resist.

It is fortunate that those who object to the manipulation of behavior feel free to manipulate minds, since otherwise they would have to remain silent.[7]

Thus, those who confine themselves to changing minds are doomed to changing nothing, perhaps because they find their advantage in changing nothing. Appealing to "restored confidence in democracy" as a remedy for the crisis of democratic systems is likely to leave things as they are; what has to be changed are the conditions of practice of democracy, a question of political contingencies, not of state of mind.

In most cases, those who maintain others in the myth of freedom and dignity are altogether experts in controlling their behaviour in a more direct and efficient way, to their own advantage. Political leaders and arms dealers cooperate in celebrating patriotic virtues, while conditioning military obedience in the most practical style. Those holding economic power make use in their advertising campaigns of slogans evoking freedom, the individual's right to satisfy desires, to assert his or her will, etc. while establishing deliberately, and by resorting expertly and perversely to laws of behaviour control, practices of consumption focused on their products. Great spiritualist religions never failed to base their authority on highly practical rules for the conduct of daily life. In all these cases, the art of power consists in disguising to the individuals the real determinants of their acts, by having them believe that they proceed from their own free mind. Never are consumers more strongly under control than when persuaded that they are kings. Never is a doctrine more firmly imposed than when its believers feel endowed with free will.

Now, if people are happy with the illusion of autonomy, why should one worry? Why should one insist on making them aware of real, hidden controls? The answer for Skinner is straightforward: nothing less is at stake than the survival of human culture, or more simply of mankind. The mixture of an illusion of freedom and of cleverly disguised controls, bringing each other reciprocal support, cannot help us solve the frightening problems we are confronted with. By satisfying ourselves with the current state of affairs, we leave mankind to the type of controls actually in use, and expose it to the most uncertain future.

A seemingly simple solution would be getting rid of all controls, so that true freedom can blossom. This has been the classical proposal of anarchist movements, and of various sorts of idealists. This would work if humans were creatures whose actions could depend on nothing and nobody. But if they are no less dependent than other organisms on those conditions that have contributed to their history, as a species and as individuals, the solution amounts to abandoning their destiny to chance. Skinner does not hesitate here to use a formula that has irritated many of his readers, and has provoked the accusation of being a prophet of established order: "What we need is not less control, but more control". More control, but of a totally different type. "We cannot choose a way of life where there is no control. We can only change the controlling conditions".[8]

It would be absurd, indeed, not to put to work our knowledge of how to induce human behaviours that would solve some of our most serious problems. Wouldn't we blame medical doctors for not applying their knowledge of the causes and prevention of a disease to stop its propagation? If scientific knowledge presents any advantage to mankind, it is precisely in enabling us to identify determining factors that control our lives, and thus providing us with the only way to control them in turn. This is the only true meaning of freedom at the present stage of evolution.

When Skinner suggests "more control", he does not mean increasing negative aversive controls. He consistently denounced these, throughout his writings, to the point that he has been blamed occasionally for being more a moralist than an experimenter. He means increasing explicit, clearly identified controls, adequately designed to reach clearly stated goals, and modified as necessary after lessons of experience; and, most important to him, a generalisation of positive controls. We recognise here the principles in operation in Walden Two. Nothing could be further from maintaining the established order. In fact, Skinner's proposals are nothing less than subversive in comparison with our current habits. If implemented, they would sweep out equally: governments mainly based on aversive controls, only tempered by the pressure, in its turn aversive, from groups of citizens; educational systems, from which, in spite of pretensions to attractiveness, most pupils would drop out were they not obliged to attend; economic systems inciting us to waste resources on the grounds that needs must be satisfied, needs that have been created on purpose to encourage consumption. Skinnerian control would begin with deep changes, indeed. It would certainly bring in a kind of order, but drastically different, as outlined in the Utopian Walden Two community: the order of a society made up of happy people, satisfied as far as their vital needs are concerned, productive of art and science in their leisure time, and with a sense of responsibility for the future of their descendants. If there is any objection to such type of control it is only because of a generalisation from order based on coercion to all sorts of order, however positive the controls involved. This is to forget that life, including social and historical life in human animals, is nothing but order, and possibly a very transitory order in the universe, the preservation of which might now be in the hands of mankind.

## SURVIVAL AS ULTIMATE VALUE

Skinner was aware that designing social order cannot be achieved without reference to some criteria, and although positive controls should normally produce happy individuals, he was not naïve enough to believe that the "pursuit of happiness", as it is phrased in the American constitution, could be a safe value.

Concerned as he was for the vital problems of our time, he could not think of any more decisive criterion than the survival of the species, which means, mankind being an essentially cultural species, survival of culture. He did not care for the perpetuation of one particular culture. If he has been accused of working to the triumph of American model of life, it is only by crude misreading of his words (Spiro Agnew, in his day, was not mistaken on that point[9]). Human cultures, as living species, do not, from an absolute point of view, have more value one than the other. They cannot be judged by any other criterion, except survival. And survival is never eternally guaranteed to any of them: what appears an advantage today may turn out to be a threat tomorrow. Skinner's social philosophy is clearly grounded in biology.

The fact that a particular culture perpetuates itself by changing or by maintaining the same structure depends on numerous conditions, usually impossible to disentangle. There is little doubt that any cultural system contains mechanisms inducing its members to behave in a sense that favours its survival. If these mechanisms, as is often the case, are mainly based on aversive control, they are likely sooner or later to generate opposition from individuals or groups, which will struggle for their own interests at the expense of the culture. In some sense, resorting to aversive controls is probably inevitable. Social life perhaps always implies some sort of compromise between the demands of collective organisation and the interests of the individual. It implies some renouncement of positive individual reinforcers. Freud thought that culture, which is the distinctive feature of mankind, cannot develop unless individual drives are repressed, unless the principle of reality takes over the principle of pleasure, with the consequence that culture is, by definition, a source of conflicts, both inter- and intra-individuals.

Skinner shares with Freud the idea that there is no way out of compromise between the ends of society and the individual's satisfaction. But whereas for Freud repression was at the basis of civilisation, for Skinner it is only one of the possible forms the compromise can take, be it the most widespread, perhaps because it is the most simple and obvious. There is however nothing essential about it, only historical. Other forms can be described, in which collective goals would be reached through positively reinforcing individual behaviours. Whereas Freud shows absolute pessimism, Skinner adopts conditional optimism. Conditional because there is no guarantee whatsoever that mankind will eventually engage in that course of action: progress, as we know, is not inherent to evolution, be it cultural or biological. But at least what we know about behaviour does not exclude some sort of balanced compromise based on positive reinforcement. This has little to do, of course, with freeing humans from the force of pulsions—the concept of human nature is not linked, for Skinner, with libido— it is essentially reciprocal adjustment between the individual and the social. Repression is replaced with regulation.

## DEFENCE OF THE INDIVIDUAL

Can we expect from a designed culture, even one based on exclusively positive control, anything other than robotisation, than a general levelling of individuals, and finally negation of individual rights? Skinner, of course, has been very much concerned with that important issue. Not only because it was a central one in his scientific as well as philosophical reflections, but because he was himself, very deeply, an individualist. We already know, from our visit to Walden Two, what his answer was. And we also know that the answer is in line with his view of a science of humanity, shaped after biological philosophy. Any sound cultural design must aim at preserving and stimulating diversity. The theme of diversity is a recurrent one in Skinner's scientific writings. It is clearly stated in *Beyond freedom and dignity*, as illustrated by the following passage:

> If a planned culture necessarily meant uniformity or regimentation, it might work against further evolution. If men were very much alike, they would be less likely to hit upon or design new practices, and a culture which made people as much alike as possible might slip into a standard pattern from which there would be no escape. That would be bad design, but if we are looking for variety, we should not fall back upon accident. Many accidental cultures have been marked by uniformity and regimentation. The exigencies of administration in governmental, religious, and economic systems breed uniformity, because it simplifies the problem of control. Traditional educational establishments specify what the student is to learn at what age and administer tests to make sure that the specifications are met. The codes of governments and religions are usually quite explicit and allow little room for diversity or change. The only hope is *planned* diversification, in which the importance of variety is recognized. The breeding of plants and animals moves toward uniformity when uniformity is important (as in simplifying agriculture and animal husbandry), but it also requires planned diversity.[10]

Skinner is critical of current civilisation, which appears as a gigantic enterprise of standardisation, under the disguise of individual freedom. Looking at cultural evolution in terms similar to biological evolution, he sees variety as the best "survival insurance".

Planned diversity, of course, does not mean programming each individual in detail, but arranging the conditions under which variety is favoured, as it has obviously been in some privileged periods of human history, notably in the field of arts, with emulation prevailing over competition, and the social context providing ample opportunities for art production at all levels of competence.

In culture as in biology, diversity is the condition of individuality. It is also, from the most elementary stages of living organisms, the universal rule. Strict reproduction of the same is the exception (although man has succeeded in producing it experimentally), but it has low, if any, survival value. As Skinner points out, uniformity can recommend itself in some situations, as in facilitating agriculture or animal husbandry. But genetic engineers wisely preserve the seeds of species not currently used, because they could save the world if current species, in use because of their present advantages, were to be victims of some future disaster.

Diversity as a deliberate cultural project has become all the more important in a world where people tend to be shaped in the same mould, because distances have been abolished, and because political or economic power has been progressively concentrated in the hands of one single cultural tradition. Until the twentieth century, cultural diversity was as conspicuous as biological diversity, and anthropologists could describe a large range of cultural patterns. They eventually succeeded in drawing attention to the interest of such variety and even to the concept of cultural relativism, but paradoxically at a time when variety was disappearing from the surface of earth and when cultural relativism had almost lost all but touristic relevance.

## THE TIME DIMENSION

Another major source of difficulty in the design of a culture that would meet the requirements of mankind's survival is the conflict between the individuals' immediate interest and the necessity to take into account, in any sound social project, long term consequences. Immediate reward seems more natural, and more efficient than delayed satisfaction. Clearly, the problems we are facing do not, in most cases, affect individuals immediately, perhaps not even during their lifetime. Although there is no problem in bringing behaviour, human or animal, under the control of immediate reinforcement, deferred reward is very much more difficult. Animal species are amenable to it only within very restricted time limits, and through a very systematic history of contingencies. Fortunately, humans have developed, with the use of language and symbolic representations in general, unprecedented capacities to evaluate rewards in such a way that deferred satisfaction will often be preferred to a more immediate one, provided that the former is valued more. Humans have learned to live with time perspectives that extend to their whole individual life and even to future generations. Many factors are involved that make for long term anticipation of human action, including compared benefits of both types (immediate *vs* delayed) of rewards, the strength of social approval or disapproval of both conducts, the probability that delayed reward will be obtained and will be enjoyed, etc. Religious and political ideologies have traditionally resorted to the threat of eternal punishment, or the promise of future happiness, to induce people to behave in certain ways for delayed satisfaction while renouncing immediate reward. In both cases, immediate punishment and threat have been added to ensure control. Heretics were condemned to eternal fire, but they were, to make things more certain, also subjected to immediate torture. Citizens of Stalin's Soviet Union were promised the triumph of the classless happy society, but were sent to the Gulag if they showed little zeal for taking their share of present effort. We know that humans tend to free themselves from such aversive controls, as recent history has showed once more. Religious and political controls of that sort have collapsed, and could have survived only by the blind use of force.

We cannot really hope to solve the world's problems today by resorting to the same practices, but we are left with the awfully difficult task of having humans act as a function of long term contingencies, when they have freed themselves in the recent past from many of the controls similarly aimed at far delayed consequences. The task is not easy in itself. It is complicated further by the fact that modern society, while praising in some contexts anticipation of the future— investing in various insurance schemes, for instance, or in education— encourages, in many respects, immediate satisfaction. Hire purchase has become general practice, providing for immediate possession of desired goods without calculating how to pay for them. Political action is essentially under the control of the next elections, producing a time perspective rarely extending beyond three or four years, when most important issues require long term anticipation and planning. It took years until alarms from ecologists were eventually taken seriously, and they are still given only lip-service by many politicians. There are few signs that we are really heading towards a society that will find its own present equilibrium—and its members their happiness—in functioning under the control of long-term contingencies. Skinner was aware that this is indeed one of the most crucial issues in the world today, and he insistently pointed to it; he might not have formulated fully satisfying practical solutions, but who will, given the prevailing factors now at work?

## COUNTERCONTROL

The solutions inevitably imply long-term planning, and the word planning in its turn implies some sort of control, by those who design plans over those who will be exposed to them. Who is going to control? Skinner has in no way suggested another form of totalitarianism. On the contrary, his analysis aims at outsmarting abuses of power by a lucid knowledge of behavioural processes. He has certainly never proposed that a new class of rulers, technocrats of behaviour, should take over political responsibilities. His cultural design has no place for a permanent caste of untouched specialists. He has only proposed that all policy, dealing with people by definition, should take into account what science tells us of human behaviour, instead of ignoring it or even going in the opposite direction, as is often the case.

Skinner warns us: while we are discussing who should control, or objecting to the idea of control, others do control, without deferring action, and they benefit from our procrastination. The choice is not between control and freedom, but between overt and covert control. Does that inevitably lead to despotism?

Let us recall that the social organisation of Walden Two guaranteed harmonious functioning independently of the personality of the founder, or of the managers at any time. Life-long careers in managing responsibility have been widely ruled out by limiting time in office; individual abuse of power has been avoided by giving all decision agencies a collegial structure and by eliminating all possibilities of personal profit from holding public office. These are elementary measures of countercontrol.

This is, indeed, the core of Skinner's social philosophy. Making the controls at work explicit is the prerequisite to any social organisation if it is to correct itself and exert countercontrol:

> The designer of a culture comes under fire because explicit design implies control (if only the control exerted by the designer). The issue is often formulated by asking: Who is to control? And the question is usually raised as if the answer were necessarily threatening. To prevent the misuse of controlling power, however, we must look not at the controller himself but at the contingencies under which he engages in control.[11]

> The great problem is to arrange effective countercontrol and hence to bring some important consequences to bear on the behavior of the controller.[12]

> All control is reciprocal, and an interchange between control and countercontrol is essential to the evolution of a culture.[13]

> Attacking controlling practices is, of course, a form of countercontrol. It may have immeasurable benefits if better controlling practices are thereby selected. But the literature of freedom and dignity have made the mistake of supposing that they are suppressing control rather than correcting it. The reciprocal control through which a culture evolves is then disturbed. To refuse to exercise available control because in some sense all control is wrong is to withhold possibly important forms of countercontrol. We have seen some of the consequences. Punitive measures, which the literature of freedom and dignity have otherwise helped to eliminate, are instead promoted. A preference for methods which make control inconspicuous or allow it to be disguised has condemned those who are in a position to exert positive countercontrol to the use of weak measures. This could be a lethal cultural mutation.[14]

History offers many examples of mechanisms and agents of countercontrol. Confronted with power based on aversive methods, countercontrol itself often takes on aversive characteristics, in insurrection, violent strike, or fraud. These threaten power, and eventually succeed in limiting it, but they usually contribute overall to maintaining its repressive techniques. In parliamentary regimes, opposition plays a more positive role in countercontrol. Freedom of the press, or generally of expression and information, has a function of countercontrol each time it unveils abuse of power. Consumers associations, when boycotting a product, exert countercontrol on unscrupulous producers. In a more subtle way, pupils exert countercontrol over their teachers, the latter (ideally) adjusting their methods if the former do not understand what they have to learn. The laboratory rat similarly shapes the behaviour of its experimenter! Such reciprocal regulation is possible only if the actions of the controllers continue to depend on the consequences they produce in the controllees. If teaching depends more on a centralised organising agency, itself remote from daily school life and with no direct contact with pupils, the latter will lose all countercontrol influence:

> Control and countercontrol tend to become dislocated when control is taken over by organized agencies. Informal contingencies are subject to quick adjustments as their effects change, but the contingencies which organizations leave to specialists may be untouched by many of the consequences.[15]

Some categories of people completely lack any means of countercontrol. Social measures supposedly in their favour may very well go for a long time in an aberrant direction without any correction. Countercontrol can only come from a third party:

> Some classical examples of a lack of balance between control and countercontrol arise when control is delegated and countercontrol then becomes ineffective. Hospitals for psychotics and homes for retardates, orphans, and old people are noted for weak countercontrol, because those who are concerned for the welfare of such people often do not know what is happening.[16]

A government exclusively based on positive methods would have no reason to fear that its methods of control might be discovered: on the contrary it would benefit from disclosing them. In its turn, overtness of controls is a condition for countercontrol. Countercontrol implies on the one hand that the actions of those in government remain as closely as possible under the control of the consequences they have in the people controlled. Political responsibility is no virtue; it derives from adequate arrangement of the relations between those who govern and those who are governed. The search for such an arrangement appears to be central in the current crises observed in Western nations. Skinner suggests that it will be reached only if those in power stop entertaining the citizens of their illusion of freedom, and if citizens stop sacrificing to that illusion the real control of their lives.

## EXPERIMENTAL POLITICS

After this admittedly very sketchy presentation of Skinner's views on social reality, or social Utopia, how can we conclude? I hope that those who knew Skinner only second-hand will have discovered an approach to human affairs quite different from the image conveyed by detractors like those quoted in Chapter 1. Misrepresentations have been especially numerous and distorting with respect to Skinner's socio-philosophical writings. Perhaps the critics were sometimes sincere, and misunderstood mainly because of a lack of preparation. One of them complained about the use of the expression "contingencies of reinforcement" in *Beyond freedom and dignity*. This is like complaining about the use of the term "relativity" in a physicist's essay, or "selection" in a biologist's popularised book. Others might have been biased by incorrect presentation of Skinner's scientific thinking gathered from psychology handbooks, and they should not be blamed for taking for granted what authorities in the field have written about Skinner. However, the true reasons why Skinner's political ideas raised such violent opposition are to be looked for in another direction. It is simply that they are disturbing to all existing ideologies or practices. In fact, none of the political schemes now in power (or in power at the time he wrote *Walden Two* or *Beyond freedom and dignity*), or current candidates to power, escapes his critique. His criticisms disturb those who hold control, as well as those who seek it, or those who like to think they are not controlled, but free. All this is an emotional reaction, and should not blur the main issue.

A question must, however, be raised: are Skinner's views scientifically based, as he claims? If so, is the scientific basis a serious one? And if this is the case, does it necessarily and legitimately lead to that conception?

There is no question that the data, methods, and concepts referred to by Skinner are part of the domain of science, as opposed to religion, art, or magic. Data can be verified or rejected, methods improved or changed, concepts elaborated or abandoned, as the result of normal scientific activity, and of course without respect to what Skinner himself thought. Whatever the importance of individual contributions, science is depersonalised, and its progress is not directly linked to respect for those who made it. Skinner referred to serious science, which does not mean, of course definitive or complete science, simply because there is no such thing as definitive and complete science. Scientific work is always an approximation, and scientists know that what they discover is nothing but the next approximation, or errors eventually corrected. Is the serious scientific basis, in this case, sufficient to found the practical conclusions that Skinner draws from it? Do the socio-political ideas legitimately, if not necessarily, derive from empirical data and theoretical concepts?

This is not an easy question, because it amounts to nothing less than a judgement on the validity of a proposal for scientific application in a specific case. The only convincing validation would of course consist in trying, but one would like to have validation before a trial. Any scientific application involves risk, as compared with its experimental reference, because it always takes place in a context that has not been, and cannot be, purified of all factors that are eliminated in the laboratory. An estimation of risk is of course crucial, but risks must be taken, if action is to be carried out. It sounds reasonable to defer application if the distance between basic knowledge and application appears too large. One might think this is the case with Skinner's project; one might argue that, whatever his sincerity and goodwill in helping mankind, his scientific foundations are too fragmentary, too restricted to laboratory animals, and too little integrated in knowledge from other sources to legitimise applications. One might like to suggest that they should first be consolidated, that they should be made convergent with other trends of human sciences, so that a more general theory might eventually emerge that would authorise extrapolation to human culture. There is little to object to in such a prudent position, both modest and respectful. But it could contain more risk, in fact, than the opposite view. For some situations cannot be solved if one does not take the risk of interfering with whatever limited information is available. Perhaps the probabilities for success are rather limited, but the certainty of disaster is total if nothing is done.

To those who choose to defer action, one must ask the question: at which point, at what level of information, will you feel it convenient to put to work scientific knowledge about behaviour in human affairs? Should students of behaviour pursue their basic research indefinitely, and see what happens? In the meantime, problems will have become worse, and the world will have continued to change under the influence of other sciences that do not have the same concern for the misuse of their technologies. Modern medicine progressed by small steps, reducing infection by trivial hygiene habits long before antibiotics were discovered. Should one have waited for Fleming before advising surgeons, obstetricians, and nurses to wash their hands?

For others, the decision not to engage in applications of psychology to human affairs is not temporary, it is definitive. They contend that the distance between scientific knowledge and the complexity of social life will never be bridged. Science can observe, describe, maybe explain, but nothing more: human history escapes all prediction or control, including scientifically based control. This contemplative position is widespread among psychologists today. It has multiple origins, which I shall not comment on here. Suffice it to point to one of its consequences. It feeds a trend that has gained some strength in the last few years, which is opposed to the scientific adventure and more generally to human attempts towards rationality. Along those lines, the objection to applying scientific knowledge to social life is not that our current knowledge is insufficient, but that scientific knowledge is dangerous (and the more developed it is, the more dangerous).

No one would deny that progress in science has indirectly brought a number of unforeseen (although not always unforeseeable) difficulties. But there is no indication that they will be solved by turning our back on science. Science could also be the only way out. In any case, science has played a minor role in the conduct of human affairs. Should we be satisfied with that state of affairs? Should we "carry on, as we have in the past, with what we have learned from personal experience or from those collections of personal experiences called history, or with the distillations of experience to be found in folk wisdom and practical rules of thumb? These have been available for centuries, and all we have to show for them is the state of the world today".[17]

Skinner does not hesitate between choosing science or refraining from any application of it, as expressed in the following text, that is altogether a reply to the accusation of oversimplifying:

> The interpretation of the complex world of human affairs in terms of an experimental analysis is no doubt often oversimplified. Claims have been exaggerated and limitations neglected. But the really great oversimplification is the traditional appeal to states of mind, feelings, and other aspects of the autonomous man which a behavior analysis is replacing. The ease with which mentalistic explanations can be invented on the spot is perhaps the best gauge of how little attention we should pay to them. And the same may be said for traditional practices. The technology which has emerged from an experimental analysis should be evaluated only in comparison with what is done in other ways. What, after all, have we to show for nonscientific or prescientific good judgment, or common sense, or the insights gained through personal experience? It is science or nothing, and the only solution to simplification is to learn how to deal with complexities.
>
> A science of behavior is not yet ready to solve all our problems, but it is a science in progress, and its ultimate adequacy cannot now be judged. When critics assert that it cannot account for this and that aspect of human behavior, they usually imply that it will never be able to do so, but the analysis continues to develop and is in fact much further advanced then its critics usually realize. The important thing is not so much to know how to solve a problem as to know how to look for a solution. The scientists who approached President Roosevelt with a proposal to build a bomb so powerful that it could end the Second World War within a few days could not say that they knew how to build it. All they could say was that they knew how to go about finding out. The behavioral problems to be solved in the world today are no doubt more complex than the practical use of nuclear fission, and the basic science by no means as far advanced, but we know where to start looking for solutions.[18]

Let us now suppose that the scientific basis claimed by Skinner lacks seriousness, or that, at best, it does not authorise, in any reasonable sense, the conceptions of humankind and society he drew from it. How should we, in that case, evaluate his socio-philosophical writings? A number of Skinner's critics have proposed to see them as pieces of a pseudo-scientific argumentation in favour of the establishment. This interpretation is difficult to uphold after reading the texts honestly. How many Americans, especially in the intelligentsia, shortly after the Second World War, would have ventured to question their political system and their society as Skinner did in *Walden Two?* What political party would take the risk of proposing to its members a reflection on *Beyond freedom and dignity* without exposing itself to unbearable internal criticism? We have found no more grounds for the opposite accusation of corrupting the basic values of American society—remember Spiro Agnew's judgement quoted in Chapter 1. The reasons why Skinner's views have been so strongly attacked, or so obstinately ignored, are to be found in the fact that they do not easily fall into usual political and ideological categories.

Skinner's social philosophy was, in his own view, anchored in scientific knowledge, with all the relativism implied. As such, it was argued very strictly in the frame of the psychological theory he had developed, and altogether presented as tentative, subject to revision, as is any scientifically based endeavour. It was also the answer to an anxiety born from observing our society, affluent as it is, but unable to cope with major problems, although they have been clearly identified. Skinner was not naïve enough to believe that his ideas could ever be implemented completely in real life. He did hope, however, that humans would be wise enough, in a time when science is apparently so much revered, to apply part of his message. He would have been happy at least with some experimental tests, in real life, of some of his suggestions. One of his last papers revealed, instead, disenchantment. We can only repeat the question he used as a title: Why are we not working to save the world?

## NOTES

1. *A matter of consequences*, pp.310–311.
2. The paper has been reprinted in *Reflections on behaviorism and society*, Chapter 18.
3. *Beyond freedom and dignity*, p.77.
4. Ibidem, pp.76–77.
5. Ibidem, p.84.
6. The original UNESCO statement is: "Wars begin in the minds of men". Skinner has commented with an elaboration on that text phrased as follows: ". . . hence it is in the minds of men that the defense of peace must be constructed", pointing to the fact that wars have many identifiable causes, that could be changed more easily than the minds of men, plausibly shaped after those conditions. See *Reflections on behaviorism and society*, p.91.
7. *Beyond freedom and dignity*, pp.91–92.
8. *About behaviorism*, p.209 (see note 8, Chapter 7).
9. See the quotation from the then Vice-President of the USA in Chapter 1.
10. *Beyond freedom and dignity*, p.162.
11. Ibidem, p.168.
12. Ibidem, p.171.
13. Ibidem, p.182.
14. Ibidem, p.181.
15. Ibidem, p.171.
16. Ibidem, p.171.
17. Ibidem, p.4.
18. Ibidem, pp.160–161.

# 16 Conclusion

The present book is intended as an introduction to Skinner's work. It is now time for readers to explore the rich production of the last behaviourist, as some insist on calling him. I hope that the simplistic representations of Skinner's contributions to psychology, that have been the rule in many circles for some years, will give place to a more balanced evaluation. The argument, throughout the preceding chapters, has been abundantly illustrated by quotations from Skinner's writings, which convey rigorous and subtle thought, often provocative, and, when it comes to social matters, straightforwardly generous. This is, of course, in contrast to depreciating statements by influential critics characterising Skinner's prose as void of scientific substance, obsolete, or socially dangerous. There is nothing to be gained in condemning with such crude judgements a scientist whose place in the history of psychology cannot be denied. If he was wrong (and in a way no one in science would claim to be completely, or definitively, right) this can be discussed only by examining closely what he wrote and did. I hope the reader is now better prepared to undertake an unbiased analysis of what Skinner had in mind, and disclosed in his overt verbal behaviour.

I feel it most important that psychologists, especially young psychologists, put their current work in perspective and develop awareness of the historical roots of their field. All too often, as I have pointed out earlier, psychologists are inclined to regard the present as an exceptional epoch of evolutionary breakthrough. Perhaps psychologists of all generations had the same feeling, disciples of Skinner being no exception. No doubt, current psychology is exciting, and I would certainly not discourage those who are in that fascinating science from enjoying it. However, this should not prevent them, be it only for the sake of scientific accuracy, from correctly appraising their links with the past.

221

With respect to Skinner, this means taking his contribution for what is has been—that is, one important step in the building of modern psychology, rather than an obstacle to its development.

As a member of the behaviourist movement, Skinner participated in the methodological austerity that made for later re-examination of issues which introspective psychology, at the turn of the century, had led into blind alleys. As the main representative of radical behaviourism, who elaborated to their extreme logical consequences the basic behaviourist tenets, he could be credited with having presented to his opponents' criticisms clearcut positions against which to argue, and on which they could perhaps build and polish their own counter-theory. Their self-confidence and their enthusiasm should not hide the fact, however, that many of the issues to which Skinner has devoted his theoretical and methodological writings, are by no means definitely solved by contemporary trends that have adopted an opposite stand. The status of mental events, of purpose and intentionality, of the relations between brain, behaviour, and mind, has not been elucidated once and for all: these and many other questions are still with us, and are likely to be for some time, even if, admittedly, some progress has been made in dealing with them technically. Skinner's formulations remain good and tough material for those who prefer in-depth treatment of difficult issues to self-satisfied assertion of their own beliefs.

As an outstanding experimenter, Skinner has provided the psychological laboratory with unprecedented multiple-purpose procedures, and was a pioneer in automating experimental control, long before personal computers became the popular gadget they are now. In so far as technical advances play a crucial part in the progress of a science, and in so far as the "Skinner Box" has penetrated laboratories in a variety of behavioural and biological specialities, the present state of behavioural studies owes something to Skinner.

Although one could have extended the exercise further to other scientists and to other schools of thought, the parallel we have drawn with Pavlov, Freud, Piaget, and Lorenz has shed some light on the relations between Skinner's work and some of the major trends of European psychology in this century. Commentaries on Skinner's conceptions have, as a rule, too narrowly confined him within the behaviourist constellation, with little attention to his singularities compared with other behaviourists, and complete neglect of overt or hidden convergences with other traditions. We have met a thinker less close to Pavlov than is usually thought; an admirer of Freud although radically critical of some of the psychoanalyst's views; surprisingly convergent with Piaget in what could be called their interactionist selectionism; quite open to Lorenz' objections to his own account of behaviour. Although in a sense Skinner followed his line with systematic obstinacy, he continued to scrutinise territories of knowledge that others were exploring at the same time, albeit from a different angle. Instead of the left-behind thinker depicted by some of his opponents, we have met a forerunner whose fault, on some issues, has been to be ahead of his time. This is especially true of his contribution to the study of verbal behaviour, which, paradoxically, has been most violently attacked as irrelevant or obsolete, and was thus indirectly one cause of his disrepute.

Having made this balance, one might ask to what extent Skinner's contributions to psychology will survive. No one, of course, can predict this. If we adopt a cumulative view of science, rather than seeing it as a succession of destructive revolutions, we can be sure that his technical contributions will remain part of the psychologists' methodological tools. We would also expect adequate historical recognition of his theoretical contribution to the progress of psychological science, after the triumphalism of some contemporary schools of thought has calmed down. Whether psychologists of the future will return to some of the tenets of Skinner's theory as a source of inspiration—as Chomsky appealed to the grammarians of Port-Royal, or Fodor to Gall—is another question; the answer will depend, among other things, on the evolution of the current debates in cognitive and neurosciences, and more specifically on the resolution of persisting contradictions within the mind-brain issue.

The future of Skinner's social philosophy is another matter. Although his major books in that vein were for some time best-sellers, and as such produced vivid discussions, mainly in newspapers and magazines, they never really gained the attention of specialists in political, social, and economic science. Nor have they been taken, at least overtly, as sources of inspiration by active politicians. In the view of many, this is the fate they deserve. Reading them honestly and carefully, our feeling has been quite different, and we hope the reader will share, if not Skinner's ideas, our curiosity for what they actually are. Admittedly, the problems of the world today are just too complex to expect their solution to lie in some hundred pages written by a psychologist. But the blatant inadequacy of actions taken and of solutions proposed invites us, more than ever, to look at them in a fresh, different manner. In that quest, Skinner's approach is still worth exploring. We shall not resume the presentation we have made of *Walden Two, Beyond freedom and dignity* and other writings in the last chapters of this book. Suffice it to pinpoint one important aspect of Skinner's message, which is methodological rather than ideological: if we really want to solve social problems, we should look at the problems themselves, not, as politicians do in our modern societies, at the part of power they can gain or lose by taking a given stand. Democracy, if it is to survive, should engage in more rational—shall we say experimental?—approaches to the problems it faces, it should become definitely problem-centred, not party- or personality-centred. This would certainly simplify the task. After all, a scientist's view of the world essentially aims at making things simpler, so that we can understand them better, and act on them more efficiently. This can help, sometimes.

Let us leave the last words to Skinner. The first quotation is from his paper on *Walden Two revisited*, and it emphasises once more the concern for the future of generations to come. The second one is from a paper entitled *Human behavior and democracy* and is about countercontrol, which we all know is the central issue today in our democracies.

> It is now widely recognized that greater changes must be made in [our] way of life. Not only can we not face the rest of the world while consuming and polluting as we do, we cannot for long face ourselves while acknowledging the violence and chaos in which we live. The choice is clear: either we do nothing and allow a miserable and probably catastrophic future to overtake us, or we use our knowledge about human behavior to create a social environment in which we shall live productive and creative lives and do so without jeopardizing the chances that those who follow us will be able to do the same.[1]

> There will no doubt continue to be governmental and economic agencies, organizations, and institutions, for they have their proper functions, but they should not be given an exclusive franchise. A social environment functions most successfully for the individual, the group, and the species if, so far as possible, people directly control people.[2]

## NOTES

1. From *Reflections on behaviorism and society* (1978), p.66. Reprinted from a preface to a new printing of *Walden Two* (Macmillan, New York, 1976). The word between brackets has been substituted for "the American".
2. Ibidem, p.15. Reprinted from *Psychology Today*, (September 1977).

# References

Austin, J.L. (1962). *How to do things with words*. Oxford: Oxford University Press.

Ayllon, T. & Azrin, N.H. (1968). *The token economy*. New York: Appleton Century Crofts.

Bates, E. (1976). *Language and context: Studies in the acquisition of pragmatics*. New York: Academic Press.

Blackman, D.E. & Lejeune, H. (Eds.) (1990). *Behaviour analysis in theory and practice: Contributions and controversies*. Hove, UK: Lawrence Erlbaum Associates Ltd.

Botson, C. & Deliège, M. (1975). *Le développement intellectuel de l'enfant. II. Une méthode d'approche: les apprentissages sans erreurs*. Brussels: Ministère de l'Education nationale.

Boulanger, B. (1990). *La variabilité comportementale. Une approche développementale chez l'humain*. Unpublished doctoral thesis, Liège.

Boulanger, B., Ingebos, A.-M., Lahak, M., Machado, A., & Richelle, M. (1987). Variabilité comportementale et conditionnement operant chez l'animal. *L'Année Psychologique, 87*, 417–434.

Breland, K. & Breland, M. (1961). The misbehavior of organisms. *American Psychologist, 61*, 681–684.

Breland, K. & Breland, M. (1966). *Animal behavior*. New York: Macmillan.

Bronckart, J.P. (1976). *Genèse et organisation des formes verbales chez l'enfant*. Brussels: Dessart-Mardaga.

Bunge, M. (1980). *The mind-body problem*. Oxford: Pergamon.

Catania, A.C. & Harnad, S. (1988). *The selection of behavior. The operant behaviorism of B.F. Skinner: Comments and consequences*. Cambridge: University Press.

Changeux, J.P. (1983). *L'Homme neuronal* [The neuronal man]. Paris: Fayard.

Chomsky, N. (1957). *Syntactic structures*. La Haye: Mouton.

Chomsky, N. (1959). Review of Skinner, B.F., Verbal behavior. *Language, 4*, 16–49.

Chomsky, N. (1972). Psychology and ideology. *Cognition, 1*, 1–46.

Chomsky, N. & Miller, G. (1963). Introduction to the formal analysis of natural languages. In R.P. Luce, R.R. Bush, & E. Galanter (Eds.) *Handbook of mathematical psychology*, pp.269–321. New York: Wiley.

Colpaert, F.C. & Slangen, J.L. (Eds) (1982). *Drug discrimination: Applications in CNS Pharmacology*. Amsterdam: Elsevier.

Dennis, W., Skinner, B.F., Sears, R.R., Kelly, E.L., Rogers, C., Flanagan, J.C., Morgan, C.T., & Likert, R. (1947). *Current trends in psychology*. Pittsburgh, PA: University of Pittsburgh Press.

Dews, P.B. (Ed.) (1970). *Festschrift for B.F. Skinner*. New York: Appleton Century Crofts.

Dickinson, A. (1980). *Contemporary animal learning theory*, London: Cambridge University Press.

Dollard, J. & Miller, N.E. (1950). *Personality and psychotherapy: An analysis in terms of learning, thinking, and culture*. New York: McGraw-Hill.

Dollard, J., Doob, L.W., Miller, N.E., & Sears, R.R. (1939). *Frustration and aggression*. New Haven: Yale University Press.

Donders, F.C. (1969). On the speed of mental processes. *Acta Psychologica, 30*, 412–431.

Eccles, J.C. (1979). *The human mystery*. Berlin: Springer.

Edelman, G.M. (1987). *Neural Darwinism: The theory of neuronal group selection*. New York: Basic Books.

Ferster, C. & Skinner, B.F. (1957). *Schedules of reinforcement*, p.741. New York: Appleton Century Crofts.

Fodor, J.A. (1983). *The modularity of mind*. Cambridge, MA: MIT/Bradford Press.

Freud, S. (1930). *Civilisation and its discontent*. London: Hogarth.

Gardner, H. (1985). *The mind's new science*. New York: Basic Books.

Gibbon, J. & Allan, L. (Eds.) (1984). *Timing and time perception*. New York: The New York Academy of Sciences.

Glennon, R.A. Järbe, T.U.C., & Frankenheim, J.F. (Eds) (1991). *Drug Discrimination: Applications to drug abuse research*. Rockville, MD: National Institute on Drug Abuse.

Goethe, von, J.W. (1971). *Faust 1* (P. Wayne, Trans.). Harmondsworth: Penguin. (Original work published (1808). Tübingen: J.C. Cotta.

Gray, J.A. (1975). *Elements of a two-process theory of learning*. New York: Academic Press.

Halliday, M.A.K. (1973). *Explorations in the functions of language*. London: E. Arnold.

Halliday, M.A.K. (1975). *Learning how to mean: Explorations in the development of language*. London: E. Arnold.

Harlow, H.F. (1959). The development of learning in the rhesus monkey. *American Scientist, 47*, 459–479.

Hebb, D.O. (1949). *The Organisation of Behavior*. New York: Wiley.

Herrnstein, R.J. (1977a). The evolution of behaviorism. *American Psychologist, 32*, 593–603.

Herrnstein, R.J. (1977b). Doing what comes naturally. A reply to Professor Skinner. *American Psychologist, 32*, 1013–1016.

Hinde, R.A. & Stevenson-Hinde, J. (Eds.) (1973). *Constraints on learning*. New York: Academic Press.

Hirschhorn, I.D. (1978). Stimulus properties of narcotic analgesics. In B.T. Ho, D.W. Richards III, & D.L. Chute (Eds.) *Drug discrimination and state dependent learning*, pp.163–174. New York: Academic Press.

Holland, J.G. & Skinner, B.F. (1961). *The analysis of behavior*. New York: McGraw-Hill.

Hollard, V.D. & Delius, J.D. (1982). Rotational invariance in visual pattern recognition by pigeons and humans. *Science*, *218*, 804–806.

Hull, C.L. (1943). *Principles of behavior*. New York: Appleton Century Crofts.

Hunt, E. (1984). A case study of how a paper containing good ideas, presented by a distinguished scientist, to an appropriate audience, had almost no influence at all. *Behavioral and Brain Sciences*, *7*, 597–598.

Illich, I. (1970). *Deschooling society*. New York: Harper & Row.

Inhelder, B., Sinclair, H., & Bovet, M. (1974.) *Apprentissage et structures de la connaissance*. Paris: Presses Universitaires de France.

Kazdin, A.E. (1978). *History of behavior modification: Experimental foundations of contemporary research*. Baltimore: University Park Press.

Kruse, H.D. (Ed.) (1957) *Integrating the approaches to mental disease*. New York: Paul B. Boeder.

Laurent, E. (1976). Review of Boston, C. & Deliège, M. (1975). *Le développement intellectuel de l'Enfant. II. Une Méthode d'approche*. Brussels: Ministère de l'Education Nationale. Le Monde de l'Education, Sept. 1976, Paris.

Le Ny, J.F. (1985). European roots and behaviourism and recent developments. In C.F. Lowe, M. Richelle, D.E. Blackman, & C.M. Bradshaw (Eds.) *Behaviour analysis and contemporary psychology*, pp.13–32. London: Lawrence Erlbaum Associates Ltd.

Lorenz, K. (1965). *Evolution and modification of behavior*. Chicago: University of Chicago Press.

Lorenz, K. (1966). *On aggression*. London: Methuen.

Lorenz, K. (1973). *Les huits péchés capitaux de la civilisation* [The eight capital sins of civilisation]. Paris: Flammarion.

Lorenz, K. (1981). *Fundamentals of ethology*. New York: Springer.

Lowe, C.F., Richelle, M., Blackman, D.E., & Bradshaw, C.M. (Eds.) (1985). *Behaviour analysis and contemporary psychology*. London: Lawrence Erlbaum Associates Ltd.

Luria, A.R. (1969). The origin and cerebral organisation of man's conscious action. *Conférence au XIXème Congrès International de Psychologie*, London.

Macar, F., Pouthas, V., & Friedman, W. (Eds.) (1992). *Time, action and cognition*. Basle: Kluwer.

Maurissen, J.P.J. (1979). Effects of toxicants on the somatosensory system. *Neurobehavioral Toxicology*, *1*, (Suppl. 1), 23–31.

Mehler, J. (Ed.) (1969). *Psycholinguistique et grammaire générative*. N° de la revue, *Langage*, *4*, 16. Paris: Didier Larousse.

Mehler, J. & Dupoux, E. (1990). *Naître humain*. Paris: Odile Jacob.

Michon, J.A. & Jackson, J.L. (Eds.) (1985). *Time, mind and behavior*. Berlin: Springer-Verlag.

Miller, G.A (1951). *Language and communication*. New York: McGraw Hill.

Miller, G.A. & Chomsky, N. (1963). Finitary models of language users. In R.P. Luce, R.R. Bush, & E. Galanter (Eds.) *Handbook of mathematical psychology. Vol. II*, pp.419–491. New York: Wiley.

Miller, S. & Konorski, J. (1928). Sur une forme particulière des réflexes conditionnels. *Compte-rendus ds séances de la société de biologie. Société polonaise de biologie*, *99*, 1155.

Modgil, S. & Modgil, C. (Eds.) (1987). *B.F. Skinner: Consensus and controversy*. New York/London: Falmer Press.

Moerk, E.L. (1977). *Pragmatic and semantic aspects of early language development.* Baltimore: University Park Press.

Moreau, M.L. & Richelle, M. (1981). *L'acquisition du language.* Brussels: Mardaga.

Olds, J. & Milner, P.M. (1954). Positive reinforcement produced by electrical stimulation of septal area and other regions of rat brain. *Journal of Comparative and Physiological Psychology, 47,* 419–427.

Pavlov, I.P. (1927). *Conditioned reflexes: An investigation of the physiological activity of the cerebral cortex.* London: Oxford University Press.

Pavlov. I.P. (1954). *Oeuvres choisies.* Moscow: Editions en Langues Etrangères.

Perelman, V. & Olbrechts-Tyteca, L. (1958). *Traité de l'argumentation.* Paris: Presses Universitaires de France.

Piaget, J. (1967). *Biologie et connaissance: Essai sur les relations entre les régulations organiques et les processus cognitifs.* Paris: Gallimard.

Piaget, J. (1968). *Le structuralisme.* Paris: Presses Universtaires de France.

Piaget, J. (1974). *Adaptation vitale et psychologie de l'intelligence.* Paris: Herman.

Piaget, J. (1976). *Le comportement, moteur de l'évolution.* Paris: Gallimard.

Piattelli-Palmarini, M. (Ed.) (1980). *Language and learning.* Cambridge, MA: Harvard University Press.

Pickens, R. & Thompson, T. (1968). Cocaine-reinforced behavior in rats: Effects of reinforcement magnitude and fixed-ratio size. *Journal of Pharmacology and Experimental Therapeutics, 161,* 122–129.

Piéron, H. (1908). L'évolution du psychisme. *Revue du Mois, 3,* 291–310.

Plotkin, H. (Ed.) (1982). *Learning, development, and culture: Essays in evolutionary epistemology.* New York: Wiley.

Plotkin, H. (1987). The evolutionary analogy in Skinner's writings. In S. Modgil & C. Modgil (Eds.) *B.F. Skinner: Consensus and controversy,* pp.139–149. New York: Falmer Press.

Plotkin, H. & Odling-Smee, F.J. (1981). A multiple-level model of evolution and its implications for sociobiology. *Behavioral and Brain Sciences, 4,* 225–268.

Popper, K.R. (1972). *Objective knowledge: An evolutionary approach.* Oxford: Oxford University Press.

Popper, K.R. (1978). *La logique de la découverte scientifique.* Paris: Payot.

Popper, K.R. & Eccles, J.C. (1977). *The self and its brain.* London: Springer.

Proctor, R.W. & Weeks, D.J. (1990). *The goal of B.F. Skinner and behavior analysis.* New York/Heidelberg: Springer.

Richelle, M. (1971). *L'acquisition du langage.* Brussels: Dessart-Mardaga.

Richelle, M. (1974a). Le behaviorisme aujourd'hui. I. Méthodes de conditionnement et théorie du comportement. *Psychologica Belgica, 14,* 127–143.

Richelle, M. (1974b). Le behaviorisme aujourd'hui. II. Réflexions sur le behaviorisme contemporain. *Psychologica Belgica, 14,* 283–296.

Richelle, M. (1976a). Constructivisme et behaviorisme. *Revue Européenne des Sciences Sociales, 19,* 291–303.

Richelle, M. (1976b). Formal analysis and functional analysis of verbal behavior: Notes on the debate between Chomsky and Skinner. *Behaviorism, 4,* 209–221.

Richelle, M. (1976c). A propos d'apprentissage. *Bulletin de Psychologie, 30,* 341–435.

Richelle, M. (1977a). Errorless training as a method in the study of cognitive development. *Activitas Nervosa Superior, 19,* 4–5.

Richelle, M. (1977b). *B.F. Skinner ou le péril behavioriste*. Brussels: Mardaga.

Richelle, M. (1979). Psychologie et formation de l'homme. In J. Starobinski (Ed.) *Former l'homme?* pp.140–162. Neuchâtel: La Baconnière.

Richelle, M. (1982). Théories comportementales: nouveaux développements. In P. Pichot & B. Samuel-Lajuenesse (Eds.) *Nouvelles tendances en psychothérapie*, pp.125–139. Paris: Masson.

Richelle, M. (1984). Are Skinner's warnings still relevant to current psychology? Commentary on B.F. Skinner, Methods and theories in the experimental analysis on behavior. *Behavioral and Brain Sciences, 7*, 531–532.

Richelle, M. (1985). Behaviour analysis and contemporary psychology. In C.F. Lowe, M. Richelle, D.E. Blackman, & C.M. Bradshaw (Eds.) *Behaviour analysis and contemporary psychology*, pp.3–11. London: Lawrence Erlbaum Associates Ltd.

Richelle, M. (1986a). Introduction: on some varieties of cognitivisms. In P. Eelen & O. Fontaine (Eds.) *Behavior therapy: Beyond the conditioning framework*, pp.13–21. Hillsdale, NJ/Leuven: Lawrence Erlbaum Associates Inc./Leuven University Press.

Richelle, M. (1986b). Apprentissage et enseignement: Réflexion sur une complémentarité. In M. Crahay & D. Lafontaine (Eds.) *L'art et la science de l'enseignement—Hommage à G. De Landsheere*, pp.233–249. Paris/Brussels: Labor/Nathan.

Richelle, M. (1987a). Variation and selection: the evolutionary analogy in Skinner's theory. In S. Modgil & C. Modgil (Eds.) *B.F. Skinner: Consensus and controversy* pp.127–137. New York/London : Falmer Press.

Richelle, M. (1987b). Les cognitivismes: Progrès, régression ou suicide de la psychologie? In M. Siguan (Ed.) *Comportement, cognition, conscience*, pp.181–199. Paris: Presses Universitaires de France.

Richelle, M. (1988). On Skinner's disenchantment. *Counselling Psychology Quarterly, 1*, 317–320.

Richelle, M. (1990). The mental illness concept from the learning theory point of view. In C. Simhandl, P. Berner, H. Luccioni & C. Alf (Eds.) *Klassifikations-probleme in der Psychiatrie*, pp.70–81. Vienna, Berlin: Ueberreuter Wissenschaft.

Richelle, M. (1991). Reconciling views on intelligence? In H.A.H. Rowe (Ed.) *Intelligence, reconceptualization and measurement*, pp.19–33. Hillsdale, NJ: Lawrence Erlbaum Associates Inc.

Richelle, M. (1992). La analogia evolucionista en el pensamiento de B.F. Skinner. In J. Roales-Nieto, M. Luciano Soriano, and M. Pérez Alvarez (Eds.) *Vigencia de la obra de Skinner* pp.115–124. Granada: Universidad de Granada.

Richelle, M. (1993) *Du nouveau sur l'esprit?* Paris: Presses Universitaires de France.

Richelle, M. & Fontaine, O. (1986). Du comportementalisme au cognitivisme. *Confrontations Psychiatriques, 26*, 291–309.

Richelle, M. & Lejeune, H. (1980). *Time in animal behaviour*. Oxford: Pergamon.

Richelle, M. & Lejeune, H. (1984). Timing competence and timing performance : a comparative approach. In J. Gibbon & L. Allan (Eds.) *Timing and time perception*, pp.254–268. New York: New York Academy of Sciences.

Richelle, M. & Ruwet, J.C. (Eds.) (1972). *Problèmes de méthodes en psychologie comparée*. Paris: Masson.

Roales-Nieto, J., Luciano Soriano, M. & Pérez Alvarez, M. (1992). *Vigencia de la obra de Skinner*. Granada: Universidad de Granada.

Saussure, F. de (1916). *Cours de linguistique générale*. Paris: Payot.

Schorr, A. (1984). *Die Verhaltens-Therapie, Ihre Geschichte von den Anfangen bis zur Gegenwart.* Weinheim and Basle: Beltz Verlag.

Schwartz, B. (1973). *L'éducation demain.* Paris: Aubier-Montaigne.

Seligman, M.E.P. & Hager, J.L. (Eds.) (1972). *Biological boundaries on learning.* New York: Appleton Century Crofts.

Shephard, R.N. & Cooper, L.A. (1982). *Mental images and their transformations.* Cambridge, MA: MIT Press.

Sinclair-DeZwart, H. (1967). *Acquisition du langage et développement de la pensée.* Paris: Dunod.

Skinner, B.F. (1931). The concept of the reflex in the description of behavior. *The Journal of General Psychology, 5*, 427–458.

Skinner, B.F. (1938). *The behavior of organisms : An experimental analysis.* New York: Appleton Century Crofts.

Skinner, B.F. (1944). A review of Hull's principles of behavior. *The American Journal of Psychology, 57*, 276–281.

Skinner, B.F. (1945). The operational analysis of psychological terms. *Psychological Review, 52*, 270–277.

Skinner, B.F. (1947). Experimental psychology. In W. Dennis et al. *Current trends in psychology,* pp.16–49. Pittsburgh, PA: University of Pittsburgh Press.

Skinner, B.F. (1948). *Walden Two.* New York : The Macmillan Company.

Skinner, B.F. (1953). *Science and human behavior.* New York: The Macmillan Company.

Skinner, B.F. (1957). *Verbal behavior.* New York: Appleton Century Crofts.

Skinner, B.F. (1963). Behaviorism at fifty. *Science, 140*, 951–958.

Skinner, B.F. (1966). The phylogeny and ontogeny of behavior. *Science, 153*, 1205–1213.

Skinner, B.F. (1968). *The technology of teaching.* New York: Appleton Century Crofts.

Skinner, B.F. (1969a). *La révolution scientifique de l'enseignement.* Brussels: Dessart-Mardaga. (Translation of B.F. Skinner (1968), *The technology of teaching.*)

Skinner, B.F. (1969b). *Contingencies of reinforcement : A theoretical analysis.* New York: Appleton Century Crofts.

Skinner, B.F. (1970a). B.F. Skinner, an autobiography. In P.B. Dews (Ed.) *Festschrift for B.F. Skinner,* pp.1–21. New York: Appleton Century Crofts.

Skinner, B.F. (1970b). Creating the creative artist. In A.J. Toynbee et al. *On the future of art,* pp.61–75. New York: Viking Press.

Skinner, B.F. (1971a). *Beyond freedom and dignity.* New York: Alfred A. Knopf.

Skinner, B.F. (1971b). *L'analyse expérimentale du comportement.* Brussels: Dessart-Mardaga. (Translation of B.F. Skinner (1969b). *Contingencies of reinforcement: A theoretical analysis.*)

Skinner, B.F. (1972). *Cumulative record: A selection of papers (third edition).* New York: Appleton Century Crofts. (First edition published 1961)

Skinner, B.F. (1973). The free and happy student. *New York University Education Quarterly, 4*, 2–6.

Skinner, B.F. (1974). *About behaviorism.* New York: Alfred A. Knopf.

Skinner, B.F. (1976). *Particulars of my life.* New York: Alfred A. Knopf.

Skinner, B.F. (1977). Herrnstein and the evolution of behaviorism. *American Psychologist, 32*, 1006–1012.

Skinner, B.F. (1978). *Reflections on behaviorism and society.* Englewood Cliffs, NJ: Prentice-Hall.

Skinner, B.F.  (1979).  *The shaping of a behaviorist.* New York: Alfred A. Knopf.

Skinner, B.F.  (1981).  Selection by consequences. *Science, 213,* 501–504.

Skinner, B.F.  (1983).  *A matter of consequences.* New York: Alfred A. Knopf.

Skinner, B.F.  (1984a).  The shame of American education. *American Psychologist, 39,* 947–954.

Skinner, B.F.  (1984b).  The evolution of behavior. *Journal of the Experimental Analysis of Behavior, 41,* 217–221.

Skinner, B.F.  (1984c).  Canonical papers of B.F. Skinner. *Behavioral and Brain Sciences, 7,* 477–724.

Skinner, B.F.  (1985).  Cognitive science and behaviorism. *British Journal of Psychology, 76,* 291–301.

Skinner, B.F.  (1987a).  Whatever happened to psychology as the science of behavior? *American Psychologist, 42,* 780–786.

Skinner, B.F.  (1987b).  *Upon further reflection.* Englewood Cliffs, NJ: Prentice-Hall.

Skinner, B.F.  (1989a).  The origin of cognitive thought. *American Psychologist, 44,* 13–18.

Skinner, B.F.  (1989b).  *Recent issues in the analysis of behavior.* Columbus, Ohio: Merrill Publishing Company.

Skinner, B.F.  (1990).  Can psychology be a science of Mind? *American Psychologist, 45,* 1206–1210.

Skinner, B.F. & Morse, H.  (1957).  Concurrent activity under fixed-interval reinforcement. *Journal of Comparative and Physiological Psychology, 50,* 279–281.

Skinner, B.F. & Vaughan, M.E.  (1983).  *Enjoy old age: A program of self-management.* New York: Norton & Company.

Sperry, R.  (1983).  *Science and moral priority.* Oxford: Basil Blackwell.

Staddon, J.E.  (1983).  *Adaptive behaviour and learning.* Cambridge: Cambridge University Press.

Staddon, J.E. & Simmelhag, V.L.  (1971).  The "superstition" experiment: A reexamination of its implications for the principles of adaptive behavior. *Psychological Review, 78,* 3–43.

Sternberg, R.J.  (1984).  Operant analysis of problem solving: Answers to questions you probably don't want to ask. *The Behavioral and Brain Sciences, 7,* 605.

Thoreau, H.D.  (1957).  *Walden or life in the woods.* New York: Mentor Books.

Tirelli, E. (1987). L'animal toxicomane: Modèles de comportement animal dans l'étude de la tolérance et de toxicomanie. *Nouvelles de la Science et des Technologies, 5,* 19–22.

Tolman, E.C.  (1932).  *Purposive behavior in animals and men.* New York: Appleton Century Crofts.

Van Parijs, P.  (1981).  *Evolutionary explanation in the social sciences. An emerging paradigm.* Totowa: Rowman & Littlefield.

Varela, F.  (1989).  *Les sciences cognitives: Tendances et perspectives.* Paris: Du Seuil.

Watson, J.B.  (1913).  Psychology as the behaviorist views it. *Psychological Review, 20,* 158–177.

Williams, J. (1974).  Evidence of complementary afterimages in the pigeon. *Journal of the Experimental Analysis of Behavior, 21,* 421–424.

Woolf, V.  (1929).  *A room of one's own.* London: Hogarth Press.

# Author Index

B.F. Skinner has no entry in this index for obvious reasons.

# Subject Index